W9-AUL-938

DISCARD

Community College Library Instruction

Quinsigamond Community College

COMMUNITY COLLEGE LIBRARY INSTRUCTION

Training for Self-Reliance in Basic Library Use

Quinsigamond Community College

FLOYD M. CAMMACK

MARRI DECOSIN

NORMAN ROBERTS

LINNET BOOKS

Hamden, Connecticut

1979

Library of Congress Cataloging in Publication Data

Cammack, Floyd M.
    Community college library instruction.

    Bibliography: p.
    Includes index.
    1. College students—Library orientation. 2. Libraries,
Community college. I. DeCosin, Marri, 1921– joint author.
II. Roberts, Norman, joint author. III. Title.
    Z675.J8C34 027.7 79–17531
    ISBN 0–208–01825–5

© Floyd M. Cammack 1979
First published 1979 as a Linnet Book,
an imprint of THE SHOE STRING PRESS, INC.
Hamden, Connecticut 06514
All rights reserved

Materials in Part 2 and in Appendixes
may be reproduced without permission

The original activity which is the subject of portions of this report was supported in part by the U.S. Office of Education, Department of Health, Education, and Welfare. However, the opinions expressed herein do not necessarily reflect the position or policy of the U.S. Office of Education, and no official endorsement by the U.S. Office of Education should be inferred.

Printed in the United States of America

[The] major impression one receives from reviewing the literature on library service for undergraduate education is that a great deal more is said about what ought to be done than about what is actually being done. Further, there are many more plans, described in glowing terms, than there are reports on their implementation. Real evaluation of the effectiveness of new programs is almost nonexistent.

—Patricia B. Knapp, *The Montieth College Library Experiment*

Contents

Acknowledgments

The authors acknowledge with much gratitude the cooperation of those fellow staff members of Leeward Community College Library whose daily participation in the operation of the system described here has produced something worth writing about. Equal thanks are due to the students whose creative reactions and suggestions shape the process and who are, themselves, the product of it. Leeward Community College's language arts faculty, whose use has improved the system, provide the vital market for which it is designed.

Individual developers of tests and instructional materials included in part 2 have graciously consented to their presentation here. In chapter 4 Phoebe Lou Hamilton prepared the first section (Library Tour); Marri DeCosin is responsible for section 2 (card catalog); Muriel Y. King prepared section 3 (subject headings); and Laurence Goldstein developed section 4 (periodical indexes). Susan Moskala and Susan Ballam participated in several aspects of materials production and analysis. Elizabeth Mano typed the manuscript. Flow charts and performance contract forms were prepared by Blanche Klim and Elaine Nakayama.

The authors thank Pierian Press for permission to quote at length from their publications, *Academic Library Instruction* and *Evaluating Library Use Instruction,* and the Association of College and Research Libraries for permission to reproduce "Guidelines for Bibliographic Instruction in Academic Libraries."

Special acknowledgment is extended to Henry Schaafsma of the college language arts faculty for his help and encouragement during the formative stages of this project and for his continued support through the years. Dr. Jean Pezzoli helped with analysis of statistics that showed us where to seek, and how to follow the right track.

Introduction

In most undergraduate institutions throughout the country some sort of orientation to library use is given either in conjunction with a general freshman campus orientation program or in one or two hours of a Freshman English classroom lecture. Both of these methods have, over the years, proved to be largely ineffectual, primarily owing to the absence of student motivation.

The ideal motivational situation involves individual instruction in library use immediately prior to the first research paper assignment. To achieve this goal, an individualized, self-paced library instruction unit was first developed in the spring of 1972 at Leeward Community College, a campus of the University of Hawaii, to conform with the self-paced format used by Freshman English courses. The flexibility of this self-contained format has proved to be a decided asset. Whatever changes and variations occur in the English courses, the library instruction unit can still be utilized at the optimum point of motivation.

As is the case with most undergraduate institutions in this country, at some stage in his college career at Leeward almost every degree candidate is required to take at least one course in English. As an integral part of this coursework each student is directed to undertake the "library unit." Weighing of grades received for work connected with this portion of the English course varies among instructors.

The original instructional unit described here consisted of two sections. The first covered a tour of the library, the card catalog, Library of Congress classification system, and the *Library of Congress Subject Headings*. A second section covered the periodical collection and periodical indexes. Students were given the option of attending lectures, listening to tapes, reading pamphlets, or any combination of these.

During the summer of 1972 the unit was revised. Experience with the two-section format indicated that our students needed more extensive basic background instruction than had been assumed. This was substantiated by an evaluation questionnaire showing that only 1 percent of our students claimed any previous instruction in the use of a library and 95 percent felt that, after completing the unit, they had learned a great deal more about using a library. To meet the indicated need for more extensive basic instruction, the unit was expanded to four sections, retaining the same areas of coverage. The former first section was restructured into three separate sections: (1) tour, (2) card catalog, (3) subject headings. The former second section, which covered the periodical collection and periodical indexes, remained basically the same and became section 4. A workbook of examples and exercises was developed as a self-correcting, self-instructional aid, correlated with the second and third sections.

At one point an attempt was made to replace lectures with video presentations. The tour was offered in this format for both semesters of the 1972/73 academic year. The second section was developed but never produced, since use of video with the first section indicated that the "hands-on" experience provided by both the audiotape and pamphlet format produced superior results. There proved to be an added factor of reinforcement in learning through use of the actual research tools (card catalog, indexes, and so on) as opposed to seeing only a pictured reproduction of them. In essence, with the functional "hands-on" approach, the student is given a "dry-run" of the basic library research techniques.

The most common criticism from students was that too much time was required to complete the unit. In response to this, in the spring 1973 semester, a control group of 97 students kept careful account of the total amount of time they spent on the unit, including the time needed for listening to the tapes, reading the pamphlets or watching the video tape, being individually tutored on any confusing aspect, taking the tests and retesting when desired, and having their test errors explained to them. The average total time this control group took to complete the unit was eleven hours and twenty-six minutes. It was deemed desirable to reduce this time to approximately nine hours, the equivalent of one week of three-credit course time (three hours of class time plus two hours of preparation time for each hour of class time).

A possible point of reduction appeared to be section 3, the *Library of Congress Subject Headings,* and an abridged version of this section was duly prepared. During the summer 1973 sessions another control group of 90 students recorded the total amount of time they spent doing this abridged version of the third section. It was found that the average time was reduced by two hours and seventeen minutes, bring the total unit time down to the desired goal of nine hours (nine hours, nine minutes, to be exact). Both the abridged and complete versions of the third section were offered in the fall 1973 semester at the instructor's option. One other revision made at this time was the expansion of an accompanying workbook to include examples and exercises for section 4.

In its current form, the overall object of the library unit is to provide each student who completes the eight-to-ten hours of instruction and testing with a confident control of the basic techniques of library use required for successful pursuit of ordinary college courses. The authors like to compare the unit to the type of instruction and testing required for a driver's license. Its simple goal is to acquaint the student sufficiently with the techniques and some of the tools required to maneuver successfully on the road to a degree.

This book is arranged in order of increasing specialization. The first chapters treat matters of concern to all who are in any way involved in the process and goals of general education at the undergraduate level. Teachers of English, the social sciences, and the humanities, all have reason to become more aware of the changing role of libraries in today's undergraduate institutions and of the new wave of activity that has resulted in the development and application of programs such as the one described here. Community and junior colleges throughout the country have, since their period of great expansion during the 1960s and early 1970s, provided a locus for experimentation in educational techniques, some of which are destined to spread to more comprehensive institutions and to become a permanent part of America's educational framework. The program described here is even now expanding to other institutions in Hawaii, both on the secondary and postsecondary levels. Similar programs in other states are also experiencing ready acceptance. As more is learned about the effects of open admissions on America's educational institutions, the more necessary it becomes to examine and, where appropriate, alter traditional methods of teaching for today's nontraditional learners.

Part 1 of this book describes in three chapters the actual setting and rationale for a bibliographic instruction program at an undergraduate institution with an established policy of open admissions; the recommended means for designing practical goals for such a program; and an outline of the types of activities necessary to develop, maintain, and evaluate it. Teachers, librarians, and researchers should find in these chapters material of interest, as they describe the development of a notably successful solution to a problem now recognized to be common to all American undergraduate colleges, whether limited to two- or four-year curricula.

Part 2 is designed to support the descriptive chapters with actual samples of teaching and testing materials developed according to the principles, and under the circumstances, described in part 1. With minor exceptions occasioned by the regular revision each semester of some parts of the library instructional unit, these are the instructional pamphlets, the workbooks, and some of the tests that are in current use. Appended to these chapters are examples of a variety of ancillary supporting data, including a pretest, the type of computer output used for item analysis, a list of materials needed for the operation of such a system, course outlines, student comments, and sample communications between librarians and teaching faculty.

This portion of the work is designed specifically to aid those who are considering the implementation of some type of library instruction system as well as those who are already involved with the operation of a program with similar goals. Since most of the developmental work in this field over the past five years has been done by librarians, many of whom are not trained in the intricacies of test and text production and evaluation, the authors have included whole examples of materials developed over a period of several years and repeatedly checked and revised for validity, reliability, and practicality. Multiple versions of the many testing instruments involved have been excluded, and only one example of each has been included to indicate the type of question and approximate level of difficulty that has proved to be workable. New instructional materials on such topics as the location of book reviews, biographical information available in most small libraries, and botanical data have also been omitted, since current drafts have not yet been tested in actual practice. What this volume does offer, however, is material sufficient for the development of a workable system of *basic library instruction* easily adaptable to the needs of virtually any college library.

Experience has shown that, with relatively minor adaptations, these sample materials can be altered for use in libraries and learning resource centers and by interested academic departments in far less time than is required to develop a similar program from scratch. The reason for including these examples is therefore to offer them for use by any institution interested in their adaptation to a particular set of local requirements. By special arrangement with The Shoe

String Press and the developers of the Leeward Community College library instructional materials, copyright is hereby waived for all sample materials included in part 2 and the appendixes to this volume. Additional test instruments and instructional materials may be obtained from the authors, who are also available to consult with institutions or individuals who may be contemplating the establishment of a similar or related system.

Under a series of grants from the University President's Educational Improvement Fund, a detailed, step-by-step program development manual is now being prepared in response to expressions of interest by other campuses in the university system. It is designed to cover the basic areas of library instruction treated in this volume but in greater detail, with specific alternatives provided to allow application of the general system to libraries of various sizes and types of collections. Provision is also made in this new work for student-constructed responses on test instruments, as well as the machine-gradable, multiple-choice technique demonstrated in the present volume. Further information will be provided by the authors on request.

PART ONE

Chapter One

Purpose, Setting, Medium, and Materials

PURPOSE

It is our purpose to bring together in a single volume the basic materials required for a general program of course-related library instruction for beginning college students. The fundamental principles, explanations, descriptions, outlines, recommendations, and sample materials included here have been tested in actual use over a period of five years and are known to be operable, reliable, valid, economical, and yet flexible enough to meet the needs of a multicultural student population in an institution committed to a policy of open admissions. The courses to which the included instructional materials are primarily related are language arts courses, required of nearly all students entering the college. Recently developed sections designed to support courses in the humanities and in the biological sciences are still experimental but rely on the same principles and techniques employed in the more basic language arts units. These techniques are fully adaptable to courses in any subject for which library resources are the medium of discovery and mastery of a body of information.

We intend this work to be more than a manual for the development of a reasonably simple answer to the standard problems of instructing undergraduates in the basic use of a library. At its core is the description of a system which has proved, even in its developmental stages, to be economical, acceptable to students and faculty, and effective enough to merit the attention of numbers of institutions throughout the country that are facing (or avoiding) what the authors are convinced is a common challenge. The materials presented here are designed to be adaptable, with minor alterations, to the needs of any comparable institution, with no requirement for any equipment more complex than a typewriter. The system can be implemented with the cooperation of one librarian and one faculty member, without recourse to curricular variation or upheaval. Its growth and acceptance at Leeward Community College was a gradual process, involving no external support or funding. Variations of it are now spreading to other institutions in the state of Hawaii (including some secondary schools), and observers have visited from institutions as distant as the University of Maine and the University of Guam.

The pattern of open admissions at the college level presumes a commitment on the part of the institution to find a means of making accessible to the many what was for so long comfortably reserved for the privileged few. The ability to acquire, evaluate, process, and transmit information at an academic level is about all that a liberal education was ever designed to accomplish. When successful, such education provides the ability not only to handle information but to treat it critically and to be able to evaluate sources as well as the product of the process. In no way is this process limited to the goals of liberal arts education. The same abilities are required equally to manipulate successfully the information found in an auto parts catalog, a table on chemical bonding properties, instructions for small business tax returns, or the draft of a legislative bill. It is our contention that the measure of anyone's ability to participate fully in the society and subcultures of which he chooses to be, or to become, a part is his degree of control of the information networks operative in that society. The often self-imposed ignorance of these communicative tools and the conventions by which they operate is a pretty good guarantee of lifelong exclusion from meaningful participation in that society.

Libraries are the depositories of by far the greatest number of these tools, at least in their printed form. If academic libraries are to justify their cost of maintenance and operation, they must be more than passive depositories, reserved for an elite whose background and credentials make them party to the arcane conventions of their operation and utilization. The attitudes of librarians such as Patricia Breivik concerning the "teaching library"[1] seem to us to hold great promise, particularly in a period of declining enrollments, when it is possible to think of major priority changes in response to different types of need. In all of the recent concern over the efficiency of academic library operations and collections, we have yet to see a measure of effectiveness based on the amount of library activity that is *self-generated.* It is perfectly possible for undergraduate college libraries to "make their own market" by actively engaging in the teaching process. The cooperation of librarians and teaching faculty which made possible the breaking of this barrier at the college described here has given the authors cause to hope that they are, perhaps, one step nearer the goals envisioned by all who are struggling toward equality of opportunity in American education.

Despite its title and much of its subject matter, this is not a book for librarians only. The concerned college teacher seeking a means to improve student performance on "research" papers may find useable ideas and materials adaptable to his need. High school teachers wishing to encourage students toward more independent initiative in their academic work may see in these pages something to suit their purpose. The system is subject to few limitations where subject matter is concerned. The samples included are only examples, chosen for their general applicability and commonality among today's collegiate institutions. The basic, elementary nature of much of the material is not a matter of the authors' caprice, but a direct response to the actual, demonstrated level of need of those students entering the collegiate world today. Careful evaluation and continuous revision of instructional and testing materials confirm the accuracy of the program's direction and are at the basis of continued student and faculty satisfaction with the system.

SETTING

The college to which we refer throughout this volume, and at which the materials and program described are currently operative, is Leeward Community College, located in Pearl City, a suburb of Honolulu, on the island of Oahu, State of Hawaii. It is one of ten institutions in the University of Hawaii system, with over 5,000 students pursuing a fairly standard variety of liberal arts and vocational/technical programs on its adequately appointed, ten-year-old campus. Its library and media center facilities are about average for an institution of its age and size, and its student body is a superbly multicultural microcosm of the population and the aspirations of the state itself. The community it serves is equally varied, containing within its borders virtually every manifestation of the modern American experience in most of its economic, social, racial, and cultural aspects.

Though a part of the western-most university system in the United States, the college is remarkable only for the absence of any dominant provincial characteristics, save possibly that of the inner eyefold. There is no racial or cultural majority on campus. The language of instruction and of most student interaction is English, as natively spoken by about 90 percent of the students and faculty.

Before proceeding, we hope the reader will permanently put away any lingering misconceptions about exotic island educational institutions or environments. The educational "door" which opened in the 1960s with the advent of the community college movement brought to the world of postsecondary education in Hawaii the same clientele that appeared on its threshold in Detroit, Dade County, and California. If, as we maintain, the local institutions, their faculties, facilities, and clientele are indeed comparable to those in other parts of the United States, then these experiences and solutions to common problems may well be applicable in other locations, irrespective of their generally less salubrious climates.

After several years of seeking official recognition of its library instructional program, the college's new Educational Development Plan, 1978–1984, includes the following passage: "Leeward will continue to provide and develop structured, course-related, instructional programs in the use of library materials for all students and equivalent services for community members." In an era of restricted budgets and prospects of possible retrenchment, such a statement is a valuable reminder of a job undertaken and a commitment made.

MEDIUM

The accuracy of national statistics about "functional illiterates" in our society is supported by our personal experience. Based on scores achieved on the Nelson-Denny Reading Test (Form D), Dr. J. A. Pezzoli, college psychometrist, reports that the percent of new students reading below the tenth-grade level jumped to 51 percent in the fall of 1978. This registers the first year in the nine-year history of placement testing that more than half of the entering students read at "developmental" levels. In 1975, for instance, the percentage was only 35 percent. The implications of these figures may be tempered with the thought that, perhaps, in today's vastly expanded educational market, there are probably more people actively *trying* to communicate effectively than ever before. Less than a generation ago, it is doubtful if more than half of the students now attending their first year of postsecondary education would have been so engaged. That they are now so occupied has placed a heavy responsibility on institutions claiming to be able to impart such skills to develop methods of doing so which are economically viable and which produce more successes than failures. We are pretty well convinced that traditional methods alone cannot meet this requirement.

By reducing the importance of time limits for assigned tasks, by eliminating most academic gamesmanship, and by actively involving the college library and its staff, we are able to apply a type of "Skinnerian" model that allows rapid reinforcement of acceptable efforts in an atmosphere somewhat less artificial than that of the traditional college classroom course, and demonstrably more effective for the market with which we deal.

Our decision to concentrate at first on the integration of library instruction with lower-division college English courses was admittedly, in part, a case of following the path of least resistance. Proximity of purposes and similarity of interests make English classes a very practical starting point, particularly at this stage in educational history when the gap between secondary school training and collegiate expectations is a matter of national concern. English, communications, and language arts courses, under whatever rubric, are a fairly standard requirement for the majority of entering students, thus affording librarians the opportunity to establish contact with the largest possible number of students through a single series of usually coordinated courses.

The success of a course-integrated system of library instruction inevitably depends on a thorough understanding of the philosophy, structure, and techniques involved in the courses themselves. It is in this area that librarians attempting a course-related system of instruction may fall short. While it is probably safe to state that every American academic librarian has, at some time or other, successfully completed one or more lower-division courses in English, it is also true that the teaching of English at the college level has changed enough to deserve our careful attention. Perhaps more than the material itself, the assumptions, expectations, and techniques of language teaching have varied over the years. Before proposing or imposing any system of library instruction, a thoughtful examination of the language teachers' own goals and needs should be undertaken. Even if the results indicate that *Plus ça change, plus c'est la même chose,* the process will highlight the areas where opportunity exists for productive cooperation toward the achievement of the *teacher's* goals, to which the librarian's objectives must, we believe, remain subordinate and supportive.

Here, then, is a description of the medium—the *whole*—of which our library instruction unit is an integral *part*.

The program in expository writing which several Language Arts Division instructors designed and are presently implementing concentrates on the language and writing aspects of the traditional freshman English course. They feel that it is the function of the college, including its library, to provide the springboards for thinking and writing, not merely the composition course. They want to introduce to the student the forms of several types of expository essays, so that when he gets an idea from whatever source, he will have a place to put that idea and a way to express it. As it is presently constituted, the one-semester program consists of four units and is completely individualized. These four units are: (1) language and usage; (2) basic expository writing; (3) library use; and (4) advanced expository writing. The guiding principle of this program is "Do it till you do it right."

Before discussing the nature of the experimental freshman English program, it seems appropriate here to attempt to explain the rationale behind the particular choice of language, library, and writing assignments that were selected for the expository writing program. First of all, we carefully examined college catalog descriptions of basic freshman English courses. It seemed that the majority of these course descriptions called for four things: grammar and usage review, library work, expository and research writing. Knowing that not all students need the same kind and amount of grammar review, and that it is difficult to review what one has never learned, made the choice of a programmed grammar and usage text the most practical solution to the problem of the language-study portion of the course. Each instructor who has run the experimental English 100 program has worked through the text and has taken all the tests. A variety of programmed grammar and usage textbooks is available, any of which would probably serve adequately. A programmed text has the advantage over the more traditional workbook exercises because it presents an explanation of the lesson the student is expected to practice. The traditional workbook depends on the teacher explaining the exercises, and such explanation is frequently omitted, with the result that the student who does the exercise may never learn precisely what skill he is exercising.

In selecting the kinds of expository papers to be written, the instructors drew on their actual college writing experiences, not on their recollections of the freshman composition course they survived in years gone by. Close observation shows that most college writing consists of essay exams, book reports or reviews, and term papers. The longer students stay in college, the more important writing, particularly critical and research writing becomes. Analysis of essay exam questions shows that the kinds of answers the questions call for are the following: enumeration, comparison, cause-effect, and definition. Occasionally an argumentative piece is required. Narrative and descriptive writing are omitted from the program because there is not much use for either in any courses *except* freshman composition, sophomore composition, or creative writing courses. In general, history, social science, and other courses, when they require writing, ask for essays that explain something in specific terms. There is little reason to believe that the college writing requirements of today differ significantly from the writing requirements of a decade, or even a century, ago.

Transfer students who go on to upper-division and perhaps eventually to graduate work will have to know how to write the essays, critical reviews, and research papers on which their grades will depend. Terminal students who will enter the lower ranks of management need to know how to write instructions that workers can follow. In upper-division and graduate school writing, it is craftsmanship and scholarship in explicit expository writing that earn honor grades. Let anyone who disagrees with this rationale examine the assignments and examinations for upper-division and graduate courses at any college or university in the country.

Each entering student (following placement via Nelson-Denny testing) takes the pretest designed for use with the programmed review text, *English 3200,* second edition.[2] Students who score over 80 on the pretest may immediately begin unit two, basic expository writing. If the student's work indicates that he already has the requisite writing ability, he is encouraged to move rapidly on to the advanced expository writing unit and the library unit. Highly motivated and capable students have completed the whole program in six weeks; most students take all semester, however, and some have been working away at the program since it was first started. In most cases, fewer than five or six students score higher than 80 on the pretest, and so most students work through the whole program which is described in detail below. The student keeps his own record of accomplishment on his performance contract (see appendix 3).

The *English 3200* portion of the course consists of a pretest, a halfway test, eleven unit tests, and a posttest. Some students can do one unit per class day, some even more, but in practice a large number of students do as little as one unit per week. Most students are encouraged to begin unit two, basic expository writing, as soon as they have completed the third *3200* test. After the first composition is accepted, the student is urged to begin the library use unit. Teachers recommend that students spend one day per week on the *3200* work, one day on the library unit, and one day per week on composition. For many students the *3200* is a great chore. If one has never learned grammar and usage, one must study the programmed text and frequently must take the unit tests several times before a passing score is attained. Eighty is considered a passing score and is justified on the basis of the "Do it till you do it right" approach. Teachers do not coerce; rather, in keeping with the philosophy of the institution, they recommend what they think the students should do.

Few students follow the recommendations, however, preferring to do one thing at a time or perhaps to find a "better way" or a shortcut through the program. If there are any shortcuts, we are not aware of them. The program is individualized and performance-based; therefore, to complete the course to the A level, the students must average 80 on the *3200* material, must average 80 on the library use tests, and must have written nine acceptable compositions. Quite a few students drop out before they complete the *3200* grammar and usage review and never begin the basic writing unit. A number of these dropouts show up the following semester because, in the words on one student, "I know what I have to do to finish."

Unit two, basic expository writing, consists of the following expository types: enumeration, comparison, contrasts, cause-effect, and definition. Instructions for writing these essays and examples of model essays are printed in a locally produced manual, "Model Essay Booklet," which is mimeographed by the college and placed on reserve in the library, the writing laboratory, and the language laboratory. Completion of unit one, the *3200* grammar-usage review and unit two, basic expository writing, brings the student to C level. Students may then elect to take the C and go their way, or may decide to work for a higher grade. Unless it is near the end of the semester, most students try for the B or A.

There is an option for students who do not complete the cause-effect and the definition papers. They may elect to receive credit for remedial English by examination. In such a case, the students formally withdraw from English 100 and receive a grade of C in remedial English. Near the end of the semester many students make a herculean effort to complete as much as half a semester's work in two or three weeks. That many of these late bloomers actually succeed in getting credit for remedial English is a testimony to the learning abilities of marginal students. We have had few native speakers of English who have been unable to do adequate work in our program; we have, however, had a large number of students who have chosen to do little or nothing for reasons of their own.

Unit three, library use, is described in detail in the following chapters and is administered entirely by the library staff. There are four subunits (called sections by the librarians): (1) Library Tour; (2) Card Catalog; (3) Library of Congress Subject Headings; and (4) Periodicals and Periodical Indexes. Students study the special instructional pamphlets or listen to recorded tapes covering the same material, make their way through a series of workbook exercises, and are tested on completion of each of the four sections, progressing always at their own pace and with options for repeating sections not completed satisfactorily. The entire library unit takes between eight and ten hours, and although students tend to grumble about the amount of time they spend in the library, most students feel it worthwhile. The entire library unit is not longer than four of the *English 3200* subunits, since there is no homework required. Like it or not, most liberal arts students come to realize that college is a world of books and is likely to remain so, at least during their lifetimes. Some students have indicated that the library unit is the most worthwhile aspect of the whole freshman English program.

Unit four, advanced expository writing, consists of the following papers: an argument, a piece of critical writing, a research proposal, and a research paper. Completion of the first two papers places the student at the B level. Completion of the last two papers places the student at the A level. Needless to say, standards are high for the quality of these advanced papers, and students quickly find out that things are not as easy as they seem. There are no shortcuts to quality so far as we know. Students who would achieve a B or an A in English 100 must not only demonstrate that they can follow explicit instructions, but their papers must also show craftsmanship and scholarship.

The result of this approach is a reasonable freshman composition course. We have no reservations about the performance levels of students who complete the program, and we are certain that their newly acquired library skills have better equipped them for adequate performance in any subsequent liberal arts courses they may attempt.

MATERIALS

Included in part 2 are copies of the actual instructional materials in use at the college. The pamphlets presented are also available in tape form, with so few changes that we have chosen to omit samples of the actual tapescripts. Both pamphlets and tapes are edited frequently, and since both are produced in-house, revisions are a relatively simple matter. The decision to maintain basic instructional material separate from the workbook material and to make it available only from the Reserve Desk distinguishes this system from several similar ones now in use at various colleges and universities throughout the country. Through this process it is possible to assure that students will, in fact, study the material on-site, with actual hands-on use of the materials explained in the texts. While convenience would argue for combined text and workbook, we maintain that the pedagogical advantage outweighs the additional labor involved.

Reading-difficulty levels have been established for the materials used, with the first section at a ninth-grade reading level and the remaining sections at eleventh- and twelfth-grade levels according to the Edward Fry Readability Test. While section 1 is necessarily restricted to our own institutional configuration, the remaining sections on the card catalog, subject heading list, and periodical and newspaper indexes are of more general applicability. While far from experts at text and test production, we are no longer rank amateurs, and our experience now leaves us reasonably confident that the items included and the areas treated are defensibly those covering the areas of greatest need for our current student population. Elegance of format and production are necessarily sacrificed to ease of revision. We find that ten copies of each pamphlet and each tape are quite adequate for a typical semester's group of 600 or so learners.

Each section (workbook, supporting instruction, and tests) is the responsibility of a single individual. Though perhaps somewhat primitive in format when compared with professionally prepared, programmed texts, we nevertheless find that monitoring the effectiveness and daily operations of the library unit a complex enough procedure to require the continuing attention and proprietary interest of individuals willing to devote consistent attention to the creation and maintenance of their particular sections. Pride in authorship is genuine and justified.

Experience, supported by statistical evidence, indicates that these workbook exercises are crucial to the successful completion of the unit. If they are done well, consistent with and supportive of both instructional materials and tests, they appear to provide a necessary (for most learners) bridge between the presentation of a concept in expository form and the testing of an actual interpretation of that concept. For sections involving the use of library materials such as indexes, the card catalog, and the subject headings list, we find that thorough revision on at least an annual basis is necessary, largely to prevent wear and tear on the individual pages and cards involved. Substitutes and replacement pages are kept on file, but few problems other than those associated with heavy use have occurred.

The writing of these exercises has proved to be a particularly exacting process, for the accidental inclusion of even one ambiguous phrase or an oversight of even minor import will be quickly brought to our attention by the conscientious students who are constantly ready to remind us that the writer's intention and the reader's interpretation are allowed to meet only through carefully written and carefully edited prose. We are seldom allowed to forget for long that cleverness is no substitute for clarity, no matter how boring or obvious the materials may appear to the casual reader.

The sample tests included in part 2 were those in actual use at the college during a recent semester. Item analyses and related scoring information appear with them. The numbering system consists of the last two digits of the calendar year, followed by the number of the appropriate section. The number following the decimal indicates the particular version of the tests for that section. For in-house purposes, we add another decimal and number from 1–20 to indicate a particular item. Thus, 783.3.7 refers to the seventh question on the third version of the test for section 3 used in 1978. These numbers can then be keyed to objectives and instructional material in both pamphlets and workbook to develop an item-bank to which we can refer when preparing new versions of the tests or to evaluate a particular approach to a learning problem.

Each of these tests is systematically revised each semester, and we continue to find this system simpler and more flexible than one involving multiple editions of a workbook or other known variations on the basic system we have chosen to employ. Tests reproduced here are slightly reduced versions of the actual format. Two or three copies of each test are laminated on light cardboard, trimmed to legal size, and hinged with color-coded tape. They also carry hidden Tattle-Tape to prevent their leaving the library building. The slightly awkward size serves also to prevent the unintentional inclusion of a copy with other materials ordinarily carried by students. Earlier, "subjective" versions of tests were prepared on ditto masters and reproduced in the familiar purple form, with the idea that more enterprising students would then not be able to copy them at will. The current, multiple-choice versions, which have the advantage of being machine-gradable, are theoretically subject to being copied by anyone so inclined. In fact, we have not found this to be a problem, perhaps because of the number of alternate versions, which tends to discourage attempts at cheating. Nor, during the period that the present system has been in operation, have we experienced a theft of any version of any test.

We have experimented with two machine-scoring systems. One of them employs a 3M scanner readily available on campus, which proved fast, convenient, and efficient. We could not, for local reasons, obtain the desired computer analyses of these scores without transferring by hand all scoring data to IBM 507 forms. At this writing, we are utilizing the IBM answer forms, but this involves hand scoring with locally prepared templates, an awkward and time-consuming process which is subject to some degree of human error. These limitations, together with our reasons for particular decisions regarding them, are covered more completely below.

The main point to be made here is that, while machine scoring and computer-produced analyses are a major convenience, neither is absolutely essential to the operation of a high-quality system of instruction. Depending on the numbers involved, hand scoring of test materials is a good way of keeping abreast of student performance and of locating problems as they occur. In other words, when and where the requisite machinery is available at a cost that can be met, it provides definite advantages. Where it is not so available, a perfectly workable system can be implemented without it.

There has been no difficulty in maintaining a 24-hour turn-around time for grading and reporting results to students and faculty. This ability to respond rapidly to student curiosity about their individual performances is well worth the effort required to maintain it. Being able to provide additional, personal instruction and advice at this point-of-need has proved to be particularly effective and appreciated by students. These conference sessions held at the "moment of truth" offer the opportunity to delve quickly, with the student, into the precise area of his misunderstanding while his curiosity still creates a reasonably receptive atmosphere.

"Conference copies" of each version of each test are kept at the reference desk, where all library instruction materials are handled. These copies have the correct answers marked and contain notes to the student explaining why each alternate answer is incorrect. Relevant pages from indexes, subject heading list, etc. are also included and marked appropriately. These conference copies are great foot- and time-savers, for while it is possible to go with the student to find the correct answer and to explain it from the particular page or tray of catalog cards, it is much faster and more convenient to do it with all the needed material immediately visible and available at the desk. Again, there has been no problem with theft of these answer "keys."

Two file drawers at the reference desk are sufficient to handle all materials and supplies necessary to operate the system. Original answer slips for earlier semesters are kept on file elsewhere for several years to accommodate students who begin the series in one semester, drop out for one reason or another, then resume at a later time. It is possible in a few minutes to locate their earlier scores, report them to current instructors, and put the student back on the track if there are remaining sections to be completed. This degree of simplicity and ease of operation means that, at most times, one person at the reference desk can handle ordinary reference traffic plus the demands of the library instruction unit: no special or separate facilities or manpower are needed. During especially busy periods, an auxiliary desk is manned adjacent to the main desk but with no need for additional equipment or supplies.

Notes

1. Patricia Senn Breivek, "Leadership Management and the Teaching Library," *Library Journal*, October 15, 1978, pp. 2405–48.
2. Joseph C. Blumenthal, *English 3200: A Programmed Course in Grammar and Usage*, 2d ed. (New York: Harcourt, Brace, Jovanovich, 1972).

Chapter Two

Guidelines, Goals, and Objectives

During the first years of the library instruction program, it was necessary to develop a set of goals and objectives, keyed naturally to a small, new collection and very tentatively geared to the estimated needs and abilities of a student body whose demographic characteristics were unknown. The process of pitting one's professional training and aspirations against an educational challenge that was (and to some extent continues to be) without easily recognized precedents or traditions is certainly invigorating and has, in retrospect, a good deal to recommend it. Guidelines, goals, and objectives so developed are perforce closely aligned with perceived needs and available tools. Inevitably, they lack the comparability with more broadly based statements toward which local efforts can be targeted.

The "Guidelines for Bibliographic Instruction in Academic Libraries," developed by the Bibliographic Instruction Task Force of the Association of College and Research Libraries and approved as policy by the ACRL Board of Directors on January 31, 1977,[1] came as a welcome confirmation that our efforts were, indeed, in line with recommendations made by expert representatives of our profession. To begin this chapter on the selection and presentation of objectives for specific programs, we present these guidelines as they appear in the above citation.

Several years earlier, the same task force had developed and issued its excellent "Academic Bibliographic Instruction: Model Statement of Objectives," providing the needed distillation of national professional experience to allow us to measure our activities against broader norms and to pull our program into conformity with what we had hitherto only assumed to be the probable direction of other collegiate efforts. At approximately the same time, Stoffle's delineation of "Library Goals and Objectives" for the Parkside campus of the University of Wisconsin appeared,[2] giving a detailed, multidimensional example of the possible application of clear objectives to the needs of undergraduate students.

In our opinion, any college library contemplating the creation of a library instruction program, or the adaptation of an existing one,

Guidelines for Bibliographic Instruction in Academic Libraries

Developed by the Bibliographic Instruction Task Force of the Association of College and Research Libraries. Approved as policy by the ACRL Board of Directors on January 31, 1977.

The college and university library performs a unique and indispensable function in the educational process. It bears the central responsibility for developing the college and university library collections; for extending bibliographic control over these collections; for instructing students formally and informally; and for advising faculty and scholars in the use of these collections.

In order to assist college and university libraries in the planning and evaluation of effective programs to instruct members of the academic community in the identification and use of information resources, the following guidelines for bibliographic instruction in academic libraries are suggested:

The library should:

(1) assess the needs of its academic community for orientation to the library's facilities and services, and for instruction in the use of the library's collections and bibliographic structure;

(2) prepare a written profile of the community's information needs;

(3) develop a written statement of objectives of bibliographic instruction which:

   (a) includes immediate and long-range goals with projected timetables for implementation;

   (b) is directed to specific identified needs within the academic community, and permits various methods of instruction for all segments of the academic community who have a need to use library resources and services;

   (c) outlines methods by which progress toward the attainment of instructional objectives can be measured. Methodology must provide for measures of learning, attitude and cost.

(4) provide continuing financial support for bibliographic instruction,

   (a) clearly identifiable within the library's budget program and statements;

   (b) sufficient to provide the professional and supportive staff, equipment, materials and facilities necessary to attain the delineated objectives.

(5) employ librarians and other qualified staff to plan, implement and evaluate the program,

   (a) inclusive of persons with training in: various academic disciplines, the identification and use of library resources, teaching skills, preparation and use of audiovisual and other instructional materials, preparation and use of evaluative instruments, clerical skills;

   (b) in sufficient numbers necessary to attain the delineated objectives;

   (c) clearly identifiable and of a status similar to persons responsible for planning, implementing and evaluating the other major functions of the library.

(6) provide facilities, equipment and materials

   (a) to accommodate the preparation of instructional materials and the presentation of various modes of instruction (individual, small or large group, lecture, discussion, media, etc.);

   (b) of sufficient size, number and scope to accommodate the attainment of the delineated objectives.

(7) involve the academic community in the formulation of objectives and the evaluation of their attainment.

(8) evaluate regularly the effectiveness of the instructional program, and demonstrate substantial attainment of written objectives. ■■

Reprinted from the April 1977 issue of College & Research Libraries News, a publication of the Association of College and Research Libraries.

should at least be aware of both outlines. We present both in this chapter, with commentary resulting from our experience in writing and administering materials designed, in large part, to achieve the goals and objectives listed in, first, the ACRL Task Force statement, and then the Wisconsin outline. Any operable system which encompasses workable means to meet the goals and objectives included in these two outlines will almost certainly be well directed toward meeting the needs of the vast majority of today's college students, irrespective of whether they begin their collegiate experience in a two- or a four-year institution.

ACADEMIC BIBLIOGRAPHIC INSTRUCTION: MODEL STATEMENT OF OBJECTIVES

ACRL Bibliographic Instruction Task Force

(Note: T stands for Terminal objective; E for Enabling objective)

General objective:

> A STUDENT, BY THE TIME HE OR SHE COMPLETES A PROGRAM OF UNDERGRADUATE STUDIES, SHOULD BE ABLE TO MAKE EFFICIENT AND EFFECTIVE USE OF THE AVAILABLE LIBRARY RESOURCES AND PERSONNEL IN THE IDENTIFICATION AND PROCUREMENT OF MATERIAL TO MEET AN INFORMATION NEED.

T1. *The student recognizes the library as a primary source of recorded information.*

E1. Given a list of information needs and services which can be best handled by a variety of campus units, the student correctly identifies the library as the best unit for at least 85% of the appropriate listings. For example, given a list of 25 information needs or services of which 14 are best handled by the library, the student correctly suggests the library for 12 of those 14 items.

COMMENT: At a time when the function and services of academic libraries, learning resource centers, media centers, and various learning laboratories are as multifarious as their designations, it is little wonder that a student fresh out of high school or returning to college after a career or other nonacademic experience is often confused about just what to expect from the changing institution(s) once comfortably designated "library." Assumptions about library users' expectations and prior experience are therefore to be carefully examined. The disarray and wide local variations in the provision of academic support services in today's colleges more than justify a clear explanation of just what functions an academic library/ learning resource center is, in fact, designed to provide. In our experience, over 95 percent of entering students admittedly had had no significant experience with libraries in their elementary and secondary educational experience, hard as that is to imagine. Our surveys definitely support the high probability that most of the students we deal with are having their first real contact with libraries, and are consequently quite naive about what to expect. In providing instructional material, it is good to concentrate on services and functions specific to a given institution, with lesser provision for imparting an idea of the types of services which can be expected from *any* academic library, irrespective of designation or local variations. It is surprisingly easy to prepare students for the use of a specific institutional library, which, after all, is designed to meet his immediate needs, while ignoring the high mobility of current generations of students. Two-year institutions should be particularly sensitive to this need for general applicability of library skills acquired in the first years of college life.

T2. *The student recognizes the library staff, particularly the reference staff, as a source of information, and is comfortable seeking assistance from staff members.*
E1. Given a map of the library, the student is able to locate key service points (e.g., circulation, reserve, periodicals). The student can identify the location of information and/ or reference area(s) of the library.
E2. The student can identify the members of the reference staff by sight and locate their offices.
E3. (If applicable) the student can identify by name the members of the reference staff best qualified to assist him in his subject major.
E4. The student asks the reference staff for assistance whenever library-related information is needed.
E5. When asked about library services, the vast majority of students will respond positively to questions such as: "Are there people within the library who are willing to give assistance in locating needed information?" "Do these people give competent assistance?"

COMMENT: While these matters are dealt with in more detail elsewhere in this volume, it is worth noting that such behavioral objectives are some of the trickiest to measure, yet utterly crucial indicators of the degree of success or failure of any library instruction program. They are so completely interlocked with the actual provision of services and the manner of their provision that it is difficult to separate the knowledge that a certain service is potentially available from a given source and the actual utilization of that resource with regular ease and confidence. In institutions where an active, successful library instruction program is in operation, librarians on public service duty can observe and participate daily in the type of behavior on the part of students which indicates that this terminal objective has, in specific instances, been adequately met. What we cannot measure, but can certainly sense in many ways, is the number of instances in which the objective has not been met. The student who avoids the library, the one who is too shy to ask, the one who "has a friend get it for him"—these are the ones for whom library instruction programs should be designed, and they are the reasons why we emphasize so strongly the techniques of "structured indirection" in any instructional system.

T3. *The student is familiar with (or has knowledge of) the library resources that are available to him.*

   a. *The student knows what library units exist on his campus and where they are located. The student knows what major information resources and collections are available in these units.*

E1. While seeking information from the library, students will use most campus library units which contain substantial material relevant to their topic.

E2. While using the library, students will use a variety of collections within the central library: Documents, pamphlet file, microfilm, etc., as appropriate to their topic.

   b. *The student understands the procedures established for using these facilities.*

E1. A student can sign out a library item correctly (as defined by each institution).

E2. The student can interpret library forms (e.g., overdue notices, search forms, hold requests, etc.).

   c. *The student knows about the off-campus information facilities available and how to approach their resources.*

E1. A student will ask the reference staff for advice about the possibilities of other information resources outside the "official libraries" of his college or university when those sources do not meet his needs.

E2. A student who has need of materials which the library does not have will request that they be borrowed from another library.

COMMENT: With the proliferation of cooperative library systems and networks of information sources, this goal presents a particularly difficult challenge in any library instruction program. Theoretically, the toal public information resources of the nation are, in some manner or other, available to any student, together with some international sources, should he have need of them. On-campus sources and procedures for their utilization tend to present the fewest problems, though ever-developing types of student services should keep the public service librarian very much aware of new information outlets developing from sources as divergent as computer science departments and offices of institutional research or psychometry. Campus publications of even small institutions are not always up-to-date on new information sources developing in one's own institution. Certainly, the librarian should be aware of these sources and their potential for the students' needs.

Necessary forms and procedures for utilization of immediately available library resources can be quite mystifying to the novice, obvious though their function and use are to the initiated. Off-campus resources are an ever-changing and apparently expanding source of potentially useful information to the college student. "Sunshine laws" in many states have opened up sources of primary data formerly out of reach to most students and even professional researchers. New "information and referral" services in many metropolitan areas are now legitimate information sources for the adult student, irrespective of his present state of sophistication. The extent to which these can, or should, be included in a program of library instruction is, we believe, too subject to local variation to merit any firm recommendations regarding inclusion or exclusion. It is possible to make distinction between "immediate" and "removed" sources of information whereby emphasis in first-level library instruction should be on the former. Hopefully, a sufficiently thorough presentation of immediate resources should imply and provide access to such "removed" sources as are germane to the educational process at hand.

It is easy to "drown" a naive student in the very information media in which one is attempting to teach him to swim. If the principle of providing keys for individual discovery is maintained, it should be possible to instill a conviction, and perhaps even the habit of conceiving that one piece or source of information can unlock another. In actual practice the exigencies of limited time and span of student interest will determine which potential sources of information are secondary and to be left to the student's own process of discovery. If instruction is limited to those materials and techniques which are basic and common to all information discovery processes, the student can, by analogy and the pressure of immediate need, apply the techniques already mastered to achieve a specific goal.

T4. *The student can make effective use of the library resources available to him.*

   a. *He knows how to use institutional holdings records (such as the card catalog and serials holdings lists) to locate materials in the library system.*

E1. Given a map of the library, the student can correctly identify the location of the library's catalog (e.g., card catalog, book catalog, public shelf list) and other holdings lists in 3* minutes

E2. The student will correctly identify and explain the purpose of selected elements on a sample catalog entry in 5* minutes. The selected elements will include: The author, title, place of publication, publisher, date of publication, series title*, bibliographic notes, tracings, and call number.

E3. Given a topic or list of topics, the student will accurately list the items found in the catalog on those topics in a specified period of time. The topics will include items which require the student to use the U.S. Library of Congress *Subject headings used in the dictionary catalog of the Library of Congress.* The student will also have to demonstrate his knowledge of form subdivisions, and subject filing rules such as (that governing) historical subdivisions filed in chronological order.

E4. Given a list of materials, the student in a specified time, can correctly identify and locate those materials which the library owns. The list shall include incomplete citations, (and citations which are listed under entries other than the "main entry." It will also include:

    Book (individual author)
    Book (corporate or institutional author)
    Journal (recent issue)
    Journal (older or discontinued title)
    Newspaper
    U.S. Document
    Pamphlet
    Nonbook materials
    Microform
    Other, as appropriate to the institution

This list will include items which require the student to demonstrate his knowledge of selected filing rules such as: initial articles are ignored in filing, abbreviations are filed as if spelled out, Mc is filed as if spelled Mac, numerals are filed as if spelled out.

b. *He knows how to use reference tools basic to all subject areas.*

E1. Given a map of the library, the student can correctly identify the location of the reference department (and its catalog) in a specified time period.

E2. In a specified time period, the student can identify major reference tools (encyclopedia, dictionary, index) in an unfamiliar field using a guide to the literature such as *Winchell's Guide to Reference Books,*

E3. In a specified time period, the student can list five periodical titles (and the indexes which cover them) in an unfamiliar subject field using a directory such as *Ulrich's International Periodical Directory.*

E4. In a specified time period, the student will list five titles available on an unfamiliar topic using a bibliography such as *Subject Guide to Books in Print, Bibliographic Index,* Library of Congress *Books' Subjects.*

E5. Given a topic with which the student is unfamiliar, in a specified time period, he will locate a general introduction to that topic and at least two references to further information, using an encyclopedia. The topic as stated should require the use or the encyclopedia's index to locate relevant materials.

E6. Given a sample entry, the student will correctly identify selected elements of a typical periodical index entry in a specific period of time. These elements will include: title of article, title of journal, volume date, author pages.

E7. Given a list of topics and a list of indexes (such as *Reader's Guide, SSHI, ASTI, PAIS*), the student will select the index which best covers each topic. At least 85%* of the students' selections should be correct.

E8. Given the author and title of a book, the student will locate a review of that book in a specified time period using a book review index such as *Book Review Digest* and *Book Review Index.*

E9. Given a specific topic of current interest, in a specified time period, the student will locate two newspaper articles on that topic, using a newspaper index such as the *New York Times Index.*

*E10. Given the name of a witness who has appeared before a Congressional Committee, the student can locate a complete citation to that testimony, using *CIS Index* in a specified time period.

*E11. Given a topic of recent concern to the federal government, the student can locate citations to information issued by both Executive and Congressional branches using the *CIS Index* and the *Monthly Catalog*.

*E12. Given a specific need for statistical information on the U.S., the student can locate the requested statistics and identify the agency publication from which the statistic was taken using *Statistical Abstract of the United States* in a specified time period.

   c. *The student knows how information is organized in his own field of interest and how to use its basic reference tools.*

   d. *The student can plan and implement an efficient search strategy using library, campus, and other resources as appropriate.*

   d. *The student can plan and implement an efficient search strategy using library, campus, and other resources as appropriate.*

   e. *The student is able to evaluate materials and select those appropriate to his needs.*

E1. Given a topic within his major field of interest, in a specified time period the student will compile a quality bibliography using an efficient search strategy and keep a diary of his search. A librarian and/or classroom faculty member will judge the quality of the bibliography on the following factors:

   1 80% of the entries shall meet one or more of the following criteria:

     (a) be written by recognized authorities in the field.

     (b) be represented in standard bibliographies on the topic.

     (c) appear in a recognized journal in the field.

   2. bibliographic format will conform to accepted standards in that subject field.

A librarian will judge the efficiency of the search strategy as evidenced in the diary. The diary should show that:

1. The student clearly defined his topic before or during the initial stages of the search.

2. The student considered and effectively used alternative search terms throughout his research.

3. The student consulted an encyclopedia or handbook or other general source to obtain standard data or information on his topic early in his search.

4. The student searched for and used available bibliographies on his topic.

5. The student searched relevant indexes or abstracts to update his information.

6. The student used the subject card catalog.

7. The student used bibliographies and/or footnotes in relevant materials found during his search.

8. The student used book reviews, biographical aids, or other sources to help him evaluate materials.

9. The student made accurate complete bibliographic notes and avoided repeated searches to locate or check citations.
10. The student located materials of interest to him outside the library.
11. The student consulted librarians and faculty members for aid and suggestions whenever appropriate.

(Note: Objectives marked with an asterisk are suggested, not recommended.)

COMMENT: Of the four terminal objectives, the last, of course, encompasses what should be the central body of instructional material in any library instructional program. If the objective itself is almost axiomatic, the potential means of achieving it are as varied as the aspirations of the library users who are given an opportunity to attempt it. While the wording of this, and perhaps other objectives in this statement are subject to some caviling, their sense is clear enough, in our estimation, to require little argument. In assessing the possible means of achieving this objective, it is important to return to the general objective and note its opening clause: "by the time he or she *completes* (our emphasis) a program of undergraduate studies. . . ." This should allow us to infer that acquisition of the skills enumerated in this list of objectives is a process which can be extended over a four-year undergraduate program. If so, well and good, for our experience shows that a careful, thorough program which covers all the enabling objectives listed in this outline is subject to numerous practical objections when attempts are made to fit it into a course-related system. It can quickly develop into so large a body of material that both classroom faculty and students begin to view it as an end in itself, and not as a tool for improved performance in both undergraduate and graduate educational pursuits.
As explained more fully elsewhere in this volume, we have therefore found it necessary to divide these terminal goals into *primitive* and *derivative* sections, concentrating on the former, where necessary to the exclusion of the latter. In the first two years of the undergraduate experience, a good deal of soundly based opinion holds that subject specialization, as implied in T2, E3 above, is neither necessary nor desirable. Within the limitations of what we know to be the tolerable time limit for administration of the library instructional program at our college (about ten hours, in its present form), we concentrate only on those skills which cannot be derived from prior knowledge. In other words, given an either/or choice, we eliminate or postpone introductions to specific reference titles in favor of concentration on use of the card catalog and *Library of Congress Subject Heading List* through which any reference book in our library can be located.

We have further examined and discarded the imposition of time limits in the actual application of our instructional system. We can understand their utility as a convenient measuring device both for establishing the validity and the reliability of text/test materials, but in the cultures with which we deal, time limits tend to have a negative psychological effect on the learning process. By thus increasing the stress under which a tentatively acquired skill is being demonstrated, we run the risk of pressuring the student into desperate strategies and increasing the temptation to short-circuit the system by guessing his way to a response—any response. We do keep a continuing check on the actual time required for both learning and testing aspects of our program, making adjustments as necessary at the end of each term. Though cognizant that in real life time is undoubtedly an all-important factor, (against which we are all constantly measured), in introducing new material to students whose grasp of the total learning process is tenuous at best, we feel that the artificial removal of time as a measure of performance seems worth the cost. By so doing, we eliminate one possible excuse for giving up.

Were it possible to introduce the element of *play*, where competitive timing could be used to educational advantage, we would be more than willing to employ it. Our current impressions are, however, that the introduction of such a factor should be delayed until a level of confidence is established on which this type of motivational technique can be solidly based. As with objectives *d* and *e* under T4, which involve the demonstration of critical, evaluative, and organizational skills, we fully concur with their inclusion as basic goals for any undergraduate curriculum. The unlimited exploration possible through use of virtually any American academic library is the ideal area for demonstration of the acquisition of these skills. The complexity of the skills involved, however, should result from the total educational experience at the college level rather than a "crash" course in utilization of library resources. "Intensive courses" in bibliographic techniques are about as effective as "intensive courses" in language, particularly those imposed on generations of graduate students trying to get past a language requirement for their degree. The impression may have been a strong one, but the *habit* was never formed, nor were the skills acquired under artificial pressures ever adequately integrated into a meaningful pattern for continued activity. The successful library instructional program must assiduously avoid "force feeding" and be adapted, with whatever exclusions necessary, to the level and degree of motivation available. Since levels of motivation are never constant, and in a healthy institution should presumably be seen to rise, a good library instructional program will remain flexible enough to permit adaptation and adjustment to the needs, if not of the moment, at least of the semester. The minute a program loses such flexibility, through the complexities of administration or preparation of materials, its utility quotient drops drastically and it should be placed under review for major overhaul.

SPECIFIC OBJECTIVES

Useful as any general set of goals and objectives is for both the creation and the evaluation of any educational program, in an operational program more specific, targeted objectives are necessary. Inevitably, a final degree of specificity must be achieved, and a definite, clearly stated objective must be set—for a specific group, in a specific place, at a specific time. In practice, such objectives are usually generated for a single institution at a particular time in its development and with a particular clientele in mind. The more closely these objectives can overlap with general goals such as those elucidated above, the better for all concerned. The requirement to state them in measurable, behavioral terms, as the ACRL objectives are, can occasionally impose its own operational constraints to the degree that they become, in practice, counterproductive.

What is, in our opinion, a fine statement of "multilevel," targeted objectives is presented by Stoffle as an appendix to her article in *Academic Library Instruction,* entitled "Library Instruction: The University of Wisconsin—Parkside Experience."[3] Though the program is designed for a four-year institution, we find it of sufficient interest to discuss here because of its recognition of the necessity for identification of four different target groups (students, faculty, staff, and community) and its graduated scale of content, designed to provide as nearly as possible what is needed by each group in a multilevel progression along a scale of "library sophistication." Terms such as "acquaint" and "make aware" are admittedly less subject to behaviorist measurement, but the recognition of different levels of need and provision for them in this approach seemed to us to argue persuasively for its presentation here. At each level and in each instance it would be possible, we surmise, to evaluate any application of this outline in behaviorist terms, but there may well be methods of determining the educational value and cost effectiveness of the program which are justifiably deemed more efficient and perhaps more revealing than those of the social science "laboratory" methods so often adopted by librarians and educators for this purpose. When a decision is to be made between the application of laboratory experimental controls for the production of reliable data on the one hand, and the production of a viable educational system or tool on the other, we opt for the latter—remembering that corollary of Murphy's Law which states that "under the most carefully controlled experimental conditions, the laboratory animal [read *student* in this case] will react exactly as it damned well pleases."

With these considerations in mind, we present here with minor commentary the Stoffle outline of goals and objectives as a well-stated and highly useful checklist of people and things to be considered in any system of academic library instruction. (The careful reader will note that the terms *goal* and *objective* are not distinguished as in section 1 above. There seems no reason to attempt to impose consistency where none exists.)

LIBRARY INSTRUCTION GOALS AND OBJECTIVES
(University of Wisconsin—Parkside)

The following objectives and goals are based on the following premises:

1. The library has a dual instructional role in the university setting:
   (a) supplementing existing classroom instruction and research
   (b) teaching information gathering skills which will enable patrons to continue education beyond the formal classroom setting
2. Library instruction should be designed to meet the immediate needs of the patron
3. Library instruction is a continuous process

MAJOR OBJECTIVES

1. To make faculty, students, staff, and community aware of what the library has and what it can do for them
2. To increase faculty, student, staff, and community skill and self-sufficiency in the use of the library

SPECIFIC OBJECTIVES

1. To increase awareness of the library as an educational (instructional), recreational (noninstructional), and cultural facility
2. To prepare patrons (faculty, students, staff, and community) to find and use library materials and facilities
3. To reinforce or provide supplementary instruction in research methods
4. To bring to the attention of library patrons specific materials, new items, and new services available in the library
5. To develop instructional programs that would provide new learning opportunities for all students, including the educationally disadvantaged and the gifted

GOALS

These are broken down, first, by patron category and, second, by library sophistication level within each patron category.

FACULTY

LEVEL I

Goal 1: To acquaint faculty members with the facilities and services of the library available for their use:
  a) interlibrary loan
  b) instructional program activities
  c) special workshops and programs
  d) literature searches
  e) circulation and reserve privileges
  f) order information and procedures
  g) displays
  h) current awareness activities
  i) telephone reference service
  j) photoduplication service
  k) posted bulletins of events and cultural "happenings" in the area
  l) seminar rooms and study rooms for conferences and special meetings
  m) functions of library departments

Goal 2: To acquaint faculty members with the physical layout of the library, that is, the location of:
  a) book stacks
  b) current magazines
  c) general magazines
  d) microformat materials
  e) microformat equipment
  f) government publications
  g) indexes and abstracts
  h) typing rooms
  i) special collections

j) maps and atlases
k) college catalogs
l) pamphlet file(s)
m) card catalog
n) periodical files
o) rest rooms
p) smoking rooms
q) reserve collection
r) checkout desk
s) information desk
t) phone books
u) seminar rooms
v) calculators
w) catalogs and lists from other libraries
x) browsing collection and arrangement of
   (1) the card catalog
   (2) periodicals printout
   (3) periodical location file

Goal 3: To acquaint faculty members with a "library contact person" who would be readily identifiable and would act as a friendly liaison in library-faculty interactions.

LEVEL II

Goal 1: To acquaint faculty members with the specialized research tools in their disciplines which are available in the library and, when appropriate, to demonstrate the use of each. Specific types of tools to be included would be:

a) guides to the literature
b) reviews of the literature
c) abstracts and digests
d) bibliographies and indexes
e) dictionaries
f) encyclopedias
g) directories and biographical sources
h) government publications
i) atlases and pictorial works
j) handbooks and manuals
k) yearbooks and almanacs
l) statistical sources
m) major monographic series
n) periodicals

Goal 2: To acquaint faculty members with library research tools and, when appropriate, demonstrate their use. Specific tools considered here are:

a) *Library of Congress Catalog Books: Subjects*
b) *National Union Catalog* (also, all subject divisions and

foreign counterparts)
c) *Books in Print* (also British, Canadian, French, and German counterparts)
d) *Cumulative Book Index*
e) *Union List of Serials and New Serial Titles*
f) *Ulrich's International Periodicals Directory* (also *Irregular Serials and Annuals*)
g) *Magazines for Libraries*
h) *Subject Headings Used in the Dictionary Catalogs of the Library of Congress*
i) *National Union Catalog of Manuscript Collections*

STUDENTS

Level I

Goal 1: To acquaint interested students with the physical layout and facilities of the library, so they can locate:
a) book stacks
b) current magazines
c) general magazines
d) microformat materials
e) microformat equipment
f) government publications
g) indexes and abstracts
h) typing rooms
i) special collections
j) maps and atlases
k) college catalogs
l) pamphlet file(s)
m) card catalog
n) periodical files
o) rest rooms
p) smoking rooms
q) reserve collection
r) checkout desk
s) information desk
t) telephone books
u) seminar rooms
v) calculators
w) student telephones
x) browsing collection and arrangement of
   (1) the card catalog
   (2) periodicals printout
   (3) periodical location file

Goal 2: To acquaint interested students with the library's facilities and services available for their use.
a) interlibrary loan
b) displays
c) telephone reference service

d) calculators and typewriters
e) photoduplication service
f) "bitch tickets"
g) posted bulletins of events and cultural "happenings" in the area
h) seminar rooms and study rooms for conferences and special meetings

LEVEL II

Goal: To teach beginning students how to:
a) develop search strategies based on their information needs
b) use the card catalog to be able to locate specific books by author, title, and subject
c) use the LC subject heading list to locate alternative subject headings for specific topics
d) use the *Monthly Catalog* to locate government publications
e) use the *Readers' Guide, Social Science and Humanities Index, Public Affairs Information Service Bulletin, Essay and General Literature Index,* and the *New York Times Index* to locate specific periodical articles
f) cite and evaluate sources of information used for a research paper

LEVEL III

Goal: To teach students enrolled in research- or bibliography-oriented courses the bibliography of their discipline and the mechanics of the various search strategies useful in their subject area. Specific topics dealt with would be:
a) types of sources, that is:
   (1) guides to the literature
   (2) reviews of the literature
   (3) .abstracts and digests
   (4) bibliographies and indexes
   (5) dictionaries
   (6) encyclopedias
   (7) directories and biographical sources
   (8) government publications
   (9) atlases and pictorial works
   (10) handbooks and manuals
   (11) yearbooks and annuals
   (12) statistical sources
   (13) major monographic series
   (14) periodicals
   and to demonstrate the use of the examples of each type.
b) the principles of good bibliography—citations and

sources evaluation

c) specialized techniques for locating major research materials on a particular topic, that is, the use of bibliographies and footnotes in secondary works and the use of bibliographic notes and tracings on card catalog cards

d) search techniques for preparing bibliographies, annotated bibliographies, speeches, short reports, and research papers

e) skills necessary to use bibliographic sources such as *Books in Print, Cumulative Book Index, National Union Catalog,* and the *Library of Congress Books Subjects,* the *Union List of Serials, New Serial Titles,* and *Ulrich's International Periodicals Directory* to locate materials available in a given discipline

LEVEL IV

Goal: To teach advanced students with library-related assignments the specific search strategy necessary to complete the course assignment and the specific skills necessary to use the complex tools which apply to the assignments.

STAFF

LEVEL I

Goal 1: To acquaint interested staff members with the physical layout of the library, that is, the location of:

a) book stacks
b) current magazines
c) general magazines
d) microformat materials
e) microformat equipment
f) government publications
g) indexes and abstracts
h) typing rooms
i) special collections
j) maps and atlases
k) college catalogs
l) pamphlet file(s)
m) card catalog
n) periodical files
o) rest rooms
p) smoking rooms
q) reserve collections
r) checkout desk
s) information desk
t) telephone books
u) seminar rooms
v) calculators

w) catalogs and lists from other libraries
x) browsing collection
y) arrangement of
   (1) the card catalog
   (2) the periodicals printout
   (3) the periodical location file

Goal 2: To acquaint each interested staff member with the facilities and services of the library available for his use:

a) interlibrary loan
b) special workshops and programs
c) circulation privileges
d) displays
e) order information and procedures
f) telephone reference service
g) photoduplication service
h) posted bulletins of events and cultural "happenings" in the area
i) seminar rooms and study rooms for conferences, special meetings
j) functions of library departments

LEVEL II

Goal: To teach interested staff how to use specialized tools that would help them do their jobs. Examples of types of tools considered essential:

a) directories
b) bibliographical sources
c) book trade sources

LEVEL III

Goal 1: To acquaint staff involved in specialized research or personal educational activities with the research tools available from the Library in their discipline and, when appropriate, to demonstrate their use. Specific tools considered here are:

a) *Library of Congress Books: Subject Catalog*
b) *Library of Congress National Union Catalog* (also, all subject divisions and foreign counterparts)
c) *Books in Print* (also British, Canadian, French, and German counterparts)
d) *Cumulative Book Index*
e) *Union List of Serials and New Serial Titles*
f) *Ulrich's International Periodicals Directory* (also Irregular Serials and Annuals)
g) *Magazines for Libraries*
h) *National Union Catalog's Manuscript Collections*
i) *Subject Headings Used in the Dictionary Catalogs of the Library of Congress.*

COMMUNITY

LEVEL I

Goal 1: To acquaint interested community members with the physical layout of the library, that is, the location of:

a) book stacks
b) current magazines
c) general magazines
d) microformat materials
e) microformat equipment
f) government publications
g) indexes and abstracts
h) typing rooms
i) special collections
j) maps and atlases
k) college catalogs
l) pamphlet file(s)
m) card catalog
n) periodical files
o) rest rooms
p) smoking rooms
q) reserve collection
r) checkout desk
s) information desk
t) telephone books
u) seminar rooms
v) calculators
w) catalogs and lists from other libraries
x) browsing collection
y) arrangement of
 (1) the card catalog
 (2) the periodicals printout
 (3) the periodical location file

Goal 2: To acquaint each interested community member with the facilities and services of the library available for his use.

a) photoduplication service
b) special workshops and programs
c) circulation privileges
d) displays
e) order information and procedures
f) telephone reference service
g) posted bulletins of events and cultural "happenings" in the area
h) seminar rooms and study rooms for conferences and special meetings.

LEVEL II

Goal: To teach interested community members how to locate books and magazines in the library, acquaint them with the facilities and services peculiar to the different types of libraries in the area, and demonstrate the use of general bibliographic tools, such as *Books in Print.*

LEVEL III

Goal: To acquaint special-interest groups in the community with the services and facilities pertaining to their interests available in the library (education, business, etc.).

The above Parkside outline is as good an example as we have come across of an attempt to cover the materials and the market for library instruction that provides for the degree of potential interest for each. Repetitive and "obvious" as it may appear at first reading, it is nevertheless a highly useful checklist against which to measure the coverage of any library instruction program. It seems important that at any stage of development or review of library instruction the potential breadth of the possible market at least be considered. For community colleges this is crucial, since today's well-served community member is quite likely—in fact almost certain—to be next semester's student. If the instruction program is kept modular in form, and an adequate item bank is available, good advantage can be taken of the repetitive character of both the materials and the services to be explained and of the target market, under whatever label or form it may occur.

LEEWARD'S GOALS AND OBJECTIVES

The following are sample goals and objectives our system strives for during regular semesters. All four sections are outlined here as they might appear, after staff consultation, at the beginning of the test-revision process that precedes each semester. The authors are convinced that the development of workable goals and objectives (both the enabling and terminal varieties) is a matter of successive approximations. The finished product, as presented in works such as *Writing Objectives for Bibliographic Instruction in Academic Libraries*[3] may appear a bit forbidding to the beginner, and we freely admit that ours has undergone many alterations throughout the years and continues to be revised in the light of our experience with a constantly changing market. The quality of an objective, if clearly stated in measurable terms, is just as subject to evaluation as are the student attempts to reach it. In some cases, we have discovered that a particular objective was, in fact, not necessary since it seemed to be automatically attained as an ancillary, unexpected by-product of another. Others have turned out to be inadvertently "compound" and therefore subject to division into two or more objectives. In general, our more useful objectives tend to be structured somewhere between what the ACRL Task Force on Bibliographic Instruction defines as a terminal objective and those defined as enabling objectives—something like a tightly constructed terminal objective or a loosely structured enabling objective. We think of our objectives as "learning outcomes." This format enables us to use them as constant guides as we change the situation or conditions under which the behavior or action is to be performed and as we vary test questions. As the item analysis of test questions proceeds, the feedback serves to allow us to reevaluate the objectives each semester and to adjust them accordingly.

As a matter of policy, we do not include time limits as criteria for student performance. We find that in the vast majority of cases, there is a natural fatigue, or concentration-span limit which determines a student's most productive and rewarding pace, and we prefer to identify the instructional unit more with the process of discovery (usually not subject to competitive time limits) than with some mystical point on an imaginary bell-curve. From a more selfish point of view, we find that too tightly structured objectives tend to eliminate the type of unexpected feedback from students' responses which can throw light on any number of aspects of the total instructional system. A tightly structured, programmed path toward a highly specific objective should—and does—eliminate the possibility of some fortuitous revelation of an area of linguistic ambiguity or of a cultural reaction for which provision should be made or of which advantage should be taken. The change in our system from "subjective" to "objective" test-answer forms for purposes of grading efficiency was made, and is now occasionally regretted, for this very reason. However, in the workbook exercises where learning takes place, we do retain the preferred student-constructed responses. Our opportunities to learn from our students are reduced in direct proportion to their potential opportunities for error. Wherever numbers and manpower allow, it may be worth the effort, particularly at the beginning of an instructional project, to leave the learner at least some opportunities for creative error. His efforts, however accidental, can be very useful.

Here, then, are the goals and objectives as they appeared during preparation for the autumn semester of 1978. They are presented as a set, with commentary following section 4.

LEEWARD COMMUNITY COLLEGE LIBRARY
LIBRARY INSTRUCTION UNIT

Statement of Goals and Objectives
Section 1—Library Tour
GOAL

The student will demonstrate ability to locate pertinent resources, facilities, and services of the library, show awareness of their potential uses and of the policies and procedures governing their use.

OBJECTIVES

Given appropriate cues, the student shall:

1. correctly identify/locate the:

card catalogs	bibliographic indexes
reference desk	periodical indexes
circulation services	print collection
reserve services	portrait collection
general book collection	vocational guidance pamphlets
Hawaiian/Pacific collection	newspapers
innovation collection	rest rooms
reference collection	individualized listening/ learning carrels
kit collection	microfilm readers
tape collection	map stand
government document collection	college catalog collection

current periodical
collection
back-issue
periodical
collection
phonorecord
collection
microfilm
collection

closed shelf
collection
dictionary stands

2. correctly identify call number prefix codes for special collections;
3. identify those services available to students in the library;
4. interpret correctly library policies that pertain to student utilization of library materials and services;
5. demonstrate knowledge of procedures for checking out reserve and general library materials.

CRITERION

On any given test of the above objectives, the student should demonstrate mastery of at least 80% of them before continuing to succeeding sections of the program.

Section 2—The Card Catalog

GOAL

The student will achieve a working knowledge of the purpose and function of the card catalog, learn through practice to use it effectively, and know how materials are arranged by call number on the library shelves.

OBJECTIVES

The student shall:

1. identify an accurate statement describing the function of a library card catalog;
2. identify/arrange a correctly alphabetized list of authors/ titles/subjects according to word-by-word filing;
3. identify/arrange a correctly alphabetized list of authors/ titles/subjects containing punctuation marks and locate cards in the card catalog which involve such punctuation marks;*
4. identify hyphenated words filed separately/combined and locate cards including such words in the card catalog;*
5. identify/arrange a correctly alphabetized list of titles/sub-jects involving articles and locate title/subject cards with such articles in the card catalog;
6. identify/arrange a correctly alphabetized list of author/ti-tle/subject cards involving "Mc, Mac, and M" and locate cards for such items in the card catalog;*

7. identify the correct filing form for numbers and dates and locate specified cards containing such forms in the card catalog;*

8. identify/arrange a correctly alphabetized list of authors/ titles/subjects involving abbreviations and locate cards for such items in the card catalog;

9. identify the following items on a catalog card: call number, author's name, title, joint author, edition, place of publication, publisher, date of publication, copyright date (when it differs from date of publication), pagination, illustrative matter, size, series, notes, tracings;

10. select the correct definition of "bibliography" vs. "biography";

11. locate the author card for material by an individual author;

12. locate the main entry card for a corporate author;

13. locate the main entry card for a pseudonymous author;

14. locate the main entry card for an editor/compiler;

15. locate the main entry card for nonbook material;

16. locate the card for a specified item in the title catalog;

17. locate cards for specified materials in the subject catalog;

18. locate card(s) for a given item in all three catalogs;

19. select the appropriate catalog to use—author, title, or subject—to locate cards for specified materials for given examples in each catalog;

20. demonstrate understanding of correct shelf order by LC call numbers of materials in the library by:
   (*a*) arranging at least four groups of LC call numbers in correct shelf order, with each designed to illustrate one of the four necessary points of comparison, and
   (*b*) retrieving a specified item from the library collection.

*Optional objective; not included every semester.

CRITERION

On any given test of the above objectives, the student should demonstrate mastery of at least 80% of them before continuing to succeeding sections of the program.

Section 3—Subject Headings
GOAL
The student will achieve a working ability to locate materials and discover alternate library resources using the *Library of Congress Subject Headings*.

OBJECTIVES
Given appropriate cues, the student shall:

1. select an accurate statement of the purpose and function of *Library of Congress Subject Headings;*
2. demonstrate a knowledge of the arrangement of entries in *LCSH* and the uses of standard and boldface types;
3. trace a see-reference to a usable subject heading and thence to a specific card in the subject card catalog;
4. identify see-references which refer to several different subject headings;
5. interpret 'sa' and trace reference to a specific card in the subject card catalog;
6. interpret 'xx' and trace reference to a specific card in the subject card catalog;
7. interpret '–' and trace reference to a specific card in the subject card catalog;
8. interpret '– –' and trace reference to a specific card in the subject card catalog;*
9. select examples of geographic/time/form subdivisions as they occur in the subject card catalog;
10. identify usable (and only usable) subdivisions of a specific subject;
11. select examples of local references in the subject card catalog.

*Optional objective; not included every semester.

CRITERION
On any given test, 80% of the questions on the above objectives should be answered correctly.

Section 4—Periodical Indexes

GOAL
The student will demonstrate an ability to utilize correctly and efficiently local and general periodical/newspaper indexes as approaches to the discovery of material on specific subjects not lending themselves to treatment in standard monographs.

OBJECTIVES
Given appropriate cues, the student shall:
1. locate a specified subject heading, subdivision, and sub-heading in the *New York Times Index* and identify citations under these headings;
2. identify the total number of citations under a specified subject heading and its related (see also) headings in the index to local newspapers;
3. identify the location of the current (prepublication) source of indexing for local newspapers;

4. interpret the subscription dates and format symbols contained in the list of periodicals available in the library;
5. differentiate the symbols designating volume, page, section, and column as they appear in periodical and newspaper indexes;
6. locate specified subject headings, subdivisions, and sub-headings with related (see also) headings in the *Readers' Guide to Periodical Literature* and identify described citations under these headings;
7. identify the complete title of a periodical indexed in the *Readers' Guide to Periodical Literature* from the abbreviation for that title;
8. indicate that the *Readers' Guide to Periodical Literature* is a subject/author index and identify a correct description of its scope;
9. indicate whether or not a specified periodical is indexed in a particular periodical index;
10. indicate which specialized subject periodical index is most likely to contain coverage for a specific subject;
11. locate an article on a specified subject in a particular periodical index, interpret the citation described, and indicate whether or not the article described is available in this library.

CRITERION:

On any test of the above objectives, 80% should be correctly answered before satisfactory control of the goal can be assumed.

We have found that, more than any other section of the instructional unit, section 3 (subject headings) has undergone extensive revision over the years. Beginning with a much more complete coverage of the topic, the original version was first reduced, then simplified and further reduced, with test results and student performance still indicating that there is a general absence in the background of most students of conscious experience with the manipulation of hierarchical orders as applied to abstract concepts—or even concrete examples, for that matter. Coupled with an equally general lack of facility with analogical reasoning techniques, the results are debilitating, if not actually crippling, to any facility for the discovery of an "unknown" through the manipulation of a given number of "knowns." Paralleling the problems many English teachers experience in training students to outline a theme before trying to write it, it is increasingly evident to us that for large numbers of our students there is no conscious relationship between—say—ice cream and the dairy industry, or between steel production and automobiles. Each verbal concept seems to be considered as discrete and not as a part of a system of divisions, subdivisions, sub-subdivisions, etc.

Were we to single out a primary instructional function of the library unit, it would be the opportunity offered by the system to allow the student to discover the patterned relationship inherent in any *system* of knowledge organized for use. The related difficulty that many students encounter in comprehending the decimal system which they must meet in section 2 (card catalog) is obviously connected with the general problem and demonstrates how integral is the basic thought-process involved in library organization to the daily requirements demanded of students in English classes, mathematics classes, and perhaps even their lives beyond the walls of any formal classroom. Another intriguing example continues to occur in responses to certain questions in sections 3 and 4, where the correct answer requires the turning of a page. Many students do not exhibit either the persistence, or the recognition of an incomplete "set," which should lead them to the correct answer. How very mystifying must be a world in which partials are not recognized as being recurrent and in which each "piece" appears to belong to a different puzzle.

While the breadth of coverage of these objectives may seem limited to the average librarian or scholar, as they do on occasion to us, they have nevertheless proved to cover the better part of the immediate needs of our students for information-handling tools. They are "primitive"—perhaps in several senses of the word—but when achieved by the student, they provide the common denominator from which most of his subsequent searches for information sources can be derived with minimal guidance from a professional librarian. When the actual process of paper writing occurs, the librarian is available and, by this time, a familiar and natural source of aid when and as needed for specific purposes. While satisfaction with individual scores for each section is doubtless important, as evidenced by the number of students who try for, and achieve, perfect "100" averages, it is the individual pride in mastery over the material itself that is consistently mentioned in student evaluations.

Notes

1. *CRL News,* no. 4 (April, 1977), p. 92.
2. Kirk, Thomas. "Bibliographic Instruction—A Review of Research." In *Evaluating Library Use Instruction,* ed. Richard J. Beeler, p. 18. Ann Arbor: Pierian Press, 1975.
3. Stoffle, Carla J. "Library Instruction: The University of Wisconsin—Parkside Experience." In *Academic Library Instruction,* ed. Hannelore B. Rader, p. 36. Ann Arbor: Pierian Press, 1975.

Chapter Three

Program Production and Evaluation

Librarians are well aware that the average high school student or college freshman does not know how to use a library effectively, nor does the prospect of learning generate much enthusiasm. We believe this is so because most library instruction programs have been ineffective. They have not been integrated with course work, and therefore appear irrelevant to the student. A conscious attempt to make the content meaningful—concerned with problems students frequently encounter—has been lacking. Our experience has been that, when relevant motivation is provided, the students participate willingly and feel that they have had a very meaningful learning experience. There is absolutely no question that library instruction is worth the effort involved. An overwhelming majority of the students who take our unit claim it to be the single most valuable learning experience they have had and feel that it should be required of all entering students.

The unit described here is *basic* library instruction. It does not cover individual reference books, as we feel the time to do that is when the student has a specific need that such reference materials will answer. As we continue to develop additional units in conjunction with other courses, we plan to cover the major reference sources that are of value to those particular courses and necessary for the completion of assignments therein. We intend also to develop instruction in research techniques geared to the particular course (see Introduction).

The preliminary elements that we consider essential to an effective program of library instruction are *student motivation* and *staff enthusiasm*. To our way of thinking, the most viable means of stimulating student motivation is to make the instruction part of a curriculum requirement. We suggest determining those areas of the curriculum to which a unit of library instruction seems most appropriate and approaching the respective faculty members with suggestions. Bearing in mind that some faculty members are apt to be defensive, a useful approach might be to ask the faculty member what assistance he would like to have the library provide to help his students obtain the maximum benefit from his course. Working directly with the instructional faculty to gain a full understanding of how they perceive the relation of the library to their courses seems to us to be the best way to develop a unit to meet their needs. The working relationships that evolve in such undertakings need to be sustained, both because the continued cooperation of the faculty is necessary in allowing adjustments and revisions in the unit, and because student attitudes often reflect those of the instructor.

Where cooperation is not forthcoming, the library staff might prepare in draft form a unit appropriate to a particular course and suggest that something along those lines might help students achieve the course objectives. The suggestion of accepting the unit as extra credit or as an optional course objective is frequently quite attractive to an instructor. In many cases he will provide additional input to develop the unit to meet the specific needs of the situation. Even if the draft unit is not acceptable, all is not in vain, because much of it can probably be adapted to another selected area. Approaching an instructor with the offer of an idea to be developed cooperatively is a particularly useful strategy.

The second essential, staff enthusiasm, may not be as responsive to promotional endeavors as the first. Administrative support is, of course, fundamental. Another requirement is staff acknowledgment that the promotion of efficient, effective use of the library's resources is a primary function of an academic library. Realization of the futility of offering a variety of services and a fine collection of resources when the potential user of these services and resources does not know how to avail himself of either, should help to generate staff enthusiasm for the project. Our purpose here is to provide a proven, effective framework, and our hope is that there are service-dedicated library staffs who will find adaptations possible for their needs. We recommend involving as many as possible of the professional staff in the instructional function of the library. In some situations it may be necessary to settle for only one or two enthusiasts supported by a few others with varying degrees of interest, but at the very least there must be a good core of enthusiasm for the project.

These two preliminary essentials are interrelated; staff enthusiasm must be present to secure the faculty cooperation necessary to acquire the course relevance requisite for student motivation. In addition, total administration of the program by the library staff is related to the presence of these two essentials. Faculty acceptance of a library instruction unit as an intrinsic aspect of a course is greatly facilitated when there is total administration of the unit by the library staff. Staff willingness to absorb the operational tasks will, of course, be proportionate to their enthusiasm for the unit. Total administration requires that a healthy portion of staff time be allocated to this function; without such conditions it is doubtful that staff enthusiasm can be encouraged and maintained. Such an allocation of staff time (30 percent in our case) obligates the library to a major commitment to its instructional role.

This commitment to the instructional role of the library must exist, staff enthusiasm must be generated, and student motivation through faculty cooperation must be fostered in order to insure a successful program. From this nurturing base, the basic tenets and restricting parameters within which the program is to be developed can be formulated. These tenets and parameters will, of course, vary with the individual situation, but the guidelines which follow can provide the basic elements.

First of all, it is necessary to establish the needs of the target group. These needs should be listed in order of priority so that judicious eliminations can be made if time restrictions so dictate. The instructor of the course may want to determine the average amount of time his students should spend on the unit. If the library staff determines this time parameter, care should be taken to be reasonable. Avoid a tendency to plan for more time than the instructor would want to allocate. It is best to present a small amount of material well. Skimming through a mass of material is not usually productive of much student learning. One is, after all, dealing with an instructional unit that is a small part of a course, not a complete course in itself.

As we stated above, when designed as a small portion of a regular course the unit provides to the greatest degree one of the essentials of the program—student motivation. A separate course for credit tends to attract only those students who need the instruction least. This situation is particularly true in a community college. We have found that those students who at the outset resist library instruction often become the ones who are most deeply appreciative of the experience once they have completed the unit.

When the instructional needs have been identified and reduced to a workable package, the instructional objectives can be stated. And their statement leads to the identification of enabling objectives. Before we proceed further in the discussion of objectives, we shall discuss the determination of the teaching strategy or instructional format. This issue has great bearing on the form that the means for evaluating student learning will take.

In our case, the determination of instructional method was limited primarily by the fact that we worked within the regular library budget. This condition has had its positive aspect, for we now know that any library should be able to afford to adapt the program to its needs within existing budget constraints.

We first agreed that the method should be based on the following precepts:

1. Within course-related time frames, students should be able to start, stop, and resume the instruction at their own discretion any time during regular library hours.

2. Instruction should take place in the library, thus affording the student realistic experiences.

3. Whenever possible, students should be actively involved in handling, observing, examining, and using those things about which they are being instructed.

4. Students should be given the option of receiving the instruction via audio or visual means.

5. Students should be able to self-evaluate their comprehension of everything they are taught, bit by bit as they progress through the instruction, by means of workbook exercises.

6. There should always be a professional librarian close by from whom students should be encouraged to request any assistance they may wish.

7. Students should be given a test to evaluate their learning on the completion of each section of instruction. Tests should be given in the library, unobtrusively monitored by the librarian. As in the instruction, tests should involve the student in actually using library resources. The tests should parallel the self-tests of the workbook.

8. There should be a battery of at least three versions of each test, and their distribution should be rotated in order to diminish the likelihood of two students taking the same test at the same time.

9. If a student is not satisfied with his test score, he should be able to retest with a variant version of the test, and if still not satisfied, retest again with yet another variant version of the test. His highest score should be considered the final one.

10. Tests should be corrected within twenty-four hours. Students should be directed to report to the reference desk for their test results, thereby affording what we believe to be an extremely valuable aspect of the program: individual tutoring on each student's errors.

11. Based upon test item analysis, all instructional and testing materials should be revised each semester.

After considering various methods of instruction, we chose to use cassette tapes for the audio option and printed materials for the visual one. The factors that influenced the decision were low cost, ease of production and revision, and compatability with the criteria set forth above.

Of the many possible ways in which library instruction can be presented, selection depends upon the particular situation, the particular target group, the particular aspect of the subject, and even the particular group of librarians involved. There is no one best method. Each situation needs to be independently appraised, with the appraiser keeping in mind the characteristics, advantages, and disadvantages of each method. The following comments on some of our considerations may, however, be of some benefit in determining a proper approach.

The library lecture has been the traditional approach to library instruction, and whether accompanied by audiovisual aids or not, it has many disadvantages. For example, the student is not actively involved, however carefully he may attend. The lecture method uses up far too much professional time in repetitious activity. Moreover, there is no assurance that each lecture group will receive uniform content and quality of instruction.

Slides are widely used in library instruction, both in the lecture and as a slide-tape presentation. These are easy to use, to make, to revise, to store, and, most important for the budget, are quite inexpensive. The fact that the sequencing of slides is not unalterably fixed makes them flexible and quickly adaptable to various needs. Because ease of revision is an important consideration in library instruction, slides are preferable to filmstrips, whose fixed sequence precludes easy revision.

Motion pictures have had limited success in self-produced library instruction. Their cost is one disadvantage. Their usual advantage of giving the illusion of reality is not necessary, since one has the actual materials at hand in a library; and their advantage of showing motion is shared with television, which is both cheaper and easier to revise. The revisions frequently necessary in library instruction would cause most films to go out of date too fast to justify their expense, and making revisions in a film is far too difficult and costly. A few topics, not subject to frequent revision, and that would benefit by the use of motion, would be well-suited for motion-picture presentation. Our recommendation in these cases is to preview what is commercially available before attempting a self-produced film. For local production, we would be prone to choose videotape, with its relatively low cost, capability for immediate replay (including retaping if necessary), and ease of duplication, rather than film, even though film has the advantage of more viewing flexibility and generally better quality.

Videotaped programs offer a vehicle for presenting all other media and when used as such are very effective. The televised lecture, however, does not exploit television's potential. It is not visual enough, and too often it results in the lecturer's talking too much and at too fast a rate. A program that uses a variety of media can be very effective, however. The limitations are the lack of face-to-face relationships which enable the student to interact, the difficulty of organizing a discussion or other follow-up activities, the absence of consideration for individual differences in students, and the considerable amount of time, staff commitment, and money necessary to produce an effective presentation. Holley and Oram advise that "a year is not too long to prepare a finished script from its committee and planning stage until it is filmed."[1] If motion is a necessary element, videotape appears to be more feasible for library instruction than does the motion picture.

Programmed instruction, whether it is presented by machine or nonmechanized means, is especially well suited to any step-by-step type of instruction. Library instruction conforms to this type of requirement and thus adapts very well to programming. The advantages of individual pacing, active participation of the student, and receipt of immediate reinforcement, as well as a thorough evaluation by the developer of the complete instructional program (forced by the programming process), all contribute toward making programmed instruction not only a viable but a preferred method of library instruction. The obvious advantage of nonmechanized, programmed instruction is its low cost. A programmed unit can be self-produced on a nominal budget and can be very effectively presented in book form.

Teaching machines for programmed instruction have the advantage of being able to present quality visuals in color, but there is no reason to show a picture when it is possible to have the student observe the actual thing. Some disadvantages of teaching machines are that only one student at a time can be accommodated, danger of loss, mechanical difficulties, and high initial expense.

Teaching machines, however, are relatively inexpensive compared to the computer. Cost is a prime consideration with computer-based teaching systems. Some of their many fine advantages are aptly enumerated by Axeen.[2] More versatility and flexibility than other types of teaching machines possess enables programmers to present a variety of materials in an interesting manner to a variety of learners. The learning sequence of the student is carefully controlled by the computer, which prevents cheating and forces the student to comprehend each frame. Every constructed response is judged immediately for accuracy, which leaves no student wondering whether his response is correct or incorrect. In addition, a complete record of student learning responses is tabulated by the computer for further analysis. Parts of a program can be easily changed or modified without disturbing the entire program. A computer can reduce the time required to bring a student to a satisfactory level of performance.

Some disadvantages of computers are the necessity for initial operational instructions and slow achievement of ease of use, mechanical breakdowns of terminal equipment, computer "downtime" due to malfunctions somewhere within the system, and time-sharing problems. The extremely high cost, however, is the prime deterrent. Except in cases where computer/terminal access is essentially free of charge, computer-based instruction is generally not economically feasible.

The audio-tutorial approach is a very effective method for library instruction, whether it involves tape in combination with slides, with printed material, with other media formats, or audiotape alone. For the initial portion of any library orientation or instructional program (a tour of the facility), we have concluded that the audiotape is the most effective approach. With the use of a small portable tape cassette player, students can be guided through the tour individually, be free to stop and examine any aspect, repeat any portion desired, and of course, may do so at their own pace.

For the more substantive aspects of library instruction, it is advisable to combine the audiotape with another medium. The slide/tape is one of the most common methods.[3] It has the advantage of being relatively inexpensive to produce, and the cost of required equipment is comparatively low. The equipment is also durable and easily operated, making it appropriate for individual student use. Both slides and tape are easily revised—an important point for library instruction.

Literature on the subject reports very little on the use of audiotape combined with printed material, which we finally concluded was the method most compatible with our proposed criteria. Gardner tested the production difficulties and effectiveness of three types of audio combinations: tape/filmstrip, slide/tape, and tape with printed material.[4] He concluded that the latter was the most successful from the users' standpoint, and that it was also the easiest and least expensive to produce and present.

We agree with Barbara Phipps, who found some fault with all library instruction methods commonly used and who feels that only through individual aid can the student really be helped.[5] Of course, giving individual aid in basic library use to all who need it is unrealistic considering the enrollment figures of most institutions. We have, however, retained this "best" method in a workable and logical form by having students learn on an individual, self-paced basis with easy access to a librarian for one-to-one assistance with any difficulty they may encounter, plus one-to-one tutoring on test errors. The bulk of the instruction is handled by the student himself, leaving only areas of confusion or misunderstanding for the one-to-one method to clarify.

For the instruction the student receives on an individual, self-paced basis, we have combined what we consider the best attributes of two methods that appear to be well suited to library instruction: the audio-tutorial approach and programmed learning. The format is not programmed learning in its purest form. However, it does use the step-by-step presentation of information followed by a workbook exercise requiring a response by the student at each step to test the level of achievement. It also retains the programmed advantage of immediate reinforcement, which assures a high level of success. The student knows he is learning correctly, and the instructor is ensured that the student is learning. Our program contains the self-pacing advantage of both programmed and audio-tutorial methods. It also provides for the active participation of the student, who must respond physically as well as mentally to every step in the instruction.

The entire library unit now consists of four sections and takes an average of eight to ten hours to complete. Librarians present a short introduction to the unit in the classrooms of each participating instructor. They describe the purposes of the unit and recommend procedures for undertaking it. A short pretest (see Chapter 6) is also administered at this time. The student picks his own time to begin and completely manages all his time involved in completing the entire unit. Each of the four sections has its own cassette tape and pamphlet (see chapter 4), so that the student has the option of learning by listening or by reading, or both. These tapes and pamphlets are kept on reserve for use within the library—a logical restriction because of the "hands-on" method of instruction. Each student is given a workbook containing examples and self-correcting exercises (see chapter 5). Each workbook question covers one point of instruction or one enabling objective.

On completing the preparation for an exercise, either by listening to that portion of the tape or by reading that portion of the pamphlet, the student is directed to test his understanding by doing that particular exercise in the workbook. Both the instruction and the exercises employ a "hands-on" technique in which the student is required to use the actual library resources he is learning about. He self-corrects his workbook exercises, using the answer sheets in the workbook, and if he finds that he has not comprehended the instruction, a "doublecheck" exercise is provided so that he may retest himself after reviewing the instruction. A reference librarian is always available to give whatever assistance is wanted.

After the student completes each of the four instructional sections, he is given a test (see chapter 6) that parallels the workbook exercises. These tests, administered within the library, also require that he use the actual library resources. Tests are graded within twenty-four hours of completion. Students are instructed to return for a review conference when their papers have been graded and before they undertake the next section of the unit. In the event that this review shows a continued lack of understanding of the material in the tape/pamphlet, the student is advised to review the instruction and retest before moving on to the next section. The student may retest twice and is given a variant version of the test each time. So far, this measure has proved to be sufficient. With three versions of each test available, rotation of alternates assures that at virtually no time is more than one version of a test in use, and students cannot predict which version will be given them.

Scores are reported regularly to each instructor as each student progresses through the unit. No pressure is placed on the student (by the librarian at least) to complete any section by any given time. To assure smooth operation, instructors are requested to advise their students to complete the unit prior to the time they will require its application in doing research paper preparation. This has so far proved to be sufficient to stagger the volume of students within the four-part cycle and to avoid end-of-semester pile-ups.

Involving the student in real experiences—relevant "hands-on" learning whereby he is actually using the library resources he is learning about—is an important aspect of the program. There is a reinforcement factor involved, and the learner's ability to retain information and skills is maximized for those tasks actually performed. It also assures proof of competence—or need for remedial review.

The use of this strategy creates a few additional tasks for librarians, but it is well worth that price. A bank of clean replacements is kept for all catalog cards, index pages, and so on, involved in the instruction. Replacements are also necessary for cards and pages containing recurring wrong answers and those cards and pages preceding and following that are subject to wear. Annual replacement is usually sufficient.

It is also necessary to keep student dispersal in mind when designing the involvement activities to avoid overcrowding in one area. For example, an exercise that requires the student to use the "L" section of the card catalog should be preceded and followed by exercises that place the same student at another area of the card catalog. When the exercise involves indexes, a variety is used to obtain this dispersion.

A checklist is kept of any information contained in the instruction that needs periodic checking. For example, if the students have been directed to look up a particular subject heading and to determine that there are x number of cards that list it, someone will need to check periodically to determine that this number of cards has not changed. If it has changed, revisions must be made. This requirement does not, in our experience, occur frequently enough to be a problem.

With freshman English students established as the target group, their library needs identified and listed in order of probable degree of usefulness, we then reduced the list to fit within a workable time framework. Our approximate goal was nine hours for the total package, the equivalent of one week of freshman English course time (3 credit course: 3 hours of class time plus 2 hours of preparation time for each hour of class time). We had chosen the instructional method, thus our next step was to write the terminal objectives and the enabling instructional objectives to meet the established needs.

In writing objectives, one must be sure that they are in logical sequence. Sometimes additions are necessary to form sequential bridges. For example, one may have an objective that meets the need for the student to know how to obtain material on reserve in the library, but in order to meet that objective one must first add another that will cover his knowledge of where the reserve collection is and what it is. Behavioral objectives should be very specific and, of course, measurable. This sequential list of objectives becomes a program or unit outline and the guide for the development of all phases of the unit.

Our unit is composed of three phases: instruction, workbook examples and exercises, and post-tests. (Although a pretest is part of the unit, we consider it an optional adjunct.). Each of the three phases uses "hands-on" experiences as much as possible. We considered combining the instruction with the workbook exercises but decided against doing so for two reasons. We felt it would discriminate against and discourage the student who may prefer to learn by listening to the tapes. The second reason is that by keeping the instruction and the workbook separate we gain the advantage of controlling an essential factor—we force the student to work *in the library* for the hands-on experience. If the instruction were in a student-owned book, our past experience indicates that he would bypass this essential aspect, thereby diminishing the effectiveness of the unit.

The student keeps his workbook, and it becomes a future guide and reference for him. These workbooks are inexpensively produced, frequently revised, and distributed free of charge. Where this system is possible, it is recommended, particularly for new instructional programs where the establishment of a precedent is involved. The ready availability of instructional tools foils the procrastinator("I left my book at home, so I can't work on it today") and removes some potential objections (cost to student) by concerned faculty. The persistent disadvantage to this type of in-house production of materials is, of course, the limitation imposed by production facilities. Professional typography, layout, and design contribute a great deal to the effectiveness of learning materials. For the imaginative developer with some budgetary flexibility, modern offset techniques do allow the interspersing of professionally produced graphics, for instance, with locally produced and frequently altered text. Once a particular design has proved to be a useful teaching device, it should be considered for more elaborate format as a permanent aspect of the system. In approaching this stage, however, the flexibility of low-cost local design seems to outweigh the merits of more elaborate, less flexible software. For decisions affecting both form and content, a consistently applied system of evaluative criteria and techniques is absolutely crucial, and it is to this matter that we now turn.

MEASUREMENT AND EVALUATION

Use of the library instruction unit by the Language Arts Division faculty has increased steadily over the past five years, despite a stabilization and slight drop in the total number of students registered. The total number of sections undertaken, as measured by the tests graded and recorded, rose from 4,526 to 4,715 during the academic year 1977–78, and the trend continues. Tables 1–4 below indicate the distribution of first attempts and retests for each section of the unit. Within these totals are a very few individuals who, for personal reasons, chose to pursue the unit on their own and not for course credit. Over 99 percent, however, represents students engaged in one stage or other of the language arts (English) course requirements.

TABLE 1

LIBRARY INSTRUCTIONAL UNIT

FALL SEMESTER, 1977

Test #	First Attempts	Retests	%	Total
I	656	101	15	757
II	544	76	14	620
III	419	67	16	486
IV	401	50	12	451
Totals	2020	294	15	2314

TABLE 2

LIBRARY INSTRUCTIONAL UNIT

SPRING, 1978

Test #	First Attempts	Retests	%	Total
I	551	110	20	661
II	428	84	20	512
III	393	55	14	448
IV	375	34	09	409
Totals	1747	283	16	2030

TABLE 3

LIBRARY INSTRUCTIONAL UNIT

SUMMER, 1978

Test #	First Attempts	Retests	%	Total
I	101	19	19	120
II	79	23	29	102
III	68	11	16	79
IV	63	7	11	70
Totals	311	60	19	371

TABLE 4

LIBRARY INSTRUCTIONAL UNIT

FALL SEMESTER, 1978

Test #	First Attempts	Retests	%	Total
I	722	170	24	892
II	510	87	17	597
III	443	140	32	583
IV	409	60	15	469
Totals	2084	457	21	2541

As basic steps toward the ultimate goal of evaluating the instructional/testing system as a whole, the type of basic tabulation illustrated in these simple tables indicates not only probable workload for staff, but something of the activity that is taking place. Attrition figures in the column First Attempts, for instance, conform closely to those for the English classes as a whole (as they should). Retests as a percentage of First Attempts is a good indicator of the level of difficulty of that section compared to its counterparts and to the whole. For new instructional programs and for those without access to elaborate, computer-produced analyses, a minimum of common-sense statistics will often provide useful guidelines and indicators of effectiveness.

Two types of evaluative procedures have been in effect since the very beginning of this library instruction program. Students who undertake the instructional program are asked, as they complete the final section, to fill out a short questionnaire, an example of which (with a typical sample of results) is included below. These student appraisals are circulated regularly to library staff engaged in preparing and revising materials, so that there is amost no lag between the discovery of an error, or of an area requiring attention for other reasons, and its remedy. Requests for evaluation of the unit by faculty

LIBRARY UNIT EVALUATION

To help the library staff with the continuous revision of this instructional unit, please complete this questionnaire by placing a check mark in the appropriate boxes and leaving this sheet in the red box on the mauka end of the Circulation Desk.

After completing this instructional unit, I feel:	to a large degree		to some degree		to a small degree		not at all		no opinion	
1. more comfortable and competent in using the library.	93	% 64	48	% 33	4	% 3		%	1	% 1
2. the experience will save me time and effort in the future.	100	68	39	23	6	4	-	-	1	1
3. the workbook exercises are useful.	88	60	44	30	13	9	-	-	1	1
4. the pamphlets provide adequate instruction.	91	62	44	30	9	6	2	1	-	-
5. the tapes provide adequate instruction.	24	16	21	14	5	3	2	1	94	64
6. the tests are fair.	88	60	41	28	7	5	2	1	8	5
7. my knowledge about how to use a library has increased.	96	66	39	27	8	5	2	1	1	1
8. my ability to handle class assignments has improved.	52	36	50	34	11		9	8	24	16
9. I understand why my professor assigned the unit.	94	64	31	21	5	3	7		9	6
10. the unit presents information which was new to me.	85	58	44	30	13	9	3	2	1	1

Completion of the unit required about   Mode = 8   hours
                                        Median = 8.45

COMMENTS: *In the space below, please make any comments you wish -- including suggestions concerning any area which you feel needs improvement or clarification.*

Name _____

(Optional)

who require it as part of their courses are made each semester and regularly produce little or no response. One notable exception is the reply that prompted creation of the pretest (see Appendix 2), which, though having been considered for several years by the library staff, was finally produced in response to a faculty suggestion. We frankly confess to a degree of opportunism is this instance, for previous attempts to establish separate control groups for testing had proved nearly impossible, and the opportunity to work with pre-and post-test data offered an equally valid means of measuring instructional outcomes.

Following the stabilization of instructional objectives, content, and format, the most significant development of the past couple of years has been the establishment of a system for the utilization of the University of Hawaii's facility for computer-assisted instruction called "EduComp." Prior to the availability of this service, statistical analyses of tests and test scores had been done by hand in an attempt to identify by laborious item analysis those questions and areas of instructional material requiring revision. While the more sophisticated calculations were beyond our reach at that stage, it was still worth the effort to identify measures of central tendency. With a constantly shifting body of thirteen tests and some 360 test items each semester to be evaluated and, if necessary, revised, analysis is a project ideally suited to the computer's abilities. Considerable adaptation of both logistics and materials were necessary to meet requirements for complete computer analysis of all our test materials. The two years of efforts toward that goal have proved eminently worthwhile. Summary tables for the fall and spring semesters (1977–78) are presented below. While a full analysis of their implications is beyond the scope of this volume, it is worth noting that, when reviewed by Leeward's psychometrist, attention was called to the excellent overall consistency of results for such a complex, cooperative venture, and the establishment of Kudor-Richardson and Spearman-Brown indexes of reliability for "teacher-constructed" tests.

In 1977 a statistical comparison of student performance on Nelson Denny Reading Tests and the library instruction unit was made, with predicted (and satisfyingly) high positive correlation. Efforts are now underway to allow tracking of individual student performance, including library unit scores, in an attempt to identify any patterns of learning activity peculiar to individuals or to special groups for whom particular provision should be made. In the meantime, the writing and revising of test and instructional materials has become

TABLE 5

Library Unit Fall Semester, 1977 Test Data

Form	N	Mean	Median	Mode	SD	SE of Mean	RK 20	SE	Spearman Brown	SE	3rd Quartile	1st Quartile	Range	Average Difficulty
1.5	169	80	85	80	2.54	.20	.603	1.60	.553	1.70	18.41	15.13	45–100	82.13
1.6	164	80	85	95	2.71	.21	.641	1.63	.684	1.53	18.59	14.76	65–100	81.71
1.7	161	80	85	90	2.56		.631	1.55	.593	1.63	18.59	15.22	60–100	83.51
1.8	162	85	90	100	2.70	.21	.711	1.45	.709	1.46	19.16	15.84	70–100	85.49
	656													
1–R														
2–R														
2.4	180	80	85	85	2.68	.20	.659	1.57	.685	1.50	18.17	14.89	10–100	81.17
2.5	182	80	85	95	2.97	.22	.719	1.58	.762	1.45	18.55	14.74	15–100	81.07
2.6	182	80	85	85	2.48	.18	.630	1.51	.636	1.50	18.14	15.13	0–100	81.95
	544													
2–R	67	75	75	70	2.43	.28	.525	1.67	.603	1.53	16.23	13.00	45–100	72.63
3.4	146	75	80	85	2.78	.23	.666	1.50	.715	1.48	17.48	13.69	65–100	76.68
3.5	136	75	80	80	2.99	.26	.702	1.63	.700	1.64	17.50	13.17	35–100	75.85
3.6	137	75	80	80	2.77	.24	.673	1.59	.742	1.41	17.43	14.21	75–100	77.41
	419													
3–R	67	75	80	75	2.53	.31	.643	1.51	.679	1.44	17.92	14.22	50–100	79.10
4.4	135	75	80	80/85	2.85	.24	.682	1.61	.677	1.62	17.78	13.81	65–100	78.22
4.5	130	80	90	90	2.89	.25	.739	1.48	.750	1.45	18.59	15.65	25–100	83.35
4.6	136	75	80	85/90	3.39	.29	.756	1.67	.772	1.62	17.92	13.58	10–100	77.28
	401													

TABLE 6

Library Unit Spring Semester, 1978 Test Data

Test Form	N	Mean	Med	Mode	SD	SE of Mean	KR 20	SE	Spearman Brown	SE	3rd Quartile	1st Quartile	Range	Average Difficulty
781.1	138	16.42	17.00	17	2.86	.24	.712	1.53	.696	1.58	18.32	15.25	4-20	82.10
781.2	139	15.53	16.12	17	2.77	.24	.629	1.69	.639	1.67	17.51	13.82	6-20	77.66
781.3	139	15.64	15.75	18	3.03	.26	.688	1.69	.705	1.65	18.12	13.63	4-20	78.20
781.4	135	16.72	17.41	18	2.59	.22	.640	1.55	.814	1.12	18.64	15.20	8-20	83.59
	551													
781.R1	99	16.95	17.71	19	2.92	.29	.745	1.48	.742	1.48	19.01	15.72	6-20	84.75
781.R2	11	16.91	16.63	18	2.77	.84	.754	1.38	.882	.95	18.13	16.75	9-19	84.55
	110													
782.1	141	15.71	16.10	16	2.81	.24	.644	1.67	.656	1.65	17.71	14.05	6-20	78.55
782.2	143	15.99	16.56	17	2.68	.22	.651	1.58	.679	1.52	17.99	14.33	7-20	79.93
782.3	144	16.30	16.77	16/17	2.73	.23	.666	1.58	.684	1.53	18.21	15.17	6-20	81.49
	428													
782.R	84	13.50	13.93	15	3.36	.37	.724	1.76	.732	1.73	16.00	11.68	3-19	67.50
	84													
783.1	132	16.43	17.25	18/19	3.07	.27	.772	1.46	.794	1.39	18.71	14.63	3-20	82.16
783.2	137	16.02	16.90	18	3.33	.28	.789	1.53	.825	1.39	18.49	13.98	0-20	80.11
783.3	124	16.30	16.77	20	3.02	.27	.747	1.52	.778	1.42	18.65	14.30	5-20	81.49
	393													
783.R	55	15.89	15.54	17	3.18	.43	.767	1.53	.703	1.73	17.88	14.34	3-20	79.45
	55													
784.1	124	16.41	16.89	18	2.62	.24	.652	1.54	.745	1.32	18.21	15.30	7-20	82.06
784.2	127	17.06	17.36	17	2.67	.24	.727	1.40	.766	1.29	18.96	15.90	4-20	85.28
784.3	124	16.19	16.60	17	2.77	.25	.664	1.61	.547	1.87	18.26	14.63	8-20	80.97
	375													
784.R	34	15.29	15.70	16	2.54	.44	.541	1.72	.561	1.68	16.63	14.13	5-20	76.47
	34													

much more efficient with the opportunity to rely on standard item analysis and comparison of students' performance. Aside from the problems of logistics involved, we should note here that in dealing with specialists in educational measurement, particular care was required to make it clear that our whole testing program was, and is, a "criterion referenced" program, not a "standardized" testing program for which so many measures of performance are designed. The resulting statistical "skew" is purposeful, desired, and helpful if interpreted within these definitions.

Another note of warning to those fortunate enough to be able to depend on computer-produced analyses of programs of this type may be justified at this point. The temptation, once lovely stacks of green printout paper covered with beautifully produced data and tables begin to appear, is to allow them to become an end in themselves. We ourselves, have been tempted on occasion to let a known fault remain in a particular test, for to correct it in mid-semester would certainly "blow the statistics."

As it became possible to apply these accepted statistical measures to the instructional and testing instruments, we then had within reach a means of answering such rudimentary questions as "Does the system work?" and "How well does it work?" Using the pretest mentioned above, it was necessary only to compare a sample of the efforts of students prior to instruction with those of students following instruction.

The results of tabulations of the first use of the library unit pretest showed that:

1. Out of 474 answer sheets tabulated, no one made a passing grade (80% or above) on all four test sections.

   15 people (3.2%) made 80% on section 1
   16 people (3.3%) made 80% on section 2
   15 people (3.2%) made 80% or better (2 made 100%) on section 3
   9 people (1.8%) made 80% on section 4

2. Section performance. Out of 1,896 sections (474 × 4) 55 sections (2.9%) were completed with a score of 80% or better.

3. No one among the sample of students pretested demonstrated knowledge of library use sufficient to meet even the most basic college level requirements.

4. Improvement rates. Comparison of the pre- and post-test scores show dramatic improvement. While the test instruments are not

identical, they are certainly comparable and show comparable cor-
relations for validity and reliability. Table 7 below compares mean
scores and "average difficulty" (mean expressed as a percentage,
comparable to our daily test scores).

TABLE 7

Section	Pretest Mean	Post-test Mean	Pretest Average Difficulty	Post-test Average Difficulty
I		15.53–16.72		77.66–83.59
II	0.20	15.71–16.30	1.02	78.55–81.49
III		16.02–16.43		80.11–82.16
IV		16.60–17.38		80.97–85.28

Expressed as a rounded percentile, the average student improved
from a pretest score of 1 to a minimum post-test score of 78 or a
maximum post-test score of 85. The mean range of improvement on
a scale of 100 is therefore 77–84 points. From next-to-no knowledge
about library use, the average student completing the library unit
reached the 80 percent level prescribed as the satisfactory performance objective.

To those contemplating the establishment of a library instructional system at the college level, this particular type of measurement
may have significant utility in responding to those who claim that
such instruction has already been undertaken at the secondary level
and has no place in the college curriculum. With all due respect for
the efforts of many secondary school teachers and librarians to impart
basic library use skills, the figures presented above, as well as the
claim by most of the students involved that information presented
was new to them, show conclusively that a college level program is
appropriate.

The ultimate criterion for evaluation of any instructional system,
of course, is some indication of its lasting effectiveness and its ap-
propriateness to the future needs of the students who undertake it.
Follow-up studies of the type necessary to achieve answers to the
many questions we have in these areas are today far beyond our
means. Random comments from librarians at some four-year campuses to which our students have transferred are all quite positive.
Students returning from time to time to use their old college library
occasionally stop by the reference desk to thank us and comment on

the value of what they have learned here. Some proudly relate their experiences in peer-teaching others who were not exposed to an effective program of basic library instruction. Such reactions are pleasant but hardly informational. If the potential instructional role of librarians is ever fully recognized, perhaps then a measure of its effectiveness will seem worthy of serious consideration.

Notes

1.   Holley, Edward G., and Oram, Robert W. "University Library Orientation By Television." *College and Research Libraries* 23 (November 1962): 491.

2.   Axeen, Marina Esther. *Teaching Library Use to Undergraduates: Comparison of Computer-Based Instruction and the Conventional Lecture.* p. 11. Urbana: University of Illinois, Coordinated Science Laboratory, 1967.

3.   Melum, Vera V. "1971 Survey of Library Orientation and Instruction Programs." *Drexel Library Quarterly* 7 (July/October 1971): 228.

4.   Gardner, Jeffrey J. "Point-of-Use Library Instruction." *Drexel Library Quarterly* 8 (July 1972): 281–285.

5.   Phipps, Barbara H. "Library Instruction for the Undergraduate." *College and Research Libraries* 29 (September 1968): 423.

PART TWO

Chapter Four

Instructional Materials

LIBRARY TOUR

This tour of the library will be self-conducted. It will introduce you to the various kinds of library materials available for your use and the services this library offers in support of your studies. It begins at the author card catalog (straight ahead and on the right as you enter the library), describes the main floor facilities, and then proceeds to the top floor, where the general, or "main collection" of books is located.

*When you need to move from one location to another
or to perform a task, the instructions to do so will appear
in "italics," the type of printing you are reading now.*

Actually walk around as directed by this pamphlet. During the tour, be sure to stop and examine items being pointed out to you. If you look at things being pointed out and pull out drawers to examine the items they contain, you will develop a better knowledge of the materials and services that the library has to offer. By doing this, <u>you</u> <u>will</u> <u>perform</u> <u>better</u> <u>on</u> <u>the</u> <u>test</u> following the tour.

*To begin the tour, please
go to the end of the author card
catalog which is straight ahead
of you as you enter the library.
You will see an orange and white
sign stating "Library Tours
Start Here." This is where you
will start the tour.*

The Card Catalogs

There are three separate card catalogs: the SUBJECT CARD CATALOG is against the wall under the clock; the TITLE CARD CATALOG is in the middle facing the front of the library; and the AUTHOR CARD CATALOG is in the center of the room directly opposite the SUBJECT CARD CATALOG. Each of these catalogs is arranged alphabetically from A to Z. You will learn how to use all of the card catalogs to their fullest advantage in the second section of the library unit. On top of the subject card catalog you can see some large red books. These are copies of the Library of Congress Subject Headings. You will learn how to use these books in the third part of the Library Unit. Once you learn how to use them, you will be able to find information much faster in the subject card catalog.

The card catalog is your index guide, to materials in the library. In other words, it is the key to finding information in the library's collections. The library's card catalog is the place to start your search when you need to locate specific materials or information. The catalog drawers contain 3" x 5" cards. Each item in the library is represented by at least one card in the card catalog.

Take a minute now to open any drawer and look at any catalog card.

3

At the top left
corner of each card
in the card catalog
there is a "call num-
ber." This call number
tells you where to find
the item in the library.

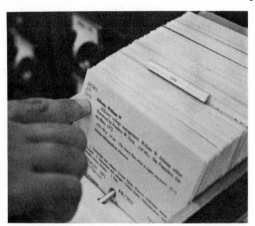

Location Symbols

A call number could be called the "address" of the item. It is composed
of letters and numbers. Often the top line of a call number is an abbreviation or word. This is a *Location Symbol* that tells you that the item can be
found in the special collection that the symbol represents. Most of the books
in the library are upstairs in the *general book collection*. The books you see
on this main floor with the card catalogs belong to *Special* collections.
Whenever a library has a large number of books with a specific emphasis or
items of a special nature, it usually organizes these things into special
collections. Here at Leeward we have nine special collections which are all
located on this main floor of the library.

4

To help you find items quickly, we have assigned location symbols to each of the special collections, as shown in the following chart:

Location Symbol	Special Collection The Symbol Represents
Ref.	Reference Collection
Map	Map Collection
Pri.	Art Print Collection
Hawn./Pac.	Hawaiian/Pacific Collection
Rec.	Phonograph Record Collection
Doc.	Government Documents Collection
Kit	Kit Collection
Tape	Tape Collection
Slide	Slide Collection

As you can see, we have made the location symbols look as much as possible like the name of the special collection they represent. That way, when you see the location symbol at the top of a call number, you know that the item is in that particular special collection and can look for it in the appropriate place. For example, if you find a book in the card catalog with a call number that starts with the abbreviation "Ref.", such as the one shown in this illustration, you will know that the book is in the Reference Collection and can go there to

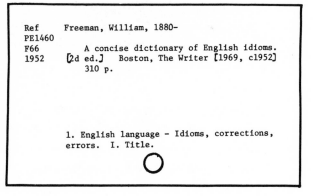

Ref   Freeman, William, 1880–
PE1460
F66   A concise dictionary of English idioms.
1952   [2d ed.]   Boston, The Writer [1969, c1952]
            310 p.

            1. English language - Idioms, corrections,
            errors. I. Title.

5

look for it instead of wasting your valuable time upstairs looking for the book in the general collection. Or, if you find an item in the catalog with a call number beginning "Rec.", you would know immediately that the item was a phonograph record album and not a book. We will review the location symbols as we come across them during the rest of the hour.

Reference/Information Desk

In the center of the card catalog area, you will see a rather long double desk. This is the place in the library to go for information and help. In most libraries this desk is called the Reference Desk or Information Desk. During library hours there is at least one librarian assigned to the Reference Desk. The librarians are there to assist you in using the library and its resources. Please do not hesitate to ask for their assistance.

Circulation Services

*Let's continue the tour now by turning to Circulation Services
at the long brown and white counter next to the library exit doors.*

Circulation Services is where you will check out materials you want to
borrow. It is also where Reserve Books, Closed Shelf material, and items in
the Kit Collection are located. To obtain any of these, you must present a
filled-out charge card to a staff member at Circulation Services. You will
need to fill out a charge card for each item you wish to borrow.

There are four items that may be checked out for three to four weeks
(depending upon the day of the week they are checked out). They are:

> Books
>
> Government Documents
>
> Pamphlets
>
> Art Prints

7

All other material may be borrowed for one to two weeks. There is no limit on the number of items you may borrow.

Any material that you have checked out may be renewed, either by taking it to Circulation Services and requesting renewal or by telephoning Circulation Services. All materials may be renewed so long as no one else has indicated a need for them.

When a library item is unavailable because a previous borrower has it, you may request at Circulation Services that it be placed on "personal hold" for you when it is returned. You will be asked to fill out a card with your name, address, and phone number. You will be informed when the item is returned, and it will be held at Circulation Services for you.

When you are returning material to the library, please use the return drops that are outside the library in the front windows beside the main exit door.

8

One drop is for records only; the other is for all other material except prints, which must be returned directly to Circulation Services since they are too large to fit through the return drops. Always return items to these drops during library hours as well as when the library is closed.

Leeward Community College Library does not charge overdue fines but remember, books, government documents, pamphlets, and art prints must be returned three to four weeks after being checked out, while all other library materials are due back in one to two weeks, depending upon the day of the week they were checked out. If you need to keep an item out beyond its due date, please *renew the loan* either by bringing it in to Circulation Services or telephoning the library and requesting that the item be renewed.

Across from Circulation Services and a few feet inside the front doors, you will see two display cases. Please walk over to them so that you will be able to have a closer view of the next areas in the library we will visit.

These cases are available for appropriate displays by students, faculty, and the general public. If you would like to display your hobby or a collection of items of interest, please see one of the librarians at the Reference Desk.

Charge-out Procedures

9

Next to the paperback exchange rack is a tall white table we call the charge-out table. The word "charge-out" is the term used for checking out a library item. Please walk over to the charge-out table for the next stop in our tour.

This table has been placed here for your convenience in charging out items from the library. If you will look under the edge of the table on either side, you will see three slots holding white cards to use when borrowing items from the library.

Most items in the library have a copy of their own catalog card attached to them. This catalog card helps you because it has all the information you will need when you are filling out a charge card. For books, we have placed

10

the card inside the front cover. If you will look at the sign holder mounted on top of the charge-out table, you will find instructions demonstrating the correct procedures for filling out charge cards.

Please take a few minutes to stop and read these signs.

When you have filled out a charge card, you present it along with the item to the person at Circulation Services. The item will be stamped with the date it is due back and given to you to take with you.

Leeward Community College Library does not issue library cards, but we request that you show some kind of identification when you borrow material. A current State of Hawaii driver's license is good when it includes your current address in raised type and can be used to imprint your identification on the charge card. If your identification does not have your name and current address in raised type, you will need to print your name and address on the charge card. We request that you use a black pen to fill out a charge card.

Reference Area 11

Right across from Circulation Services is a small room
full of books and a few carrels. This is where our tour is taking
us next so please walk over to the area shown in this picture.

This room is called the Reference Area and is the location for the
library's collection of reference books. Reference books are items such as
almanacs, directories, encyclopedias, handbooks; books that are generally consulted for a specific piece of information. They are for use only in the
library. (However, many of these books may be borrowed overnight with
special permission granted by a librarian.) When the library buys new
editions of reference books, the older edition is transferred to the general
circulation collection so that it may be borrowed. These older editions

12

still contain much information that is current. Be sure to check this alternate source before requesting special permission to borrow a reference book.

The reference collection begins on the first shelf to your left as you enter the Reference Area and continues along the shelves throughout the entire room. Notice that the beginning of the Reference Collection contains the general encyclopedias such as the *Encyclopedia Americana*. Also notice that the call numbers are typed on a white label on the spine (back) of the books. The top line of the call number has the location symbol "Ref.". All books in the Reference Collection have this location symbol above their call number. Thus, if you find a book in the card catalog with a call number beginning with "Ref.", you will know to come to this place to look for the book.

At the entrance to the Reference Area, you will see two mustard yellow file cabinets. The first cabinet contains Vocational Guidance Pamphlets, arranged in folders alphabetically by job title. If you are in doubt about what career you would like to have, this is a good place to look for information about types of jobs. Each file contains all the essential information about each job, such as the job description and training requirements. These pamphlets are arranged alphabetically by job title and may be borrowed from the library. The bottom drawer of this cabinet contains the library's Portrait Collection. The word "portrait" is the fancy (but official) description of a picture of a person. Don't confuse the library's portrait collection with the print collection. The word "print" means that the item referred to is a copy of a work of art. However, when we talk about pictures of people, we use the term "portraits." This library's Portrait Collection is of famous people throughout history. It includes portraits of U.S. Presidents, Kings, newscasters, authors, stars of the stage and many other prominent persons.

13

The portraits are arranged alphabetically by the name of the person pictured. Like the Vocational Guidance Pamphlets, items from the Portrait Collection may be borrowed from the library for one to two weeks.

The second cabinet contains course outlines of courses being taught during the current semester. These are for use in the library. The bottom drawer contains a file of Independent Study Projects done by students at Leeward.

On top of these cabinets are career announcements, including notices of current positions available with the State of Hawaii and the City and County of Honolulu.

Please stop for a few minutes and examine the items just described in the mustard yellow file cabinets. A quick review will develop familiarization with the collections they contain.

Along the back wall of the Reference Area are hung the two major local daily newspapers, the *Star-Bulletin*, the *Advertiser*; and other local newspapers, including those from the neighbor islands. The rods at the right of this section hold the most recent issues of these papers. The hanging folders contain issues of the *Star-Bulletin* and *Advertiser* for two or three months back. Issues prior to this are kept on microfilm, which you will learn more about further on in the library instruction unit. With the exception of the *Hawaii Observer* (1973-75) which is on closed shelves, the library does not retain back issues of other newspapers. Back issues of the *Star-Bulletin* and *Advertiser* may be borrowed from the library.

The carrels in the Reference Area are referred to as Bibliographic Index Carrels. They contain indexes to all types of materials available from

14

publishers and producers of audio-visual materials. If you want to buy your own book on a subject that interests you, you could use the Bibliographic indexes to see what is available, who publishes it and how much it would cost. Please feel free to ask a librarian to show you how to use these useful indexes if you are trying to track down a book or audio-visual item. We also ask that you not use the Bibliographic Index carrels for study spaces. Later on in the tour we will see many carrels set aside for this purpose. So, please leave these carrels open for people who need to use the Bibliographic Indexes.

The atlas stand is along the brick wall beside the Bibliographic Index carrels. Atlases contain maps of geographical locations in the world and, in some cases, of the universe as well. You can think of an atlas as a bound volume of maps. Atlases are classified as Reference books and are for use in the library. The reason they are kept in this special place is that atlases are usually too large to fit on the regular book shelves.

Next to the atlas stand is the map case. It contains individual maps, most of which may be borrowed from the library. A few maps are for use only in the library. The call number for each map has the location symbol "Map" as the first line.

Just before you leave the Reference area, notice the wire basket on wheels across from the map cabinet. There are several of these baskets scattered throughout the library. Please do not put material you have used within the library back on the shelves; place it in one of these baskets and the library staff will reshelve it.

15

As you leave the Reference area, please notice the tall white table jutting out from a large round post. This is the Reserve Materials charge-out table. We will be returning to this location at the conclusion of the tour for an explanation of what Reserve is and how it works. But in the meantime let us proceed with the tour.

16

To continue the tour, we must now proceed to the back left
corner of the library.

Please leave
the Reference Area
and walk back
past the Reference
Desk and card
catalogs......

......turn left
at the end of the
subject catalog and
walk past the carrels
along the wall, all
the way over to the
last set of shelving
which contains the
library's print
collection

You should now be in the position to start viewing the
library's special collections.

Print Collection

The set of shelving next to the wall contains the library's print collection. These are reproductions of famous works of art. The back of each print
has a catalog card on it which identifies the print. The first line of the
call number, in the upper left corner of the card, is "Pri.", which stands for
Print. Prints may be borrowed for three to four weeks; we will also lend you
brackets with cords to hang the prints.

After viewing the prints, please walk around to the next set
of shelving to the books which are facing the study carrels.
You may use these study carrels to do your homework.

Innovation Collection

The set of shelving next to the Print Collection contains the
Innovation Collection. These are books and magazines about teaching and
education which have been collected for the faculty here at Leeward. Students
are also welcome to use these books. Cards in the card catalog for these
books have a plastic cover over them with the phrase "Innovation Collection"
printed in blue.

Walk back the way we came through the study carrel area to
the next set of shelving we see which contains the popular
Hawaiian/Pacific Collection. Next to the brick wall you will see
a row of carrels with AV equipment. This equipment is for use
with the Business Accounting Classes.

Hawaiian/Pacific Collection

The Hawaiian/Pacific Collection is on both sides of this range of shelving. Starting on the left by the fire door are the Hawaiian/Pacific reference books, and you will notice that the top line of the call numbers for these books has the location symbol, "Hawn./Pac." for Hawaiian/Pacific and "Ref." for References. The second part of this collection contains the Hawaiian/Pacific books you may borrow, so only the location symbol "Hawn./ Pac." is used in the call number.

When you are finished looking at this collection, then go to the set of shelving next to the Hawaiian/Pacific Collection.

College Catalog Collection

The College Catalog Collection is arranged in colored boxes and shelved alphabetically by State. Over 2,000 catalogs from mainland colleges, universities, junior colleges, community colleges and specialized institutions are in this collection for your use. College catalogs may be borrowed for one to two weeks.

After viewing the College Catalog Collection, please walk around this set of shelving to look at two more popular special collections.

19

Tape Cassette
and
Phonorecord Collections

The set of shelving you are now looking at contains two of the library's special collections. The top shelf contains the library's Tape Cassette Collection. The tapes are in plastic containers which look like books and have the call number and title on the spine of the container. All of the library's tapes are cassettes and the call numbers for them begin with the location symbol "Tape" as the top line in the call number.

The remainder of this shelving contains the Phonograph Record Collection. The location symbol on the first line of the call numbers for phonograph records in "Rec.". For your convenience in browsing, we have prepared a chart of the general call number arrangement of the collection to help you find your favorite type of music. You will find the white chart posted on the end of this set of shelving next to the title catalog. You are welcome to browse through both the tape cassette and record collections and to use them with the library's media equipment, or you may check out your selections of tapes and records for one to two weeks.

At this point you should be standing in the area of the record collection with your back to the back of the title catalog. Please turn now and look at the walled-in area next to the record and tape collections. The area which you are to view next has carrels which contain AV equipment.

Individualized Learning Center

The Individualized Learning Center, consisting of 24 learning carrels, has been equipped with a variety of audio-visual equipment. The carrels in the center have filmstrip projectors, record players and two cassette tape recorders. One recorder is for monaural recordings, and the other is for stereo recordings. Feel free to use this equipment for your own listening enjoyment or to make your own tape recordings of records. The recorders are not wired together to copy tapes. Thus, if you try to copy a tape, you will only erase your master.

The carrels along the side of the Individualized Learning Center are also equipped with monaural and stereo tape cassette players plus slide projectors. This equipment may be used for listening to tapes or sound/slide combinations. The library's phonograph records, tapes, kits, slides and filmstrips may be used on this equipment. There is an instruction book for use of the equipment in each carrel. A librarian is available if you need assistance. Headphones to use with this equipment may be checked out at Circulation Services.

Beyond the Individualized Learning Center are two sets of shelving which hold the library's Periodical Collection. That is where our tour is taking us next, so please move to that area.

Periodical Collection

The term "periodical" is used by libraries for magazines which come out on a regular basis (weekly, monthly, quarterly). The first set of shelving has the most recent or "current" issue of each periodical the library subscribes to, arranged on the shelves alphabetically by title, beginning at the rear window. The second set of shelving contains older issues of these magazines arranged in the same manner. These older or "back issues" may be borrowed for one-to-two weeks; whereas the current issues may not be borrowed. Issues older than those on these back issue shelves are on microfilm, which will be explained a little further on. If you want to see if the library has a particular magazine, you can check in "Leeward Community College Library Magazine and Newspapers." Copies can be found on top of the microfilm cabinets next to the periodical shelving.

Continue walking forward through more study carrels to the last two sets of shelving.

Government Documents
Collection

The last two sets of shelving in this area of the room contain the
Government Documents Collection. These are publications of the United States
Government. They cover a wide variety of subjects, such as reports of
Congressional activities, census reports, tax information, national park
information and reports from the Office of the President of the United States.
You will note that the location symbol in each call number for this material
is "Doc.". This library is a partial government depository and receives all
government publications in selected subject areas. This material is listed
in the card catalogs and may be borrowed for four weeks.

*Please return now the way you came, past the long gray
cabinets, to the two sided carrels full of books. These books
are Periodical Indexes, the next point in our tour.*

23

Periodical Indexes

The periodical indexes are kept in six two-sided carrels behind the
author catalog. You will learn how to use these indexes in the fourth section
of this library unit. For the time being, note only their location within the
library and that they contain listings of articles in magazines and newspapers.
You will find them to be a rich source of information for writing term papers.

Plato Terminal

A PLATO terminal, near the periodical indexes, is available for your use
during regular library hours. No special permission is required. Instructions and a reservation log are beside the terminal.

24

Microfilm Collection

On the other side of the display board you will find the microfilm section, containing four tables with microfilm readers and walled in by two rows
of gray cabinets that contain the library's collection of magazines and newspapers on microfilm. Magazines on microfilm are older than the paper issues
on the periodical back issue shelves. The library buys magazines on microfilm
because with microfilm copies we can save space and assure you that an
unmutilated copy will be available.

Frequently, newspapers can be your best source of information on both
historical and current affairs. We have provided three newspapers on microfilm for your use. Three of the newspapers deal with our locality. They are
the *Honolulu Star-Bulletin*, the *Honolulu Advertiser* and the *Hawaii Observer*
(1973-78). The fourth newspaper is the *New York Times*, which is the most
comprehensive daily newspaper in the United States. Because the *New York
Times* is so packed with information, it can be found on microfilm in many
libraries throughout the nation and we are no exception. Our subscription
goes back to January 1960. Like periodicals, these newspapers are indexed
so articles can be found quickly. You will also learn how to use them in the
fourth section of the Library Unit.

The machines on the tables between the microfilm cabinets are used to
read the microfilm. The four larger ones are reader/printers, which can make
paper copies of the image projected on the screen. Instructions for doing
this are on the machines and the cost is ten cents a page. Since almost all

of our magazines and newspapers are on microfilm you will eventually need to use these machines in your research. You are not expected to know how to use them for this library unit. However, a self-instructional manual for their use has been provided on the tables by the readers and any library staff member can assist you when needed.

Notice now the xerox machine against the wall across from the last microfilm reader. The machine is stocked with legal size paper, 8-1/2" x 14, and operates on a coin deposit basis. For your convenience, the machine will take nickles, dimes and make change for quarter coins. However, if you need to change a dollar bill to operate the machine, you may obtain coins from Circulation Services.

Just across from the xerox machine is a table with a pencil sharpener, hole puncher, stapler, and paper cutter, which are for your use.

Go now to the aisle that runs beside the xerox machine and behind the microfilm cabinets. One side is a wall, the upper portion of which is made of glass. Through the glass you can see some shelving. These shelves contain more special collections including those on "closed shelves."

Closed Shelves

Some library material is kept on "closed shelves" behind the Circulation Services counter. We want to emphasize that closed shelf material may be borrowed in the same manner as material on the open shelves.

There are two collections of non-print or audio-visual materials on closed shelves. There are the Kit Collection and the Slide Collection. The top line or the call number, or the location symbol, for these collections are: Kit or Slide.

The bottom line of the call number for material on closed shelves will be either the words "closed shelves," or the abbreviation "c.s.". Sometimes a few spaces below a call number on catalog cards you will find the phrase "also closed shelves." This means that in addition to the book being on the open shelves there will also be a copy on closed shelves. Thus, if you can't find the book on open shelves, you can ask for the closed shelf copy at Circulation Services. This is true for many of the Hawaiian books. To charge out something from closed shelves, either for use in the library or to take home, fill out a charge card and present it at Circulation Services.

Continue down the aisle to the end of the Author Card
Catalog to the approximate area where we began the tour.

Dictionaries

Notice that at one end of the Author Catalog and at one end of the Title Catalog there are dictionary stands. On top of these stands are large unabridged dictionaries for your use. There are also dictionary stands in other areas of the library. We have placed smaller dictionaries on the shelves

inside these stands. Feel free to take the smaller dictionaries to the area
where you are studying; then return them to the dictionary stands when you
are finished.

> *Let's go to the library's top floor now. Go through the*
> *door beside the beginning of the subject catalog and up the*
> *stairs. You will see yellow signs directing you to the general*
> *book collection. After entering the top floor, make a left*
> *turn and walk past the first group of study carrels to the next*
> *aisle. Go left all the way down this aisle to the corner,*
> *where you will find a door on your left. This is the next stop*
> *in our tour.*

Typing Room

One of the more popular services provided for the students by the Leeward
Community College Library is this typing room. These typewriters are for your
use at no charge to type your reports and term papers for your instructors.
However, you must provide your own typing paper.

General Circulating Collection

The General Circulating Collection begins on the shelving in this corner
of the library. Note that each set of shelving is numbered. The collection
begins on the shelving numbered "1," where the call numbers on the spines of
the books begin with the letter "A." If you will look at the top of the
shelving, you will see a yellow sign indicating the start of the collection.
From this point on, the books are shelved in three-foot sections of shelving

28

from top to bottom down each set of the shelves and then up to the next set of

shelves, moving across aisles and making "U" turns down the other side of the

shelves. This snake-like pattern is continued throughout the library from

shelf section 1, containing the books bearing call numbers beginning with the

letter "A," to the end of the collection on shelf section 6A, containing the

books bearing call numbers beginning with the letter "Z." The diagram below

illustrates how books are shelved in their snake-like pattern.

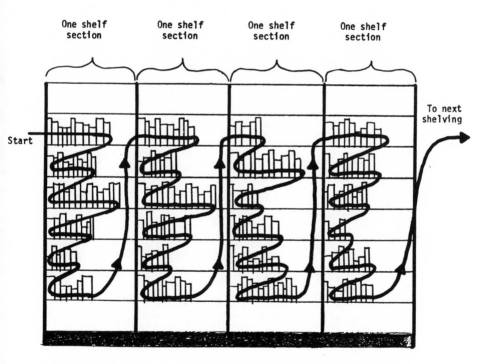

There is a diagram of the top floor of the library on the end of each range of shelves. It indicates where you are standing and the various call number locations. Notice also that there are labels on the end of each range of shelves which indicate the alphabetical section of the call numbers that are found on those shelves.

If the book you are seeking is not exactly where it is supposed to be, first check the shelves around the place where it should have been shelved. The book may have been reshelved incorrectly by another student. If you still cannot find it, and are interested in seeking further for it, go to Circulation Services and ask someone there to determine the book's location. It may have been placed on reserve by an instructor, or it may be checked out by someone else. It could also be in use in the library by another student. Keep in mind that you can always request to have a book placed on personal hold for you when it is returned by another reader.

If there are books available in our collection that are available at the Manoa Campus libraries or other community college libraries in the state, we can borrow them for you on inter-library loan. However, it will take us approximately two weeks to get a book this way for you. So, if it is possible for you to go to another library yourself, you will probably be able to get the material more quickly.

Before returning downstairs, please feel free to browse around the general book collection. You will notice that there are many study carrels provided for your use. A "superquiet" intensive study area has been designated in the far opposite corner of this floor where the end of the general circulating collection is shelved. If you will look down the aisle running from the typing room, you will see a sign hanging from the ceiling stating, "SUPERQUIET Intensive Study Area."

30

Now please return downstairs to the Reserve Materials
charge-out table at the entrance to the Reference Area where we
were during an earlier point in our tour.

Reserve Collection

The Reserve Collection is kept behind Circulation Services and consists
of all kinds of items--books, pamphlets, and audio-visual materials. Instructors sometimes put their own copies of books on reserve also. The primary
purpose of a reserve collection is to make a limited number of copies of
required reading more available for short periods to a larger number of students.

31

Instructors place material on reserve to help you, the student. For example, an instructor has 30 students in his class, and he wants all of them to read Chapter 4 of "Audiovisual Instruction" by Wittich and Schuller. He does not think his students need to buy the book, the instructor then goes to the library and finds that it has only one copy. He gives his class the assignment to read Chapter 4, tells them the book is available in the library. The first student who comes to the library would find the book and check it out for three to four weeks, so the other 29 students would not have a chance to read the assignment. To avoid this situation, the instructor goes to the library and puts the book on 2-hour reserve. This way all of the students have a chance at using the book because it is kept in the library. Each student can check out the book for 2 hours and read the assignment in the library.

Whenever an instructor places books or other items on reserve, the library will list these items in two different ways so that you can find out what is on reserve and be able to check out what you need. Now, please notice the two large notebooks on the charge-out table. Both books contain identical lists of all material on reserve for each class. In the black notebook labeled COURSE TITLES the reserve lists are filed by the title of the course. However, if you cannot remember the title of your course, then you can find the reserve list you need by the second method, which files the reserve lists by INSTRUCTOR'S NAME in the green notebook.

Take a minute now to open up one of the reserve notebooks and look at a reserve book list page. You will notice that each page contains columns for information on reserve items. Each item is listed with its call number, title, author and how long the item may be borrowed. There are only two loan periods, 2 hours and 3 days. (The instructor who places the item on reserve selects the loan period for how long an item may be checked out.)

To borrow material that is on reserve, you must fill out a charge card
for it. Charge cards are found in three (3) slots under the Reserve Materials
Charge-out Table. Directions for filling out the charge card are given on a
large white sign mounted on the pillar and an example is given on the table
top for you to follow when you need these materials.

The pamphlet you are reading from is a reserve item. Perhaps you were
assisted in getting this pamphlet by a library staff member. However, in the
future you will have to fill out your own charge card for any item you need
to check out from the reserve collection or the library's main collection.
To give you some practical experience with Reserve, do the following. Look up
the Library Unit in either the INSTRUCTOR'S NAME reserve notebook under the
name of your instructor, or in the COURSE TITLES reserve notebook under the
name of the course for which you are taking this library unit. (It is also
filed under Library Unit in both notebooks.) The page you find should list
the four sections of the Library Unit.

When you have the charge card filled out completely, take it along with
your driver's license or I.D. to the Reserve Collection Services at Circulation
Services directly across from where you are standing now. The staff person
behind the desk will use your charge card to get the reserve item for you and
charge it out to you. When you are finished with the reserve item, return it
to the Reserve Collection Services where you picked the item up. The large
white sign attached to the Reserve Materials charge-out table is a review of
the procedure that has just been described to you and you may want to refer
to it as a reminder of how the reserve system works when you have instructors
who use it.

This is the conclusion of the library tour. Please feel free to review this pamphlet before asking a librarian for Library Unit Test I. If you have any questions, please go to the librarian at the Reference/Information Desk. The librarians are there to assist you with all of the Library Unit and are trained to answer any questions you may have.

When you are finished with this pamphlet, please return it to Reserve Collection Services.

THE CARD CATALOG

The card catalog is straight ahead of you as you enter the library, it occupies a central position within the library. The card catalog is the index to the library collection. An index tells you what is available and where to find it. An index to a book tells you what is in the book and on what page you will find it. The card catalog, which is the index to the library collection, tells you what is available in the library and where in the library you will find it.

There are cards in the catalog to represent all the books, magazines, pamphlets, government documents, phonograph records, prints, tapes and other audiovisual material, cards for just about everything in the library collection. So the card catalog is what you use to find out what the library has to meet your needs. We have at Leeward a divided card catalog. That is to say, we have three separate card catalogs: an author catalog, a title catalog and a subject catalog. All library material, whether it is a book, phonograph record, tape, filmstrip, print, or whatever (we use the comprehensive term material or item to cover all types of material in the library) each item the library owns usually has at least three cards in the catalog to represent it. A card under the author's name in the author catalog; a card under the title in the title catalog and a card under each of its subject areas in the subject catalog.

There are several rules for filing that should be kept in mind when using the card catalog. These rules hold true for all three sections of the card catalog. Five of the most commonly encountered ones will be pointed out at this point.

First filing rule: All cards are filed alphabetically word by word, alphabetizing letter by letter to the end of each word. In word by word filing you apply the princple of "nothing before something", considering the space between words as "nothing". Let the symbol Ø represent nothing or the space and consider it a letter that precedes "a" in the alphabet; i.e., the alphabet starts Ø, A, B, C, D. etc. Look at the example on page 1 of your workbook. 'Every body' as two words is filed first, whereas 'everybody' as one word is filed *after* the filing of all the titles with 'every' as a separate word.

'Every body' as two words is filed as: E-V-E-R-Y-Ø-B-O-D-Y
'Everybody' as one word is filed as: E-V-E-R-Y-B-O-D-Y

Also notice 'everyday' and 'everyone' in the example in your workbook. 'Every day' as two words and further down 'everyday' as one word; 'every one' as two words and further down 'everyone' as one word.

Now you are ready to test yourself on this first filing rule by answering all the questions in the First Exercise in your workbook. After you have done the exercise, check your answers with the correct answers found on the workbook page that follows the exercise. Learn from any mistakes you may have made. If you cannot figure out why your answer is wrong and/or the workbook answer is right, be sure to ask a librarian to explain. When you are satisfied that you understand the exercise, return to the pamphlet and continue. For most of the exercises in Section Two, you will find a "Double Check Exercise" on the answer page. These extra exercises give you a chance to retest yourself, which is helpful if you had difficulty or found it necessary to review the instruction.

Each time you are directed to do a workbook exercise, follow this same procedure: do the exercise, correct it, learn from your mistakes, do the Double Check Exercise if you want to retest yourself, then continue with the instruction in this pamphlet.

At this point, put this pamphlet aside and test yourself by answering all the questions in the First Exercise on page 2 of your workbook.

Second filing rule: All punctuation is disregarded, including apostrophes. The contraction I'll is filed as Ill, we'd is filed as wed, etc. Carefully examine the three apostrophe examples at the top of page 4 of your workbook. These are arranged in correct filing order.

Third filing rule: If a title begins with one of the three articles in the English language: A, An, or The (or their foreign language equivalents) this article is omitted when filing and the card is filed by the word following the article. For example, the book "An Enemy of the People" will be filed in the title catalog under Enemy of the People and the book "The Godfather" will be filed under Godfather. When an article appears as the second word or in any position other than the first word, it is NOT omitted. Only when it appears as the first word is it omitted. Look at the initial article example on page 4 of the workbook.

Fourth filing rule: All abbreviations are filed as if they are spelled out. Dr. is filed as Doctor, Mr. as Mister, U.S. as United States, and so forth. The exception is Mrs. which is filed as the abbreviation is spelled: MRS. (See the example for filing abbreviations on the lower portion of p. 4 of the workbook.)

At this point carefully review the filing rule examples on page 4 of your workbook. Then when you are ready, test yourself on these filing rules by completing the Second Exercise on page 5 and 6 of your workbook.

(Sample extract, complete text available from author.)

LIBRARY SUBJECT HEADINGS

Subject Heading, Type Face, and See References. Atop the subject card catalog cases on the main floor of the library are several large, red volumes on revolving stands. They are titled *Library of Congress Subject Headings,* (or *LCSH* for short,) and each set includes two volumes. These books provide a very useful guide to the contents and arrangement of the subject card catalog in the cases below. Both the books and the cards are meant to be used together, and by learning how they work, you will acquire the key to discovering quickly what books, tapes, records, etc. the library has available on any subject of your choice. Virtually all library materials except contents of periodicals and newspapers are represented in the subject card catalog, and *LCSH* is the key to its use.

Suppose you are interested in finding materials on a particular subject; say, for instance, "Fishes." By checking the appropriate drawer under that heading, you will find materials available on the subject represented by cards filed *after* the guide card "FISHES," (never before the guide card.) Now, if you look in the red *LCSH* volumes for the same word, "Fishes" you will find it appears there also, in boldface (dark) type.

Now take a moment to examine these subject headings and their arrangement in the book. Please turn to page 74. First note that the headings are arranged three columns to a page, and that they appear in lightface (light) and boldface (dark) types, alphabetically down each column. Beneath some of these alphabetically arranged headings, there are indented lists of words and phrases, with each indented group arranged in its separate order. You will learn about these indented groups later in this pamphlet. Starting in the upper left column, you will find "Animal Industry" is in boldface type, followed by the lightface heading "Animal Instinct." The dark and light headings are arranged alphabetically. The indented headings are in a different order.

Turn to page 75. The subject heading, "Animal sounds," appears in boldface type in the middle column. There are eleven lines of indented headings under this heading. All of these indented headings pertain in one way or another to the boldface heading, "Animal sounds," above. The next heading in the margin in alphabetical sequence is a lightface heading "Animal stories." The difference is crucial, for only the boldface headings in the left-hand margins indicate *usable subject headings*—that is, headings which you can locate on *guide cards* in the subject card catalog below. Words in lightface type in the left-hand margins are *unusable*—that is, they do *not appear on guide cards* in the subject card catalog below.

To summarize, where the boldface subject heading is used in our subject card catalog, it is shown in caps (capital letters) on a raised, plastic guide with cards behind this guide card representing books, pamphlets, records, etc. that this library has available on the subject. It is a usable subject heading.

See references. A heading in lightface type in the column margin, with *See*_____ immediately below it is called a "see reference." It directs you from an unusable to a usable subject heading. These words are very much like "Dead End" signs on the roadway. They tell you to take another route—to *see* another heading.

If you will return to page 74, column 1 and look for the first heading that appears in the column margin in lightface type, you will find it is "Animal instinct." The phrase, "Animal instinct," is therefore the first *see* reference.

(Sample extract, complete text available from author.)

PERIODICALS AND PERIODICAL INDEXES

In this section of the library unit you will learn some basic techniques for finding information in magazines and newspapers. These techniques are similar to those you learned for subject searching in the third section about the subject catalog. Magazines and newspapers are valuable sources of information on present-day topics of interest and research in progress. In libraries, magazines and newspapers are called *periodicals.*

A periodical is a publication that comes out on a periodic, or regular, schedule. For example, the *Honolulu Advertiser* comes out daily, *Newsweek* comes out weekly, *Good Housekeeping* comes out monthly, and the *Journal of Marriage and the Family* comes out quarterly, that is, every three months.

Periodicals are important because they contain articles on up-to-date topics. Many of these topics may not be written about in books until several years later. Other topics may never be covered in book form and thus may never be available to you through the library's card catalog.

Leeward library subscribes to over 380 periodicals. No one has the time to search through all of these for information on a specific topic. And that's why a periodical index is important.

An index is a list telling where material on various subjects can be found. Indexes are usually arranged alphabetically.

A periodical index is a list of subjects (and sometimes authors) arranged in alphabetical order. Under each subject is a listing of magazine articles about the subject, also arranged in alphabetical order. Periodical indexes usually index only magazines, not newspapers. Since a daily newspaper comes out 365 times a year, many more times than a magazine, each newspaper index usually indexes only one newspaper.

Most periodical indexes are published monthly in paperbound form. Once a year all the paper issues are combined into one alphabetical sequence and bound into hard covers. This bound volume covers only the year given on the cover.

One periodical index will usually index over 100 different periodicals. That is, it will arrange by subject (and sometimes author also) all the articles written in over 100 periodicals. When an index does this for a whole year, you can see that it makes available to you articles on many subjects in many magazines in one alphabetical listing covering a complete year in one bound volume. This information would otherwise be extremely difficult to find.

Periodical indexes in this library are in the study carrels behind the author card catalog. Go to that area at this time. The magazine indexes are shelved alphabetically from carrel 1 through carrel 8.

The newspaper indexes are in carrels 9–12. Walk around these carrels, beginning with carrel no. 1, and glance at some of the titles on the spines of the indexes. The title of each index makes it fairly obvious what kind of material is indexed. For example, the *Education Index* indexes periodicals in the field of education.

Regardless of which magazine index you use, a standard order is generally used in giving the information about the magazine articles. This information is referred to as a *citation*. A citation includes title, author, name of the magazine containing the article, volume number, page numbers, and the date of the magazine issue.

(Sample extract, complete text available from author.)

Chapter Five

Workbooks

Name _____

L I B R A R Y   U N I T

WORKBOOK

EXAMPLES AND EXERCISES

SECTION TWO:
THE CARD CATALOG

Leeward Community College Library

Spring 1979

LIBRARY UNIT WORKBOOK -- SECTION TWO

This workbook is yours to keep and may be taken out of the library. Write your name on the cover as soon as you receive it. Inside are practice questions -- and the answers to those questions -- which will help you prepare for Library Unit Test Number Two.

When you are ready to start work on Library Unit Section Two, fill out a charge card for either the pamphlet or the tape, obtaining the correct call number from the Instructor Reserve List or the Course Reserve List. Present the card at the Reserve Materials Desk. The pamphlet or tape will tell you how to use this workbook. When you have completed all the exercises, bring this workbook to the Reference Desk, where you will be given test materials on request.

DO NOT PROCEED ANY FURTHER IN THIS WORKBOOK THAN THE INTRODUCTION ON THE NEXT PAGE WITHOUT THE INSTRUCTIONS CONTAINED IN EITHER TAPE TC17A OR SECTION TWO PAMPHLET BOTH OF WHICH ARE AVAILABLE AT THE RESERVE MATERIALS DESK.

INTRODUCTION

This workbook is to be used in conjunction with Tape TC17a or
the pamphlet for Section Two of the Library Unit, both of which are
available at the Reserve Materials Desk. The tape and the pamphlet
cover the same material. This instructional material will prepare
you to take Library Unit Test Two covering use of the card catalog.

To prepare yourself for Test Two, choose either the tape or the
pamphlet, depending on whether you prefer to listen or to read. As
you listen or read, you will be directed to investigate specific items
and to follow through by doing example exercises in this workbook.
Be sure to follow through as directed, for only by so doing will
you be fully prepared to undertake Test Two.

Answers to the exercise questions will be found in the workbook
at the end of each exercise section. This enables you to evaluate
your own learning and to review when necessary. In many instances,
a second exercise will follow, so you can retest your learning if you
wish. If you have any questions whatsoever, do not hesitate to seek
the assistance of a librarian.

After completing this workbook, you are prepared to take Test Two.
Allow yourself sufficient time (about an hour) to take the test. When
you are ready, present your workbook to the librarian, who will issue
you the test, *which is to be taken in the Library.* Your completed test
and answer sheet are to be turned in to the librarian who will then return your workbook, should you wish to keep it for further reference.

Be sure to complete this workbook, for it is designed to help you
prepare for the tests. The workbook exercises are similar to the questions appearing in the tests so that, in effect, they comprise a self-
correcting pretest.

Above all, do not hesitate to ask a librarian for any assistance
you may need.

FILING RULE EXAMPLE

WORD BY WORD

        Every body was embalmed
        Every day of the year counts
        Every one of them would serve the purpose
        Every zebra has stripes
        Everybody loves somebody sometime
        Everyday occurrences
        Everyone supported his nomination

Do not try to understand the above example or to do any of the exercises on the pages that follow without learning how to approach them by either listening to Tape TC17a or reading the Library Unit instructional pamphlet for Section Two; The Card Catalog, both of which are available at the Reserve Materials Desk.

FIRST EXERCISE   SECTION TWO

2

I. The card catalog is the_____to the library collection.

II. Is this statement true or false?
There are cards in the card catalog to represent only the books in the
library collection. There are no cards representing magazines, phonograph records, tapes or any other material that the library has.

    True _____ or False _____

III. Which of the following is filed first? Place an X in front of the one
which would be filed first in each of the following groups (you will
have four X's, one for each group).

  A.____To please my love   B.____Toward the East

   ____Too many people   ____To win the contest

   ____Two too many   ____Together again

  C.____Newspapers   D.____Central areas

   ____News to report   ____Centipede studies

   ____New Zealand   ____Centennial memories

IV. Arrange the following in the order they would be filed in the card
catalog by writing number 1 in front of the one that would come first,
2 for the one that comes second, etc.

  A.____Some of my friends   B.____Tender is the night

   ____Something in the air   ____Ten times ten

   ____Some basic considerations ____Tension at high noon

   ____Someone I know   ____Ten men on a horse

   ____Somewhere the sun is shining ____Tenderly

   ____Some things are scary   ____Tenderloin

   ____Somebody special   ____Ten thousand cranes

      C.____In the days of giants

       ____Image of America

       ____I met a man

       ____Inca ruins

       ____Imaginary conversations

       ____I am a camera

       ____In an unknown land

ANSWERS TO FIRST EXERCISE

I.	index						
II.	False						
III.	A.	To please my love					
	B.	To win the contest					
	C.	New Zealand					
	D.	Centennial memories					
IV.	A.	2	B.	4	C.	6	
		6		3		3	
		1		7		2	
		5		1		7	
		7		6		4	
		3		5		1	
		4		2		5	

If any of your answers were incorrect please review that portion of the instruction. BE SURE you understand your error before proceeding. Do not hesitate to ask a librarian to clarify anything that is not clear to you. Continue to do this self correction, reviewing and clarifying on each exercise throughout the workbook.

Double check -- First Exercise

Many exercises in this workbook will be followed by a second exercise on the answer sheet. This enables you to retest yourself, particularly if you found it necessary to review the material. The answers to these double check exercises will be found at the very end of this workbook on page 25.

Arrange the following in the order they would be filed in the catalog by writing number 1 in front of the one that would come first, 2 for the one that comes second, etc.

_____   Force of habit

_____   For the young in heart

_____   Forts for defense

_____   Forthcoming events

_____   For modern families

_____   Fort Sumter memoirs

_____   Forbidden fruits

_____   For the families of twins

_____   Forth we forge

_____   Forage for livestock

SECTION TWO
4

FILING RULE EXAMPLES

Each group below is in correct filing order.

PUNCTUATION (Apostrophe):

I am aware of you	I will overcome	Who'll mind the store
I mean every word	Ill feelings exposed	Whom is objective
I'm aware of it	I'll survive	Who's afraid
Imagine that	Ill winds in May	Who's who
	I'll worry no more	Whose country is this

INITIAL ARTICLES ('a, an, the' omitted):

The agent	The endless summer	Analysis of costs
Better times	Energy conservation	An analytic analysis
A cruel awakening	An evening with Arturo	Analytical art
		Anatomy of love

(Note: 'And' is <u>not</u> ommitted) ──────> And anarchy will prevail
An angel in disguise

ABBREVIATIONS:

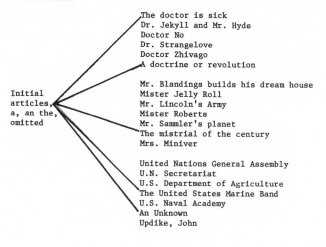

Initial articles, a, an the, omitted

The doctor is sick
Dr. Jekyll and Mr. Hyde
Doctor No
Dr. Strangelove
Doctor Zhivago
A doctrine or revolution

Mr. Blandings builds his dream house
Mister Jelly Roll
Mr. Lincoln's Army
Mister Roberts
Mr. Sammler's planet
The mistrial of the century
Mrs. Miniver

United Nations General Assembly
U.N. Secretariat
U.S. Department of Agriculture
The United States Marine Band
U.S. Naval Academy
An Unknown
Updike, John

SECOND EXERCISE

I. In the following titles to be filed in the card catalog, circle the
    words that are disregarded:

    A. A journey to the planets Mars and Venus.
    B. An enormous task and the consequences thereof.
    C. And away to the stars!
    D. To a wild rose.

II. Arrange the following in the order they would be filed in the card
    catalog by writing number 1 in front of the one that would come first,
    2 for the one that comes second, etc.

    A. ____We'll see about that

        ____Well after it happened

        ____We'll work together

        ____We will win

        ____Well water pollution

        ____We won't retreat

    B. ____Law reform

        ____Law - Digests

        ____Law, Ancient

        ____Law (Theology)

        ____Law and politics

        ____Law enforcement

    C. ____An absolute indiscretion

        ____Analog functions

        ____Ain't she sweet

        ____Andalusian summer

        ____An Anatolian war

        ____Aim for the moon

        ____Ad for murder

        ____And baby makes three

(CONTINUED ON NEXT PAGE)

D.   _____Mr. Ace

     _____Miss Adams

     _____Mister Adams

     _____Mrs. Abbott

     _____Mistress Mary

E.   _____St. Joan the martyr

     _____Saint of Bleeker Street

     _____St. Jerome's writings

     _____Saints and sinners

     _____Saint of a guy

     _____St. Francis of Assisi

     _____Saint Joan of Arc

III. In what order would the following be filed in the card catalog?

     _____U.S. National Institute on Alcohol Abuse and Alcoholism

     _____Unity House

     _____Union of Independent Colleges

ANSWERS TO SECOND EXERCISE

I. A. Only the initial article 'A' is disregarded.
    B. Only the initial article 'An' is disregarded.
    C. None of the words in this title is disregarded.
    D. None of the words in this title is disregarded.

II. A. 4   B. 5   C. 1   D. 2   E. 4
        3   3   5   1   6
        6   1   4   3   2
        1   6   8   5   7
        5   2   6   4 Remember, 'Mrs.'   5
        2   4   3   is the <u>only</u> abbrevia-   1
                          2   tion that is NOT   3
                          7   spelled out.

III. The abbreviation, 'U.S.' is spelled out and filed as 'United
     States,' therefore, it is filed after Union of Independent
     Colleges but before Unity House:

            Union of Independent Colleges
            U.S. National Institute on Alcohol Abuse and Alcoholism
            Unity House

                    Double Check -- Second Exercise

    A. _____Mr. Slugger Strikes out

        _____A Mr. Smith is here

        _____The Mr. Singer songbook

    B. _____Androcles and the lion

        _____An ancient tradition

        _____Anagrams that challenge

        _____An angel in disguise

        _____And away we go

                    ANSWERS ON PAGE 25

FILING RULE EXAMPLE

NUMBERS:

The number 150 is filed as:	One hundred fifty
The number 150½ is filed as:	One hundred fifty and one half
The number 1500 is filed as:	One thousand five hundred
The date 1500 is filed as:	Fifteen hundred
The date 1550 is filed as:	Fifteen fifty
The number 1550 is filed as:	One thousand five hundred fifty

FOLLOW THROUGH THE FOLLOWING EXAMPLE WHICH IS IN ALPHABETICAL ORDER.

Example:(listed in alphabetical order)   File as:

1984	Nineteen eighty-four
The 1950's	Nineteen fifties
The 1956 Presidential campaign	Nineteen fifty-six Presidential campaign
1914: the coming of the First World War	Nineteen fourteen: the coming ...
1900: the end of an era	Nineteen hundred: the end ...
1971 in review	Nineteen seventy-one in review
The 1968 election	Nineteen sixty-eight election
The 1963 tragedy	Nineteen sixty-three tragedy
The 1920's	Nineteen twenties
The 19th century	Nineteenth century
The 90th parallel	Ninetieth parallel
90 acres called Paradise	Ninety acres called Paradise
90½	Ninety and one half

THIRD EXERCISE

I. Example: 63 is filed as sixty-three

A. 145 is filed as _____

B. 1,100 is filed as _____

C. The date 1800 is filed as _____

D. The date 1492 is filed as _____

E. 2½ is filed as_____

F. _____ is filed as one hundred thousand

II. Arrange the following in the order they would be filed in the card catalog by writing number 1 in front of the one that would come first, 2 for the one that comes second, etc.

A. _____1700 to 1750 in English history

_____7 year locust

_____7,000 years of progress

_____The 7th wonder

_____The 7 year itch

_____The 17th summer

_____17 hours of terror

_____7,000,000 guinea pigs

B. _____1930

_____1942

_____1949

_____1953

_____1958

_____1961

_____1969

_____1972

_____1976

_____1980

ANSWERS TO THIRD EXERCISE

I. A. one hundred forty five
   B. one thousand one hundred
   C. eighteen hundred
   D. fourteen ninety-two
   E. two and one half
   F. 100,000

II. A. 6   B. 10
    4   5
    2   4
    8   3
    3   2
    7   9
    5   8
    1   7
            6
            1

Double Check -- Third Exercise

_____80 days around the world

_____Eight bells

_____82 ways to serve rice

_____88 per cent proof

_____18th century drama

_____84 household hints

_____The 1812 overture

_____87 different ways to survive

_____The 8½ week diet

_____18 year olds

_____86 questions about organic gardening

_____The eighth day

ANSWER ON PAGE 25

EXPLANATION OF A CATALOG CARD

```
   1
LB1607    2
R6      Rollins, Sidney Philip, 1920-
                          3
           Introduction to secondary education [by] Sidney P.
        Rollins [and] Adolph Unruh.  2d ed.  Chicago, Rand McNally
           [1964]        9         10         11              12
              vi, 278 p.    illus.    24 cm.   (Rand McNally education
        series)
                          13
           Includes bibliographies.
           Maps on lining papers.


                   14                        14
           1. Education, Secondary.  I. Unruh, Adolph, joint author.
           II. Title.
```

1. Call number:
      LB1607   Indicates subject
      R6   Letter and number combination for the author's name, <u>Rollins</u>

2. Author's name and date of birth. (Note inverted form: last name first)

3. Title of the item.

4. Joint authors.

5. Edition

6-8. Imprint composed of 6: Place of publication

                        7: Publisher

                        8: Date of publication

9. Paging

10. Illustrations (the item has pictures)

11. Size indicated in centimeters of height.

12. Series note.

13. Notes further explaining the item.

14. Headings for other cards in the catalog for this item.

AFTER YOU HAVE FULLY UNDERSTOOD THIS PAGE, RETURN TO WHERE YOU LEFT OFF IN THE
TAPE OR PAMPHLET. DO NOT DO THE NEXT EXERCISE UNTIL YOU HAVE FINISHED THE
PREPARATION FOR IT IN THE TAPE OR PAMPHLET.

FOURTH EXERCISE

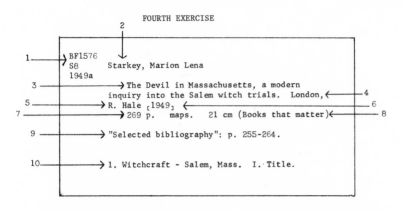

I. From the catalog card reproduced above find the following five points
   of information (A-E). Write the <u>number</u> given to that point of information in the blank.

   Example: __3__ Title

   A____ Number of pages in the book

   B____ Publisher

   C____ Author

   D____ Call number

   E____ Date of publication

II. Using the author card catalog look up the following books and supply
    the information asked for:

    A. *How Russia is ruled,* by Merle Fainsod.

       (1) What is the call number for this book?

       (2) Merle Fainsod is a joint author of <u>another</u> book. Who are the
           other joint authors of this other book?

       _____

       (3) What edition is this other book?_____

CONTINUED ON NEXT PAGE

B. The library has a number of books by Christopher Darlington Morley. Find the card for his book titled *The ironing board*. This is a collection of a certain type of Morley's writings. What type of writings are these: (The note on the card tells you.) _____

C. *Twentieth century interpretations of Hamlet*, compiled by David M. Bevington contains a bibliography. On what pages of the book will you find it? _____

D. The revised edition of a book by Donald Gordon Payne that was first published under the title, *The children*, is available in this library. What is the title of this revised edition?
_____

E. This library also has four other books by Donald Gordon Payne. Two of them have copyright dates that differ from their publication dates. What are the publication dates and the copyright dates of these two books?

Publication date _____ Copyright date _____

Publication date _____ Copyright date _____

III. Of the following, choose the one that correctly completes the sentence defining a bibliography.

A bibliography

____(a) is a list of material relating to a particular subject or author.

____(b) is the history or story of a person's life.

____(c) lists famous quotations by and about people.

____(d) tells you where you can find facts about an author.

____(e) lists topics arranged in alphabetical order

ANSWERS TO FOURTH EXERCISE

I. A. 7
    B. 5
    C. 2
    D. 1
    E. 6

II. A. 1. JN6531
            F3

        2. Lincoln Gordon and Joseph C. Palamountain, Jr.

        3. 3d ed.

    B. Essays

    C. 119–120

    D. Walkabout

    E. Publication date <u>1964</u>   Copyright date <u>1963</u>
        Publication date <u>1967</u>   Copyright date <u>1966</u>

III. a

FIFTH EXERCISE

Using the author card catalog, answer the following questions:

   I.   What is the number on the front of the drawer in the author card catalog that you should look in to find out if this library has anything by Eugene Paul? _____

  II.   What is the title of a book by the National Symposium on the Effect on Children of Television Programming and Advertising?

          _____

 III.   What name are the books by O. Henry found under? _____

  IV.   A pocket book of short stories edited by Philip Van Doren Stern contains a story by James Thurber. What is the title of that story?

          _____

   V. A. What is the call number for a phonograph record of Anton Dvorak's chamber music?

          B. What quartet performs in the first two volumes of this recording?
              _____

          C. Is there also a card in the author card catalog for this recording under the quartet's name? _____

  VI.   What is the call number of an art print of James Whistler's painting of his mother?

 VII.   A collection of essays written by various authors is represented in the author card catalog under the name of the:

     (a) author of the first essay in the book.

     (b) publisher.

     (c) editor or compiler.

     (d) author who wrote most of the essays.

     (e) each individual author.

ANSWERS TO FIFTH EXERCISE

I.   76

II. Action for children's television.

III. Porter, William Sydney

IV. The night the ghost got in.

V.   A   Rec
         RF
         D88C5

     B. Kohon Quartet

     C. yes

VI. Pri
     P12
     W45

VII. (c) editor or compiler

Double check -- Fifth Exercise

I.   Using the author card catalog, answer the following questions:

     A. What is the call number of a book by the National Secretaries
         Association?

     B. How many books does this library have by Eric Blair? _____

     C. You would like to know if this library has a recording of Artur
         Rubinstein playing the music of Edvard Grieg. What should you
         look under in the author card catalog? _____

     D. What is the title of an Andy Warhol painting that this library has?

         _____

II. A collection of poems written by various poets is represented in the
     author card catalog by a card under the name of the _____

ANSWERS ON PAGE 25

SIXTH EXERCISE

I.   Using the title card catalog, count how many editions of "Life on the Mississippi" the library has. (Note the quotation marks above. This indicates that "Life on the Mississippi" is a title. Titles are either italicized, underlined, or placed within quotation marks when they are mentioned in writing.) ANSWER: _____

II. Using the subject card catalog, how many items about John Barrymore does the library have?_____

III. The library has a book called "Handbook of electronic circuits". This book is represented in each of the three card catalogs as follows:

A card in the_____ catalog filed under_____

A card in the_____ catalog filed under_____

A card in the_____ catalog filed under_____

IV. Complete the following by filling in the blanks.

A.   For material BY John F. Kennedy you would look in the _____ card catalog.

B.   For material ABOUT John F. Kennedy you would look in the _____ card catalog.

C.   For material with John F. Kennedy as the name of the book you would look in the _____card catalog.

V.   A.   How many art prints does the library have of Paul Gauguin's paintings?_____

B.   How many items does the library have about Paul Gauguin?_____

VI. Give the complete call number for the following items in this library:

A.   The book "I'll trade you an elk".

B.   A book about how to stop smoking.

(CONTINUED ON NEXT PAGE)

C. A tape about Tennessee Williams.

D. A phonograph record of "The Glass Menagerie".

E. A document by the United States National Institute on Alcohol Abuse and Alcoholism.

F. The tape "1969: year of the mayors".

ANSWERS TO SIXTH EXERCISE

I. 3
II. 2
III. A card in the <u>title</u> catalog filed under <u>Handbook of electronic circuits</u>
A card in the <u>author</u> catalog filed under <u>RCA Service Company, Inc.</u>
A card in the <u>subject</u> catalog filed under <u>Electronic Circuits</u>

IV. A. author
B. subject
C. title

V. A. 9
B. 3

VI. A. QL31   B. RC567   C. Tape   D. Rec
G64G6   C3   TC14   RT12
                                              W5

E. Doc.   F. Tape
HE 20.2402:   TC46
AL1/972

Double Check -- Sixth Exercise

I. How many books does the library have:

A. by Albert Schweitzer _____ and in which catalog did you look to
find out? _____

B. about Albert Schweitzer _____ and in which catalog did you look
to find out? _____

C. with Albert Schweitzer's name as the name of the book _____ and in
which catalog did you look to find out? _____

II. Give the complete call number for the following:

A. A tape about John Dillinger.

B. A report of activities conducted by the Mott Institute for
Community Improvement.

III. Who wrote "The Grandfathers?" _____

ANSWERS ON PAGE 25

How Material is Arranged on the Shelves by the
Library of Congress Classification System

A library classification system groups material on like subjects together.
There are two basic library classification systems used in the United States,
the Dewey Decimal system and the Library of Congress system. Many colleges
and universities use the Library of Congress system. Hamilton and Sinclair
Libraries on Manoa Campus use the Library of Congress system and your library
here at Leeward also uses this system. It is really not as complex as it
first appears.

In this system, knowledge is broken down into classes, divisions, and
subdivisions using a combination of letters running from A-Z and numbers
running from 1 to 9999. The letters represent the broad classes of knowledge
and the numbers represent divisions. You are not expected to know these
breakdowns. It is brought to your attention because many students ask what
the purpose is and how it works. Any time you want an interpretation you can
always refer to your Library Handbook where you will find a brief outline of
the Library of Congress Classification Schedule and a comprehensive comparison
of Dewey Decimal numbers with the Library of Congress Classification. You
will also find a brief outline posted on the end of many of the ranges of
shelving throughout the library.

Each item in the library is assigned its own classification, and these
are called 'call numbers'. Material is arranged on the shelves by these call
numbers. No two items have exactly the same call number--each has its own
specific number. Most call numbers have two lines. (Some call numbers will
have more than these two basic lines to indicate the edition date, or the
volume number, or the copy number, or other similar distinguishing information.)
There are four parts to this two line call number. The first part is the
letter(s) on the first line. The second part is the number on the first line.
The third part is the letter on the second line and the fourth part is the
number on the second line.

When looking for a book with a specific call number, the first thing you
need to do is to locate the shelves where the books have call numbers that
begin with the letter(s) on the first line. When you have found that section,
you then look for the next part of the call number--the number on the first
line. Within a group of books all having call numbers with the same first
line, you then look for the next part of the call number--the letter on the
second line. If you find several books with the same letter/number combinations up to this point, then look for the last part of the call number--the
number on the second line.

Now, knowing that each call number has four points of comparison, and
that you use these four parts in sequence to locate material on the shelves,
continue through the following explanation. This explanation is not meant to
be actual, it is an explanation of the concept of the arrangement in what is
hoped to be the clearest way for understanding.

CONTINUED ON NEXT PAGE

Books are shelved first by the letter(s) on the first line--so the A's come first. A letter standing alone (such as "A") is shelved before that letter combined with another (such as "AA", "AB", etc.). The arrangement is thus:

A	AA	AB	AC	AD	AE	AF	etc. to AZ
Then	B	BA	BB	BC	etc. to BZ		
Then	C	CA	etc. to CZ				
Then	D	etc. through the entire alphabet to ZZ					

Within a letter(s) group, for example with all the books which have call numbers starting with F, the arrangement is numerical by the number following the letter(s).

F1 F2 F3 F4 F5 etc.   F25 F26 F27 etc.   F100 F101 F102 etc.

Within like first lines, when both the letter(s) and numbers are the same, for example F21, books are shelved alphabetically by the first letter of the second line.

F21	F21	F21	F21	F21	F21	etc.
A	B	C	D	E	F	

And finally, within like call numbers at this point (books that have the same first lines and same first letters of the second line) for example a whole section of F21

        A

books are further arranged by the numbers on the second line which are DECIMAL numbers. This is the only unusual thing to remember: numbers on the second line are decimal numbers (numbers on the first line are whole numbers arranged in the ordinary numerical manner).

An easy way to determine the lowest decimal number is to consider the number a digit at a time. This means that anything beginning with a 1 would come before anything beginning with a 2 and anything beginning with a 2 would come before those beginning with a 3, etc.

F21 A1659	comes before	F21 A2	because 1 comes before 2

Likewise:

F21 A1659	comes before	F21 A17	because 6 comes before 7

and

F21 A1659	comes before	F21 A166	because 5 comes before 6

Remember that this applies only to the number on the second line because the second line is a decimal number. Some people find it useful to place an imaginary decimal point before the first numeral on the second line; (A217 = A.217) which produces the same result, just as if you were to express

CONTINUED ON NEXT PAGE

monetary amounts only with cents, mills, etc.

Remember that the number on the <u>first</u> line is a whole number.

F21		F121	
A1659	comes before	A2	because 21 (twenty-one) comes before
			121 (one hundred twenty-one)

On the first line you are <u>not</u> comparing the 2 in the 21 with the 1 in the 121. You are looking at the <u>whole</u> number: 21 comes before 121.

Follow through on the following examples which are arranged in the order that these book call numbers should be filed on the shelves. Be <u>sure</u> to ask for a librarian's assistance if it is not clear to you.

Q5	QA4	QB3	QB22	QB22	QB22	QB22	QB22	QB22	QB22	QB22
C5643	C5643	C5643	C5643	E5643	E667	E77	E8	E9174	E924	E93

HN253	HN253.3	HN253.51	HN253.7	HN254
Z9	A1	A1	A1	A1

PS3545	PS3545	PS3545	PS3545	PS3545	PS3545
I5335R2	I535M39	I535M4	I535N2	I55K8	I552K7

Be sure you understand. Ask questions if you don't. Then proceed to the Seventh Exercise.

DO THE SEVENTH EXERCISE ON THE NEXT PAGE

I. Place the call numbers in each of the following groups in correct order
    according to the Library of Congress classification by using the numbers
    1, 2, 3, 4 to designate the one that comes first, second, etc.
    Example: (2)   (4)   (1)   (3)
               D   P   B   L

A. ( )   ( )   ( )   ( )   D. ( )   ( )   ( )   ( )
    E169   BC50   PE1417 BR100   E169   E169   E169   E169
    M35   D42   R8   T53   A23   M15   C64   L92

B. ( )   ( )   ( )   ( )   E. ( )   ( )   ( )   ( )
    D169   DA169 DG169 D169   DU624   DU624   DU624   DU624
    C23   A23   A22   L92   D91   D823   D6148   D231

C. ( )   ( )   ( )   ( )
    DA712 DA9   DA72   DA712
    G12   I22   H36   F54

II. A. You are looking for the book with the call number $\frac{PN4874}{G29E7}$
         Which of the following books would be right before it on the shelf?

         1. PN4875   2. PN4874   3. PN4873   4. PN4874
             G157A1   G157A1   G3F2   G3F2

                (Answer 1, 2, 3, or 4)   ANSWER:_____

     B. Which of the above books would be right after it on the shelf?

                                                 ANSWER:_____

     C. On the shelf, which of the following would be right after the book
         with the call number: Hawn./Pac.
                                  HM294
                                  B7W3

         1. HM294   2. Hawn./Pac.   3. HM295   4. Hawn./Pac.
             B8A2   HM294   B7W3   HM294
                          B71A2   B8W3

                                                 ANSWER:_____

III. Before taking Test Two you should have the practice experience of
      retrieving an item from the library. To do so, please request an
      assignment slip from the librarian at the Reference Desk. Correct your
      answers to I and II above, learn from your errors, do Double Check
      Exercise 7 if you feel it necessary and then request an assignment slip
      that will assign you a specific item to find in the library. When you
      have found that item, answer the following two questions about it:

      A. What is the call number?

      B. Inside the front cover you will find: "This is the answer to
          Library Unit Workbook, Exercise 7, Question III". What is that
          answer? _____

PLEASE REPLACE THE ITEM IN ITS CORRECT LOCATION FOR THE NEXT PERSON TO FIND.

ANSWERS TO SEVENTH EXERCISE

I. A. 3, 1, 4, 2
    B. 1, 3, 4, 2
    C. 4, 1, 2, 3 (Remember that the number on the first line is a whole
                     number)
    D. 1, 4, 2, 3
    E. 4, 3, 2, 1 (Remember that the number on the second line is a decimal
                     number)

II. A. 2
    B. 4
    C. 2

DOUBLE CHECK -- SEVENTH EXERCISE

I. Arrange the following call numbers in correct order.

    A. ( ) ( ) ( ) ( )
        PZ3   PZ3   PZ3   PZ3
        S9   S819   S89   S7787

    B. ( )   ( )   ( )   ( )   ( )   ( )
        HM343.3   HM343   HM343.2   HM343.3   HM343   HM343.2
        B423   B43   B43   B43   B423   B423

    C. ( )   ( )   ( )   ( )   ( )
        PS3651   PS3651   PS3651   PS3651   PS3651
        C212M4   C221K7   C22K8   C2112M5   C22M3

        ANSWERS ON NEXT PAGE

DOUBLE CHECK EXERCISE ANSWERS

Double Check Exercise 1	Double Check Exercise 2			Double Check Exercise 3
6	A. 2	B.	4	7
3	3		2	2
10	1		1	12
9			5	8
1			3	5
7				9
5				3
2				10
8				1
4				4
				11
				6

Double Check-- Fifth Exercise

I. A. HF5547
        N184
        1967

    B. 10

    C. Either: Grieg, Edvard or Rubinstein, Artur

    D. Marilyn Monroe

II. editor or compiler

Double Check -- Sixth Exercise

I. A. 9 - author
    B. 6 - subject
    C. 2 - title

II. A. Tape
        TC69

    B. LC4091
        T68

III. Conrad Richter

Double Check -- Seventh Exercise

I. A. 4, 2, 3, 1
    B. 5, 2, 4, 6, 1, 3
    C. 2, 5, 3, 1, 4

You should now be prepared to take Library
Unit Test Two. Allow yourself sufficient time
to take it (about an hour.) When you are ready,
turn this workbook in to a librarian who will
supply you with Test Two, which is to be completed in the Library.

When you have completed Test Two, hand it
in to a librarian who will return your workbook
to you. You can then continue with the next
section of the Library Unit by requesting from
the librarian a copy of the workbook for Sections
Three and Four. Tapes and pamphlets for Sections
Three and Four are available at the Reserve
Materials Desk.

We suggest, however, that you await the
results of your test performance on this section
and discuss them with a librarian before continuing to the next section of the Library Unit.

Name_____

L I B R A R Y   U N I T

WORKBOOK

Examples and Exercises

Section Three: Subject Headings

Section Four: Periodical Indexes

Leeward Community College Library

Spring, 1979

LIBRARY UNIT WORKBOOK -- SECTIONS THREE AND FOUR

This workbook is yours to keep and may be taken out of the Library. Write your name on the cover as soon as you receive it. Inside are practice questions which will help you prepare for Library Unit Tests Three and Four. The correct answers to each question may be found at the end of each section, on pages 8 and 21.

When you are ready to start work on Library Unit Section Three, fill out a charge card for either the pamphlet or the tape, obtaining the correct call number from the Instructor Reserve List or the Course Reserve List. Present the card at the Reserve Materials Desk. The pamphlet or tape will tell you how to use this workbook. When you have completed the exercises for Section Three, bring this workbook to the Reference Desk, where you will be given test materials on request.

The same procedure applies for Section Four exercises, pamphlets, tapes and tests. On completion of Test Number Three, this workbook will be returned to you for use in preparation for Section Four.

DO NOT PROCEED ANY FURTHER IN THIS WORKBOOK WITHOUT THE INSTRUCTIONS CONTAINED IN EITHER TAPE TC17B OR THE PAMPHLET FOR SECTION THREE OF THE LIBRARY UNIT, BOTH OF WHICH ARE AVAILABLE AT THE RESERVE MATERIALS DESK.

FIRST EXERCISE

I. In the *Library of Congress Subject Headings, (LCSH,)* a subject
    heading in lightface type in the column margin is: (Check one.)

    A. a usable subject heading._____

    B. an unusable subject heading._____

II. Define a "see reference."

    _____

III. List the see references from the following pages in *LCSH*.

    A. page 159, column 2 _____

    _____

    B. page 307, column 2 _____

    _____

    C. page 603, column 3 _____

    _____

IV. What are the subject headings that are used for the following subjects
    in *LCSH*?

    A. Babies _____

    B. Drug habit _____

    C. Evil spirits _____

V. Give the call number for books in this library on the following sub-
    jects.

    A. Japanese paper folding

    B. Ping-pong

VI. What subject headings are suggested for the following subjects in
    LCSH?

    A. Addresses_____

    B. Automobile thefts _____

SECOND EXERCISE

I. List the usable subject headings on the following pages in *LCSH*.

A. page 606 _____

B. page 695, column 3 _____

C. page 889 _____

II. Give an illustration of each kind of cross reference and sub-division for the subject, "Detergents, Synthetic," in *LCSH*.

A. _____

B. _____

C. _____

D. _____

III. Define a "see also" reference.

_____

IV. List the related, more specific references for the following topics in *LCSH*.

A. Commercial art _____

B. Friendship _____

V. Answer the following questions about the subject, "Friendship," in *LCSH*.

A. What is the more specific, related heading listed second in

LCSH?_____

B. Look in the subject card catalog under your answer to A above and give the call number on the first catalog card found under this subject heading.

VI. "x" references are not important for your purposes and may be dis-regarded. (Check one.)

A. _____ True

B. _____ False

VII. Define "xx" references.

_____

VIII. List the generally broader subject headings given for the following subjects in *LCSH*.

A. Consumer credit _____

B. Immigrants _____

C. Medicine _____

IX. A. What is the first, broader heading to which you are referred when you look under "Fruit trees" in *LCSH?*

_____

B. Look in the subject card catalog under your answer to A
above and give the call number on the first card filed
under that heading.

X. List the additional, related subject headings for the following subjects in *LCSH*.

A. Coconut _____

B. Gem cutting _____

SUBJECT - SUBDIVISIONS
(Orders of Arrangement)

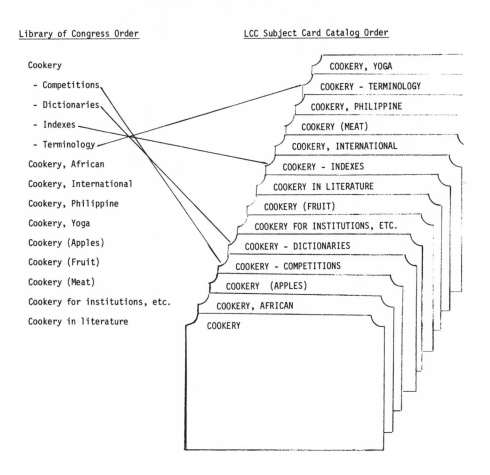

Library of Congress Order

Cookery

- Competitions
- Dictionaries
- Indexes
- Terminology

Cookery, African

Cookery, International

Cookery, Philippine

Cookery, Yoga

Cookery (Apples)

Cookery (Fruit)

Cookery (Meat)

Cookery for institutions, etc.

Cookery in literature

LCC Subject Card Catalog Order

COOKERY, YOGA

COOKERY - TERMINOLOGY

COOKERY, PHILIPPINE

COOKERY (MEAT)

COOKERY, INTERNATIONAL

COOKERY - INDEXES

COOKERY IN LITERATURE

COOKERY (FRUIT)

COOKERY FOR INSTITUTIONS, ETC.

COOKERY - DICTIONARIES

COOKERY - COMPETITIONS

COOKERY (APPLES)

COOKERY, AFRICAN

COOKERY

Section Three
5

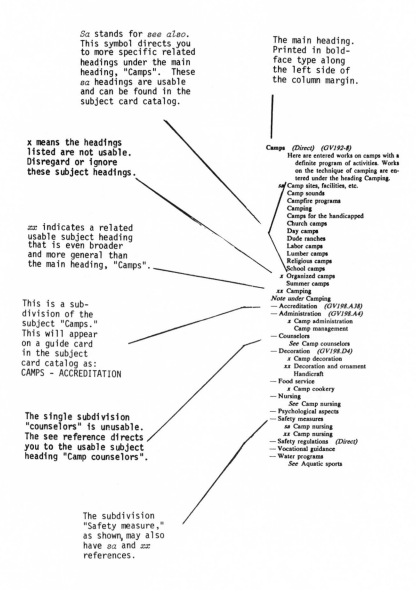

Sa stands for *see also*.
This symbol directs you
to more specific related
headings under the main
heading, "Camps". These
sa headings are usable
and can be found in the
subject card catalog.

The main heading.
Printed in bold-
face type along
the left side of
the column margin.

x means the headings
listed are not usable.
Disregard or ignore
these subject headings.

xx indicates a related
usable subject heading
that is even broader
and more general than
the main heading, "Camps".

This is a sub-
division of the
subject "Camps."
This will appear
on a guide card
in the subject
card catalog as:
CAMPS - ACCREDITATION

The single subdivision
"counselors" is unusable.
The see reference directs
you to the usable subject
heading "Camp counselors".

The subdivision
"Safety measure,"
as shown, may also
have *sa* and *xx*
references.

Camps *(Direct) (GV192-8)*
   Here are entered works on camps with a
   definite program of activities. Works
   on the technique of camping are en-
   tered under the heading Camping.
sa Camp sites, facilities, etc.
   Camp sounds
   Campfire programs
   Camping
   Camps for the handicapped
   Church camps
   Day camps
   Dude ranches
   Labor camps
   Lumber camps
   Religious camps
   School camps
x Organized camps
   Summer camps
xx Camping
Note under Camping
— Accreditation *(GV198.A38)*
— Administration *(GV198.A4)*
   x Camp administration
      Camp management
— Counselors
      See Camp counselors
— Decoration *(GV198.D4)*
   x Camp decoration
   xx Decoration and ornament
      Handicraft
— Food service
   x Camp cookery
— Nursing
      See Camp nursing
— Psychological aspects
— Safety measures
   sa Camp nursing
   xx Camp nursing
— Safety regulations *(Direct)*
— Vocational guidance
— Water programs
      See Aquatic sports

THIRD EXERCISE

I.   How can you identify a subdivision of a subject heading in *LCSH?*

_____

II. How can you identify a subdivision of a subject heading in the subject
     card catalog?

_____

III. Using *LCSH*, list all the usable subdivisions for the following subject
     headings.

     A. Alcoholic beverages   _____

     B. Oral communication   _____

IV. List the place or geographic subdivisions found in the subject card catalog
     for the following subject headings:

     A. Design, decorative   _____

     B. Shrubs   _____

V.   Which of the following (found in drawer 108 of the subject card catalog) are:

     A. Subject headings with subdivisions?

         1. Siberia - History   4. Slave-trade - Africa

         2. Sikkim, India   5. Slavery in Rome

         3. Singers, American   6. Slums - U.S.

     _____

     B. Which of the above are place subdivisions?

     _____

VI. Answer the following questions about the subject heading, "Mammals."

     A. What is the second subdivision shown in *LCSH* under the subject heading?

     _____

     B. When written out on a guide card in the subject card catalog, how does
         the subject heading with the above subdivision read?

     _____

     C. What is the call number of a book in this library found in the subject
         card catalog under that subject heading with that subdivision?

     _____

FOURTH EXERCISE

I. Give the subject headings for the following names found in the subject card catalog.

    A. President John Kennedy _____

    B. Folies Bergere _____

    C. American Stock Exchange _____

II. Give the subject headings for the following local interest subjects in the subject card catalog.

    A. University of Hawaii _____

    B. Ala Wai _____

    C. Hawaiian quilting _____

SECTION THREE EXERCISES -- ANSWERS

FIRST EXERCISE

   I. B

  II. A see reference directs you from an unusable to a usable heading.

 III. A. Bantu law
           See Law, Bantu

           Bantu marriage customs and rites
           See Marriage customs and rites, Bantu

       B. Child suicide
           See Children - Suicidal behavior

           Child vagrants
           See Children, Vagrant

       C. None

  IV. A. Infants

       B. Drug abuse
           Narcotic habit

       C. Demonology

   V. A. (See Origami)

           TT870   TT870   TT870
           D364   H32   S25

       B. (See Table tennis)

           GV1005
           M5

  VI. A. Baccalaureate addresses
           Lectures and lecturing
           Orations
           Speeches, addresses, etc.

       B. Automobile thieves
           Theft from motor vehicles

SECTION THREE ANSWERS (CONTINUED)

SECOND EXERCISE

   I. A. English language
       B. Folk-lore of bees; Folk-lore of birds; Folk-lore of children
       C. None -- heading on a preceding page

   II. A. *Sa* references 1. Detergent pollution of rivers, lakes, etc.
                              2. Detergent pollution of the sea
                              3. Synthetic detergents industry

       B. *x* reference 1. Synthetic detergents

       C. *xx* references 1. Cleaning compounds
                             2. Soap
                             3. Surface active agents

       D. subdivisions 1. - Biodegradation
                            2. - Patents
                            3. - Quality Control
                            4. - Testing
                            5. - Toxicology

   III. A see also ref. directs you to related subject headings that
         are usually more specific.

   IV. A. Art and industry
         Color in advertising
         Photography, Advertising

       B. Fellowship
         Love
         Sympathy

   V. A. Love

       B. HQ33
         F77
         1963

   VI. A. True

   VII. *xx* references are related, generally broader aspects of the
         subject heading they are listed under.

   VIII. A. Banks and banking
          Credit
          Finance, Personal

        B. None (This is a see reference)

SECTION THREE ANSWERS (CONTINUED)

    C. Human biology
        Life sciences
        Pathology

IX. A. Fruit-culture

    B. SB359
        C38

X. A. *Sa* Coconut industry
            Coir
            Copra
        xx Copra

    B. *Sa* Diamond cutting
        xx Cutting
            Gems
            Precious stones

THIRD EXERCISE

  I. By the dash, " — ," which precedes the subdivision

 II. By the dash, " — ," which separates the subdivision from the main heading.

III. A. - Analysis
        - Patents
        - Standards

    B. - Juvenile literature
        - Moral and religious aspects
          (- Research is NOT a usable subdivision. It is a see reference)

IV. A. - Africa
        - China
        - Japan
        - Mexico

    B. - Hawaii
        - New Zealand
        - U. S.

  V. A. 1, 4, 6

    B. 4, 6 (1 is a subdivision of a place, "Siberia" but not a place subdivision).

VI. A. Anatomy

    B. MAMMALS - ANATOMY

    C. QL713
        H67
        1970

SECTION THREE ANSWERS (CONTINUED)

FOURTH EXERCISE

  I. A. KENNEDY, JOHN FITZGERALD, PRES. U. S., 1917 - 1963
      B. PARIS. FOLIES-BERGERE
      C. NEW YORK. AMERICAN STOCK EXCHANGE

 II. A. HAWAII. UNIVERSITY, HONOLULU.
      B. ALA WAI CANAL
      C. QUILTING - HAWAII

END OF SECTION THREE

DO NOT PROCEED TO SECTION FOUR UNTIL YOU HAVE TESTED FOR SECTION THREE!!!

PLEASE BRING THIS WORKBOOK TO THE INFORMATION/REFERENCE DESK BEFORE
TESTING. ALSO RETURN YOUR PAMPHLET/TAPE STUDY MATERIALS TO THE
RESERVE MATERIALS DESK.

DO NOT PROCEED ANY FURTHER IN THIS WORKBOOK
WITHOUT THE INSTRUCTION CONTAINED IN EITHER
TAPE TC18 OR THE PAMPHLET FOR SECTION FOUR
OF THE LIBRARY UNIT, BOTH OF WHICH ARE AVAIL-
ABLE AT THE RESERVE MATERIALS DESK.

STANDARD MAGAZINE INDEX CITATION

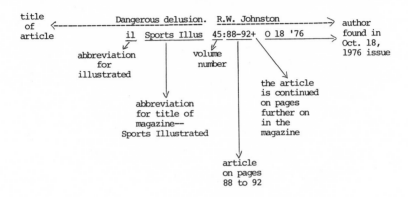

FIFTH EXERCISE

I. In the following citation identify the parts listed A through G.

Speedy gem polisher you can build. il
Newsweek 145:102+ Ja '76.

A. Speedy gem polisher you can build _____

B. il _____

C. Newsweek _____

D. 145 _____

E. 102 _____

F. + _____

G. Ja '76 _____

Answers to the questions asked in the tape or pamphlet (page 4)

1. *Sports Illustrated* for October 18, 1976 is available on microfilm.

2. *Sports Illustrated* is a weekly magazine. Like other weekly magazines, such as *Time* and *Newsweek*, it is available on microfilm about every six months. Thus, it is necessary to check the microfilm drawer or the Back Issue Periodicals shelves, to see in which form last October's issue is available. Keep in mind that back issues of magazines may be checked out of the library, so if the microfilm is not yet available, and the paper issue is not on the shelf, the issue could be checked out.

SIXTH EXERCISE

I. Leeward Community College Library: (circle the correct answer)

A. has *Fortune* magazine issues of 1972 in paper form only.

B. does not have *Fortune* magazine for 1972.

C. has *Fortune* magazine for 1972 on microfilm only.

D. has *Fortune* magazine for 1972 in both paper form and microfilm.

II. Does Leeward Community College Library have *Personnel and Guidance Journal?* (Answer each question either yes or no.)

A. in paper form? _____

B. for Spring 1963? _____

C. for the present year? _____

Section Four
15

READERS' GUIDE TO PERIODICAL LITERATURE

MARCH 10, 1976   147

1. *Subject heading*

2. *Subdivision (of Women)*

3. *Sub-subdivision (of subdivision Europe)*

4. *See also reference*

5. *See reference*

WOHLHUTER, Rick
  Wohlhuter's better half. P. Putnam. il Sports
  Illus 44:49-50 F 16 '76
WOLCOTT, Leonard T.
  In defense of missions. Chr Today 20:15-17 Ja
  16 '76
WOLMAN, William
  Economic diary. Bus W p 14+ F 9; 14+ F 16;
  15-16 F 23 '76
WOLTERS, Richard
  Pictures. il Writers Digest 56:6+ F '76
WOLVES
  Showdown on the tundra. R. Rau. il Read Digest
  108:147-50 F '76
WOLYNSKI, Mara
  What men and women should know about each
  other now. Mademoiselle 82:134+ F '76
WOMEN
  Notes from abroad (cont) Ms 4:104-5+ F '76
    Anatomy and physiology
    See also
    Menstruation
        Crime
  American women and crime. R. J. Simon. bibl
  f il Ann Am Acad 423:31-46 Ja '76
        Economic conditions
  Displaced homemaker. A. McCarthy. Common-
  weal 103:38+ Ja 16 '76
        Employment
  Job strategies '76. N. A. Comer. Mademoiselle
  82:112-15 F '76
  Women on the job. McCalls 103:68+ F '76
    See also
    Women—Occupations
        Equal rights
  Discreet victory; effects of wide-ranging laws
  in Great Britain. il Time 107:49 F 2 '76
  Due process and pregnancies. C. E. Polhemus.
  Mo Labor R 99:54-5 Ja '76
  Getting off the boat and into the power
  swim. M. Korda. Harp Baz 109:119+ F '76
  Men and women together; legal aspects; adapta-
  tion of address. R. C. Allen. il MH 59:21-5
  Fall '75
  Pregnancies and Title VII. C. E. Polhemus. Mo
  Labor R 99:55 Ja '76
  Second sex; 25 years later; interview; ed by
  J. Gerassi. S. de Beauvoir. por Society 13:79-
  85 Ja '76
        Health and hygiene
  Medical checklist for mothers. A. J. Goldberg.
  Parents Mag 51:18+ F '76
        History
  Men & herstory. J. Jaffee; discussion. SLJ 22:
  2 Ja '76
    See also
    Indians of South America—Women
        Legal status, laws, etc.
    See also
    Women—Equal rights
        'Occupations
  Emerging woman (cont) il Am Home 79:70-1+
  Ja; 55+ F '76
  Five women who began again. il por Made-
  moiselle 82:86+ F '76
  Found women; Catron County, New Mexico. M.
  J. L. Woodfin. il Ms 4:57-61 F '76
  That career quandary. J. Marks. Seventeen 35:
  25 F '76
        Social and moral questions
  Movin' on—alone. K. McLean. Am Home 79:28
  Ja '76
        Africa
  In Africa & Europe: how do women spend 1440
  minutes a day? il Sr Schol 108:18-19 F 10 '76
        Europe
  In Africa & Europe: how do women spend 1440
  minutes a day? il Sr Schol 108:18-19 F 10 '76
        Bowi
  Three faces of Celtic woman. J. Markale. il
  UNESCO Courier 28:18-22+ D '75
        Great Britain
  Discreet victory. il Time 107:49 F 2 '76
        Southwestern states
  Southwest quilters. M. Callum. il Bet Hom &
  Gard 54:68-75 F '76
        United States
  Found women; Catron County, New Mexico. M.
  J. L. Woodfin. il Ms 4:57-61 F '76
  7 women who made the right moves. il Made-
  moiselle 82:130-1 F '76
  Wheelsmart American woman. D. List. il Vogue
  166:152-7+ F '76
  Womanpower! A new American doctrine. B.
  Abzug. por Redbook 146:34+ F '76
  Women of the month (cont) il Ladies Home J
  93:79 F '76

        History
  Have-it girls; American women of style, exhibit
  at the Costume Institute of Metropolitan mu-
  seum of art. D. Vreeland. il por Vogue 166:
  160-5 F '76
  Thinking about Western thinking. J. Didion.
  Esquire 85:10+ F '76
WOMEN, Famous
  Ten most admired women. il Good H 182:14+
  Ja '76
WOMEN and men
  Persons in the office; an ardent plea for sexual
  harassment and flirting. R. Koenig. il Harper
  252:87-8+ F '76
  What men and women should know about each
  other now. M. Wolynski; R. Kramer. Made-
  moiselle 82:134-5+ F '76
WOMEN and politics
  Womanpower! A new American doctrine. B.
  Abzug. por Redbook 146:34+ F '76
WOMEN and religion
  Women in the church. T. Balasuriya. Common-
  weal 103:29-42 Ja 16 '76
    See also
    Nuns
    Women clergy
WOMEN artists
        Bibliography
  Women as artists. M. Schiller. Am Artist 40:
  22-5 F '76
WOMEN athletes
  On the beam at the young folks' home; Olympia
  Manor, training school for women gymnasts.
  A. Verschoth. il Sports Illus 44:54+ F 2 '76
WOMEN clergy
  Mr and Mrs Minister. G. Nadel. il pors N Y
  Times Mag p 14-15+ F 1 '76
WOMEN conductors (music)
  Wielding their batons too:
  Brico. A. Brico. por Opera N 40:14 F 14 '76
  Queler. E. Queler. por Opera N 40:12 F 14
  '76
  Somogi. J. Somogi. por Opera N 40:13 F
  14 '76
WOMEN in literature
  Men & herstory. C. Jaffee; discussion. SLJ 22:2
  Ja '76
WOMEN in politics
    See also
    Women public officers
WOMEN in the arts
  Defining their role; symposium. il Opera N 40:
  16-19 F 14 '76
  Viewpoint. R. Jacobson. Opera N 40:4 F 14 '76
WOMEN in the television industry
  Lady behind the lens; news cinematographer.
  J. Maple. il pors Ebony 31:44-6+ F '76
WOMEN journalists
  Common scold: Anne Royall. D. Dodd and B.
  Williams. il por Am Hist Illus 10:32-8 Ja '76
WOMEN librarians. See Librarians
WOMEN ministers. See Women clergy
WOMEN moving picture directors
  Look this way. Breathe. Brava! L. Wertmuller.
  M. Orth. por Newsweek 87:79 Ja 26 '76
WOMEN photographers
    See also
    Maple, J.
WOMEN public officers
  One quiet victory; election in Schwenksville, Pa.
  P. Span. il Ms 4:17 F '76
WOMEN sailors. See Servicewomen
WOMEN scientists
        Conferences
  Conference on minority women scientists. P. Q.
  Hall and others. Science 191:457 F 6 '76
WOMEN'S liberation movement
  What has gone wrong with the women's move-
  ment? Harp Baz 109:59+ F '76
WONG, LaVerne
  Meeting place for the total educator. il Wilson
  Lib Bull 50:390-4 Ja '76
WOOD, Leona
  Aman-Wood Shay; melting pot of ethnic dance.
  V. H. Swisher. il Dance Mag 50:63-6 F '76
WOOD, Peter
  Super bowl of birding. il N Y Times Mag p30-
  3 F 15 '76
WOOD as fuel
  Which firewood? Where to find it? What about
  cost? il Sunset 156:94 F '76
  Wood fuel crisis. Sci Digest 79:16-17 Ja '76
WOODBRIDGE, N.J. public library. See Libraries
  —New Jersey
WOODCHUCKS
  Prophet without honor; the groundhog. R. Beck.
  il Outdoor Life 157:62-3+ F '76
WOODEN, John
  Basketball's John Wooden; what a coach can
  teach a teacher. R. G. Tharp and R. Galli-
  more. bibl il pors Psychol Today 9:74-8 Ja
  '76
WOODEN boats. See Boats—Materials
WOODEN toys. See Toys
WOODFIN, Mary Jo Lass
  Found women; Catron County, New Mexico. il
  Ms 4:57-61 F '76

SEVENTH EXERCISE

DO NOT MARK THE INDEXES.

I. Using the *Business Periodicals Index* for July 1964–June 1965:

    A. Find the second citation under the subject AIRPLANES IN BUSINESS.
    What is the title of the article? _____

    B. What does "il" stand for? _____

    C. What is the complete name of the magazine in which the article
    appears? _____

    D. What pages does the article appear on? _____

    E. What is the volume number? _____

    F. What does the "+" stand for? _____

II. Using the *Readers' Guide to Periodical Literature* for March 1967–
    February 1968 answer the following questions:

    A. What subject heading is used for articles about used automobiles?
    _____

    B. What is the name of the magazine that the first article listed under
    the above subject heading appears in? _____

    C. In what issue (or date) of the magazine does the article appear?
    _____

    D. Is the article available for you to read in this library? _____

III. Using the *Education Index* for July 1967–June 1968, answer the following
    questions.

    A. What is the complete name of the magazine in which there is an article
    about spectrochemistry? _____

    B. How many citations are there under the subject COURTS and its
    related headings? _____

    C. How many usable subdivisions are there under the subject INSTRUMENTAL
    MUSIC? _____

Section Four
17

INDEX TO THE HONOLULU ADVERTISER AND
HONOLULU STAR-BULLETIN

1. **Subject heading**

                                    Section

2. **Newspaper:**   Date / Page Column
    A = Advertiser
    S = Star Bulletin
    S&A = Sunday paper   to be held

                                          . Joy' at Aala

           A4/11/74 A3:2   .n Stad S6/5/

                                          . floating festival

3. **See also reference**

4. **See reference**   . A8/2/74 D7:1

                                          .layed S8/14/74 D8:1
                                          owds S9/3/74 A1:5

                                          .s A3/5/74 A11:3

                                          al Ctr; charge exploitation

                                          ntract talks A7/23/74 A2:2
                                          A7/24/74 A7:1
                                          .on arbitration, mediation A7/

                                          rch A7/26/74 A4:2
                                          .usal A7/27/74 A3:1
                                          .par on meet S&A7/28/74 A3:2
                                          . fight against Cultural Ctr S8/3/74 C8:3
                                          .al Ctr emp may be expelled A8/5/74 A3:2
                                          .ntinue picketing S8/5/74 A10:1 A8/6/24 A5:1
                                          .End picketing A8/13/74 A3:2
                                          Family sues Polynesian Cultural Center for
                                          $500,000 A8/30/74 A6:5
                                          FILIPINO CHAMBER OF COMMERCE
                                          Sponsors Christmas show A12/26/74 B4:1
             .s&A6/16/   FILIPINO COOKERY
                                          See COOKERY, FILIPINO
                                          FILIPINO MUSIC
                                          See MUSIC, FILIPINO
                                          FILIPINOS
          .rs in Vietnam S3/4/74 A1   Ex-Huk ldr Luis Taruc on 1st U.S. visit A2/4/74
          .LIAM ERNEST, 1923-   C3:1 S2/4/74 C16:3
          .pers taken out for Senate &   Ltr: Why Filipinos migrate to the U.S. S9/19/
          / Cncl S8/7/74 C3:8   74 B12:1
          .itional restrictions on development ● **1.** FILIPINOS IN THE HAWAIIAN ISLANDS
          y Kauai Cty Plng Cmsn S12/13/74   Emme Tomimbang has "Young Sounds Philip-
                                               pines" program on KISA A1/2/74 C1:3
          .DEZ, E. K., SHOWS, INC.   Ltr: Thompson wrong in blaming immigrants for
          .ernandez takes fun seriously A4/26/74   high welfare costs by A Cahill S3/8/74 A19:4
                                               Susi Ng Pilipinas at Leeward Cmnty College help
          .ES   stus take pride in cultural heritage A3/29/74 C1:1
          .isle ferry seen sailing over setback S&A   Look at St's fastest growing ethnic gp S3/29/
          .7/74 A3:2   74 A2:1
          .wn Inter-Island Ferry System has organizing   Judge Benj Menor, who will become nation's
          .mit extended for 30 days S3/5/74 D7:6   1st Supreme Ct Justice of Fil ancestry, looks
          .c Sea Transp jetfoil due soon A3/13/74 A3 ● **2.** back A4/11/74 A3:2
          .publishes 12-stu study on ferry impact S&A   Jackery Lin Tejada wins Miss Hawaii Filipina
          .21/74 A14:1   Contest S7/1/74 B2:4
          .earl Harbor ferry eyed A7/27/74 A5:1   Kauai movie by Wm J Sollner depicts 400 yrs
          .Jan for $50 million "sea highway" readied   of Filipino culture S7/15/74 C5:1
          .10/25/74 D4:1   Most cases of Toxoplasmosis found here because
          .ee also HAWAIIAN INTER-ISLAND FERRY   they eat raw meat S8/28/74 C8:1
          . SYSTEM INC.   Immigrants looking for a better life S9/9/74
          .IYDROFOILS   B1:1
          .IYDROPLANES   Hawaii's troubled Filipino community S&A9/
          .RTILIZATION (BIOLOGY)   22/74 A3:1
          .JH scientists research in-vitro fertilization &   Immigrant assimilation discussed A9/23/74 A8:3
          .Ivlpmt of eggs outside of animal's body A2/   Meeting on school beating death S9/23/
          .!6/74 B1:1   74 A6:4
          .RTILIZERS AND MANURES   Oahu Filipino Council organizes task force to
          .5 Hunter's series on Van Geldern, man behind   work on sch tensions S10/7/74 A10:1
          .ias project S&A6/16/74 A1:1 A6/17/74 A1:2   Ad bought by Marcos govt upsets Isle Filipinos
          .16/18/74 A1:2   S11/74 D1:4 A11/12/74 A9:2

FILIPINOS IN THE HAWAIIAN ISLANDS
P.I. didn't buy ad; United Fil Council did A11/
13/74 A4:3 S11/13/74 A9:7
Series on immigrants: Hawaii's no paradise
S11/29/74 A2:3; Frustration takes heavy toll
S11/30/74 A2:2; Proud Filipinos resist going
on welfare S12/2/74 BB:1; He no longer
teaches S12/3/74 G3:1
See also OAHU FILIPINO COMMUNITY ◀—— **3.**
COUNCIL
OPERATION MANONG
FILM FESTIVALS
See MOTION PICTURE FESTIVALS
FINANCES
See HAWAII (STATE) FINANCES
HONOLULU. FINANCES
FINGERPRINTS
HB 2467 would amend law to allow suspected
juvenile felons to be fingerprinted w/out prior
Fam Ct OK A2/19/74 A5:1
FIRE PREVENTION
High-rise protection: sprinklers vs containment
A1/16/74 A4:5
Stricter fire rules urged for high rise S1/16/74 E1
E1:1
Cncl gp mandates sprinkler for high-rises A2/2/
74 A2:3
D Pellegrin's series re fire safety in high-rise Hon
A4/9/74 A1:2 A4/10/74 A1:1 A4/11/74 A1:2
A4/12/74 A1:3
City Managing Dir crit story re deficiencies in
Fire Dept A4/11/74 A1:2
Edit: Act before tragedy strikes S&A4/14/74
D2:1
Sprinkler system dampens 'flame' in Cncl A4/18/
74 A3:6
Fire sprinkler need in high-rises debates S6/26/
74 B1:1
City Council holds bill mandating fire sprinklers
A9/21/74 A4:4
City OK expected on sprinkler bill for bldgs
over 75 ft A10/26/74 A4:2 S10/28/74 A12:1
Sprinkler measure approved A10/30/74 A2:2
S10/30/74 D1:1
Fire sprinklers now required in new high-rise
bldgs S11/4/74 A20:1
New city bldg relies on smoke detection system
S11/5/74 A13:3
Edit: safety & high-rise fires A11/8/74 A18:1
FIRE SAFETY
See FIRE PREVENTION ◀—— **4.**
FIRE STATIONS
Kona dedicates fire station S&A3/3/74 A9:1
FIREARMS
City asks state for handgun ban S3/1/74 C6:1
Gun enthusiasts blast gun control bill A3/6/74
A10
Citizens Home Protective Assn urge others to
fight control bill A3/14/74 A4:1
Gun control: Pro and con S&A4/21/74 E53
Felon since '56, Saml Naumu's now cleared
S5/23/74 C24:3
Flare gun is "not a weapon" A6/14/74 C7:2
St Supreme Ct upheld conviction of M L
Tsukiyama A8/31/74 A6:1
Lori Matsukawa, Miss Teenage America, learns
to shoot S&A11/10/74 C4:1
See also SHOOTINGS
FIREMEN
More for Big Isle, Kauai asked by union S5/22/
74 B6:1
Kauai & Big Isle firemen stage "sick-ins" to
protest contract deadlock S7/18/74 A1:7
Fire fighters "sick-in" may spread A7/14/74
A6:2
Hon firemen join sick-in; all isles now affected
S7/19/74 A1:1
On duty firemen keep sidlns up S7/22/74 A1:1
Firemen still stay off jobs S7/22/74 A2:1
Relieved by new shift S7/23/74 A1:3
Ill firemen caused false alarm says City phy-
sician S7/23/74 A4:2

EIGHTH EXERCISE

Using the *Index to the Honolulu Advertiser and Honolulu Star-Bulletin* for 1972, find a list of citations for the subject, PARENTS ANONYMOUS. There are several articles on the subject. List the following information for the first and fourth citations. (DO NOT MARK THE INDEX.)

	Newspaper Name	Date of Issue	Page	Column
1st	_____	_____	_____	_____
4th	_____	_____	_____	_____

HAWAII OBSERVER INDEX - SAMPLE CITATION

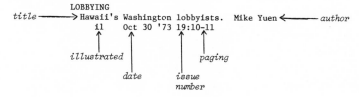

NEW YORK TIMES INDEX

Section Four
19

1. Subject heading

2. See also reference

3. See reference

4. Date, page, column

May 3, 15:4

5. Subdivision

6. Sub-subdivision (notice the black dot)

7. (S) = short article
   (M) = medium article
   (L) = long article

... see also US — Econ Co...

HARRIS, Louis, & Associates. See also Pres Elect
'76, My 13
HARRIS, Milton (Dr). See also Lubricants, My 15
HARRIS, William. See also Kidnapping, Hearst,
Patricia, My 6
HARRISON, John. See also US — Pol, My 14
HARSHMAN, Marv. See also Basketball — Coll, My 4
HART, Gary W (Sen). See also Chemical Warfare,
My 10. Coal — US, My 8. US — Econ Conditions, My 8.
US — Interior Dept, My 8. Wyoming, My 8
HART, Gary W (Mrs). See also US — Cong (Genl),
My 14
HART, Judith (Min). See also Mozambique, My 12
HARTE-Hanks Newspapers Inc
   Harte-Hanks Newspapers Inc of San Antonia, Tex,
acquires Jacksonville, Fla, TV station TV 12 Inc for
$10.4-million (S), My 14,71:5
HARTFORD Insurance Group. See also ITT, My 2
HARTKE, Vance (Sen). See also Veterans — US, My 8
HARTMAN, Arthur A (Asst Sec). See also Cyprus,
My 7

1. HARVARD Club (NYC)
   Reverses policy seeking to weaken martinis as econ
measure, following flood of protests by club members
and record drop in martini sales; restores 8-1 drink
(S). My 2,37:8
HARVARD University. See also Labor — US —
Unemployment, My 13. Rowing, My 12. Saudi
Arabia, My 11
   Harvard Law School's East Asian Center invited
Benigno S Aquino Jr, currently engaged in hunger
strike while being detained in Philippines by Pres
Marcos, to be visiting fellow (S), My 9,40:8; Harvard
Univ Bd of Overseers approves plan to give equal
consideration to men and women applying to Harvard
and Radcliffe Colls, beginning in '76; plan replaces
quota of 5 men for every 2 women admitted and is
expected to bring male-female ration to 3-2 'within
reasonable period'; plan sets as goal opening of all
prizes and fellowships to both men and women,
'substantial representation of both sexes among
teaching faculty and adm' and improvement in
physical facilities for women; recommends no increase
in size of coll, move that will cause drop in number of
males admitted and has apparently alarmed some
alumni; 2 colls will remain technically separate
institutions, but plan foresees eventual merger; vice
pres Dr Chase N Peterson comments (M), My 14,9:6

2. HARWOOD, Michael. See also Energy and Power,
My 11
HARYOU-ACT (Orgn). See also Educ — NYC —
School Adm, My 3
HASAN, Nurul (Min). See also India, My 12
HASEGAWA, Ryutaro. See also Oil — Far East —
China, People's Republic of, My 12
HASKELL, Floyd K (Sen). See also Coal — US, My 6.
US — Environment, My 14. US — Interior Dept, My 14.
Wyoming, My 14
HASSAN II, King of Morocco. See also Morocco,
My 5
HASSANEIN, Salah M. See also Motion Pictures —
US, My 11
HASSETT, William D. See also Housing — NYS, My 1

3. HATCH, Francis W Jr (Repr)
   Father dies (S), My 15,46:4
HATCH Act. See US — Govt Employes — Hatch Act
HATCHER, Richard G (Mayor). See also Gary
(Ind), My 7
HATFIELD, Ella. See also Hatfield Family, My 12
HATFIELD, Mark O (Sen). See also Numismatics,
My 11. US — Interior Dept, My 14
HATFIELD Family
   Ella Hatfield, whose marriage to Charles McCoy in
1898, schocked feuding families of Hatfield and
McCoys in W Va and Ky, dies May 9 at age 98 (S),
My 12,30:5
HATHAWAY, C F, Corp. See also Apparel — US —
Labor, My 3
HATHAWAY, Stanley K. See also Air Pollution — US,
My 7. Air Pollution — Wyoming, My 1,6. Area
Planning, My 7. Coal — US, My 1,6,7,8. Oil — US —
Offshore, My 6. US — Environment, My 1,3,4,6,14. US —
Interior Dept, My 1,2,3,4,6,7,8,10,14. Water Pollution,
My 1,6. Water — Wyoming, My 7. Wyoming, My 1,7,
8,14

H...
also
My 3.
My 10
HEALTH.
HEALTH on
NY. See also
HEALTH Insur...
indus and union...
HEALTH Organiz...
   WHO votes to a...
South and North V...
HEALTH Research Gro
HEALY, John F (Chmn).
HEARST, Patricia. See als...
My 4
HEARST Newspapers. See also .
My 2
HEART. See als. related headings, eg.
   Byron B Brenden receives patent for t...
employs sound to break through solids, metho...
to have increasing importance in med diagnosis; ...
Health Insts is sponsoring research in heart field (M),
4. My 3,15:4; Lee Roy Hargrave Jr, former nursing aide
convicted of administering lethal dose of medication to
elderly heart patient, takes overdose of amphetamines
shortly after he is sentenced to life imprisonment,
Petersburg, Va; Judge Oliver A Pollard imposed life
sentence on jury's recommendation; Hargrave worked
in Petersburg Gen Hosp coronary unit, where 6
patients died after receiving massive unauthorized
doses of heart depressant lidocaine; was tried in death
of Josephine Thomas, 73 (S), My 7,41:1
5. Transplants
   Perrin Johnson, 61, world's longest living heart
transplant patient, dies 6 1/2 yrs after receiving new
heart; developed lung complications (S), My 3,27:7
6. • Twin-Heart Transplants
   Unidentified South African man receives 2d heart in
transplant operation, Cape Town; Dr Jaques Losman
heads cardiac team (S), My 6,28:4; 3d double-heart
transplant patient condition, Cape Town, South Africa
7. (S), My 7,15:1
HEATING. See also fields of use
   NYS Atty Gen Lefkowitz opposes state legis to
eliminate preferential utility rates for electrically
heated homes, which, he says, would send already
high elec-heating bills soaring and would lead to
'widespread abandonment of homes and undesirable
hardships,' May 2 testimony to Assembly Com on
Corps, Authorities and Comms; says such a bill should
contain grandfather clause for existing all-elec homes;
opposes proposed ban on construction of all-elec
hoems but favors measure barring utilities from
paying any subsidies for conversions to all-elec
heating and requiring consumers buying such conversions to be apprised of projected costs; Jane Steben
of GET Consumer Protection says utilities should
absorb extra costs; Con Ed vp Robert O Lehrman
supports ban on 'undue or unreasonable' rate
preferences; PSC moved toward elimination of such
preferences when it revised Con Ed rate structure
change it approved in Nov '74 (M), My 3,35:3; NYC
City Council approves rent increases of up to $9 per
mo to compensate landlords of rent-controlled apts for
increased fuel costs; bill will require owners to satisfy
certain fuel-expenditure requirements; low-income and
elderly tenants will be exempt; tenant and landlord
spokesmen comment (L), My 10,18:2; Eileen O'Brien
reply to Roger Starr's Apr 27 defense of Beame Adm's
proposal for special rent increases in rent-controlled
apartments to cover landlords' increased fuel costs,
My 11,VIII,8:2
HEBERT, F Edward (Repr). See also Oil — US —
Prices, My 4
HEBREW (Organizations). See also other key words
HEBREW University (Jerusalem). See also Yeshiva
University, My 4
HECHT, Buric n G (Assemblyman). See also Courts —
NYS — Supreme Court (State), My 10

theat...
Theater
HERBERT, V...
Revs, Naughty
HERBERT H Lehm...
My 12
HERBICIDES
   Ed, commenting on pr
Vietnam, cites dispositio
harmful Orange herbicid
during conflict, My 8,38
HERDE, Thomas. See also
News — US, My 3
HERKO, Robert. See also
HERMAN, Beaumont A. '
England College (Mass),
HERMAN, Richard L. See
HERNANDEZ, Betty Cece
Addiction — US, My 7
HERNANDEZ, Martha. Se
University, My 1
HEROIN. Use Drug Addi
HERSHMAN, Mendes. Se
Corp (NYS), My 8
HERZOG, Raymond H. Se
Finances, My 14
HESS, Charles T (Dr). Se
of, My 4
HESS, Joe. See also Kara
HESTER, James M (Dr). S
My 5
HESTON, Charlton. See a
American, My 4
HEVESI, Alan G (Assemb
Homes, My 2
HEWITT, Bob. See also T
HEWMAN, Susan H. See
HEXTER, Marguerite and
See also Philanthropy, N
HEYMAN, Michael (Prof)
University of, My 11
HEYMAN, Philip B. See a
HEYWARD, Carter (Rev.)
My 15
HIALEAH Race Track. See
Thoroughbreds, My 8
HIAS Service, United. See
HICKS, Louise Day (Coun
Mass — Equal Educ, My
HIEN Luong Bridge. See a
Vietnam, My 10
HIGH Schools. Use Educ
HIGHER Education (Orga
beginning Education or E
HIGHLAND Manor Nursin
See also Nursing Homes,

NINTH EXERCISE

I. How many citations are there on discrimination in housing in New Jersey
in the *New York Times Index* for 1970? _____

II. A. In the following citation from the *New York Times Index*, what does
4:3 stand for? _____

Fire in dorm causes $75,000 damage (L), JL 14, 4:3

B. What does "(L)" stand for in the above citation?

SECTION FOUR EXERCISES -- ANSWERS

FIFTH EXERCISE

I. A. Title of article
    B. Illustrated
    C. Name of magazine
    D. Volume number
    E. Page article begins on
    F. Article continues on pages further on in the magazine
    G. Date of magazine issue.

SIXTH EXERCISE

I. C

II. A. No
     B. No (Note that on "Abbreviations Used" page at front of the list,
             "S" stands for September and "Spr" stands for Spring.)
     C. No

SEVENTH EXERCISE

I. A. Business aviation shows overseas growth
    B. Illustrated
    C. *American Aviation*
    D. 22 to 24
    E. 28
    F. continued on further pages of the magazine

II. A. Automobiles, Used
     B. Motor Trend
     C. December, 1967
     D. No (The library's subscription did not begin until January 1968)

III. A. *Journal of Chemical Education*
      B. 6 (Though the first citation under COURTS refers you to two separate
             issues of the magazine it is still considered to be <u>one</u> <u>citation</u>,
             as the indentation of the lines indicates.)
      C. 5 (Do not count the unused subdivision "Performance," which directs
             you to see another heading; do not count the italicized sub-subdivisions.)

EIGHTH EXERCISE

    1st *Star-Bulletin & Advertiser*   Sept. 3, 1972   A5   2
    4th *Star-Bulletin*   Sept. 13, 1972   E4   1

NINTH EXERCISE

I. 12

II. A. Page and column
     B. Long article

Chapter Six

Sample Tests

The Library and Its Services: Pretest / 176

DO NOT MARK THIS TEST FORM

Leeward Community College Library

LIBRARY UNIT PRETEST

Spring 1979

INSTRUCTIONS: *Please PRINT your name, last name first, today's date, your instructor's name, the name of the course (example: English 100) and the section number of that course in the spaces provided along the left-hand side of your answer sheet.*

Each item number (1 through 20) on the answer sheet corresponds to the question of the same number below. Each question has five possible answers to choose from (A, B, C, D or E), and there are five spaces for each on the answer sheet (the first space representing choice A, the second B, etc.) Mark your answer like this:

If the correct answer is C: ꞊꞊꞊ ꞊꞊꞊ ▰▰▰ ꞊꞊꞊ ꞊꞊꞊

Make a heavy dark line between the dotted lines with a number two pencil. Because of computer scanning, it is essential to use this type of pencil. If you do not have a number two pencil, be sure to request one from the person administering this test.

If you change your mind about an answer, be sure to erase completely. The scanner is sensitive to stray marks of any kind and could easily interpret them as wrong answers. DO NOT MAKE ANY MARKS OTHER THAN ONE ANSWER FOR EACH QUESTION on your answer sheet. There is only one correct answer for each question.

THE LIBRARY AND ITS SERVICES

1. The majority of books in the Leeward Community College (LCC) Library collections are found

    A. on the bottom level.
    B. in the Reference Area.
    C. on the main floor.
    D. near the Circulation Desk.
    E. on the top level.

2. Where in the LCC Library would the item with the following call number be found?

    RF284
    P42
    c.s.

    A. in the Reference Area.
    B. on the current periodical shelves.
    C. near the Super-Quiet Study Area.
    D. in the area behind the Circulation Desk.
    E. in the Colored Slide Collection

3. Which of the following is <u>not</u> available in the library for student use?

   A. Typewriters
   B. Photocopier
   C. Slide projectors

   D. Tape recorders
   E. Video recorders

4. Reserve material may be charged out for

   A. two hours or three days.
   B. one hour.
   C. overnight only.

   D. one or two weeks.
   E. immediate use in the Reserve Area only.

5. Which of the following types of material may <u>not</u> be borrowed from the library?

   A. Art Prints
   B. Phonorecords
   C. New books

   D. New magazines
   E. Cassette tapes

USING THE CARD CATALOG

6. The library card catalog tells you what materials

   A. the community college libraries in Hawaii have.
   B. LCC Library has on order.
   C. UH System libraries have.
   D. LCC Library has in its general and special collections.
   E. are currently shelved and available to borrow.

7. Which of the groups below is arranged in correct LCC card catalog order?

   A. An android aspect
      A Nanking duck
      And anteaters, too
      Andante moods
      Andy'll be here
      Andy wins again

   B. And anteaters, too
      Andante moods
      An android aspect
      Andy wins again
      Andy'll be here
      A Nanking duck

   C. And anteaters, too
      Andante moods
      An android aspect
      Andy'll be here
      Andy wins again
      A Nanking duck

   D. Andante moods
      An android aspect
      Andy'll be here
      Andy wins again
      And anteaters, too
      A Nanking duck

   E. A Nanking duck
      An android aspect
      And anteaters, too
      Andante moods
      Andy wins again
      Andy'll be here

8. On the example of a catalog card below, to what does the circled item refer?

```
ND623
V66 G53   Gnudi, Desare
               Citale da Bologna and Bolognese painting in the
          fourteenth century.  In collaboration with Robert
          Harris.  Olga Ragusa, trans.  New York, (H. N. Abrams)
          [1964]

               80 p. illus.  (part col., part mounted) plates
          (part col.)  38 cm.

               Bibliography:  p. 79-80

               1. Vitale da Bologna, fl.  1320-1359.
          I.  Title

          ND623.V66G53                    64-11579
```

A. Publisher
B. Joint Author
C. Translator

D. Illustrator
E. Editor

9. A bibliography is

A. a list of footnotes.
B. information about a particular book.
C. a list of sources.
D. the story of a person's life.
E. a book about the Bible.

10. To locate a book in the Library about John Milton's *Paradise Lost*, you should consult the

A. author card catalog under "M".
B. literature card catalog under both "M" and "P".

C. subject card catalog under "P".
D. subject card catalog under "M".
E. title card catalog under "P".

USING LIBRARY OF CONGRESS SUBJECT HEADINGS

11. In the guide to subject headings (called *Library of Congress Subject Headings*, or *LCSH*) the use of boldface type indicates

A. an outdated subject heading.
B. a usable subject heading.
C. a nonusable subject heading.
D. a subject heading for which there are subdivisions.
E. a new subject heading added since the last edition.

12. *LCSH* contains *"See"* references. These *See* references refer you

    A. to the guide book which accompanies LCSH.
    B. from an unusable heading to a usable heading.
    C. to the index of *LCSH*.
    D. from a usable heading to another usable heading.
    E. to the page number which will give you additional information.

13. The symbol, *"sa,"* refers the user of *LCSH* from one heading to another. The heading referred to is

    A. more general.
    B. preferred.
    C. more specific.
    D. not recommended.
    E. a sub-aspect.

14. What does the symbol, *"xx,"* found in *LCSH* indicate?

    A. An unusable subject heading.
    B. A more general subject heading.
    C. A heading which is particularly recommended.
    D. A subject heading not recommended for common use.
    E. A more specific subject heading.

15. Rare earth ions
    xx Ions
    — Spectra

    In the above example, "Spectra" is

    A. an unusable subject heading.
    B. a subdivision.
    C. a more general term.
    D. a usable subject heading.
    E. an additional related subject heading.

USING PERIODICAL AND NEWSPAPER INDEXES

16-17. *Use the following reference taken from a periodical index to answer questions 16 and 17.*

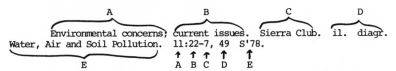

16. What letter refers to the name of the magazine in the above periodical citation?

17. What letter refers to the volume number in the above periodical index citation?

18. Which of the following statements is not true?

    The *New York Times Index*

    A. is a subject index to articles that appear in that newspaper.
    B. gives a summary of articles that appear in that newspaper.
    C. gives an indication of article length.
    D. subarranges articles alphabetically by their headlines.
    E. is an index of national and international news.

19. The correct interpretation of A5:1, taken from the *Index to the Honolulu Advertiser and Honolulu Star-Bulletin*, is

    A. April 5, section 1.
    B. column A, 5th article, 1st paragraph.
    C. the *Advertiser* of May 1 (5th month, 1st day)
    D. section A, page 5, column 1.
    E. column A, section 5, paragraph 1.

20. In the list of periodicals available at Leeward Community College Library, which of the following symbols indicates that back issues of a periodical are kept in paper form until replaced by microfilm?

    A. MFC   B. PA   C. MI   D. MF   E. BIP

Library Tour

Leeward Community College Library

LIBRARY UNIT TEST 781.1

<u>INSTRUCTIONS</u>: *Before beginning the test, please inspect this test card and the answer sheet. Each item number 1 through 20 on the answer sheet corresponds to a question on your test card. After each number are five choices. To mark your answer, make a heavy dark line through the letter of your choice with the special pencil provided with this test.*

If you change your mind about an answer, please erase it completely. We use a machine to score your answer sheet. The machine is sensitive to stray marks of any kind on your answer sheet and may interpret them as wrong answers.

Read each question carefully. Select the correct answer and mark the appropriate letter-box on your answer sheet. There is only one correct answer for each question. Guess if you must. You may take as much time as you want to work on this test. Return this test card with your answer sheet to the Reference Desk when you have finished.

<u>True or False Statements</u>: *Mark your answer sheet A for true statements or B for false statements.*

1. Circulation Services is located in front of the closed shelves.

2. The Kit Collection is shelved behind Circulation Services.

3. The Title Catalog is the card catalog standing next to the Periodical Indexes.

4. The Portrait Collection is kept in hanging folders behind Circulation Services.

5. The Subject Card Catalog is on the main floor next to the Phonorecord Collection.

6. To place an item on "personal hold" you must give a Reference Librarian a card with your name, address and phone number.

7. When you are finished with 2-hour Reserve books, return them to one of the wire baskets placed around the library.

8. The library provides four reader/printers for making paper copies of microfilm.

9. Leeward Community College Library can obtain a book for you from another library through a service called Inter-Library Loan.

10. In checking a book out of the library, one of the pieces of information you are <u>not</u> asked to put on the charge card is how long the book may be borrowed.

MATCHING: *Below this statement is a selection of call numbers that may be found in the Leeward Community College Library. Read each call number carefully. Questions are given below the call numbers. Read each question carefully. Assign a call number choice to each statement by marking the number of the choice on the answer sheet.*

Choice A	Choice B	Choice C	Choice D	Choice E
Pri	Kit	N7353	Ref	Tape
P21	K66	N613	PN44	TC156
B53	c.s.	v.2	M341	
		c.s.	1973	

Questions:

11. Which call number would lead you to the hanging folders behind the Innovation Collection?

12. Which call number would lead you to the area across from Circulation Services?

MULTIPLE CHOICE: *Select the correct answer to complete each statement. Mark the appropriate letter-box on your answer sheet.*

13. Which one of the following call number choices is an item that is on closed shelves and must be asked for at Circulation Services.

Choice A	Choice B	Choice C	Choice D
Pri	DS711	DS711	Ref.
DS711	H65	H65	DS711
H65	c.s.	1965	H65

14. The regular charge-out table is located next to:

   A. the copy machine
   B. the map case
   C. the atlas stand
   D. the paperback exchange rack

15. Older issues of magazines may be found:

   A. next to the newspapers in the Reference Area.
   B. on the Current Periodicals shelving.
   C. on the Back Issue Periodicals shelving.
   D. in the Intensive Study Area.

16. Last week's copies of the *Honolulu Star-Bulletin* are kept:

   A. on microfilm.
   B. in hanging folders in the Reference Area.
   C. in hanging folders behind the Print Collection.
   D. with Current Periodicals.

17. The Reference Desks are located:

    A. in front of the closed shelves.
    B. next to the Bibliographic Index Carrels.
    C. in the center of the card catalog area.
    D. beside the Reserve Materials charge-out table.

18. Which of the following pieces of equipment is available for your use in the Individualized Learning Center carrels?

    A. Slide projectors
    B. Television sets
    C. Movie projectors
    D. Computer terminals

19. To find out what materials have been put on Reserve by your instructor, you should check at the

    A. Reserve Materials charge-out table
    B. Reference Desk
    C. Circulation Desk
    D. Reserve Collection Services

20. The Reserve Collection is kept:

    A. in the general collection.
    B. in the Reference Area.
    C. behind Circulation Services.
    D. with the Periodical Collection.

Leeward Community College Library

LIBRARY UNIT TEST 781.Retest 1

<u>INSTRUCTIONS</u>: *Before beginning the test, please inspect this test card and the answer sheet. Each item number 1 through 20 on the answer sheet corresponds to a question on your test card. After each number are five choices. To mark your answer, make a heavy dark line through the letter of your choice with the special pencil provided with this test.*

If you change your mind about an answer, please erase it completely. We use a machine to score your answer sheet. The machine is sensitive to stray marks of any kind on your answer sheet and may interpret them as wrong answers.

Read each question carefully. Select the correct answer and mark the appropriate letter-box on your answer sheet. There is only one correct answer for each question. Guess if you must. You may take as much time as you want to work on this test. Return this test card with your answer sheet to the Reference Desk when you have finished.

<u>True or False Statements</u>: *Mark your answer sheet A for true statements or B for false statements.*

1. Circulation Services is the place to request books from the Closed Shelves Collection.

2. Atlases are kept in the General Book Collection on the top floor of the library.

3. The Author Catalog is in the center of the main floor next to the Periodical Indexes.

4. The Print Collection is shelved next to the Hawaiian/Pacific Collection.

5. When you enter the main entrance of the library, the Subject Card Catalog is straight ahead and on the left.

6. Items checked out of the library may be renewed by telephoning Circulation Services.

7. When returning art prints to the library, take them to Circulation Services.

8. Older editions of almanacs and encyclopedias in the General Book Collection may be borrowed from the library like regular books.

9. Books on the paperback exchange rack must be checked out from Circulation Services.

10. In checking a book out of the library, one of the pieces of information you are asked to put on the charge card is the call number of the book.

MATCHING: *The choices given below are typical call numbers that may be found in the Leeward Library card catalog. Look at each call number carefully. Statements are given below the call numbers. Read each statement carefully. Assign a call number choice to each statement by marking the letter of the choice on the answer sheet.*

Choice A	Choice B	Choice C	Choice D	Choice E
Ref.	GU476	Tape	Doc.	Hawn./Pac.
E174	N2813	TC66	T1.1:	P28.1
J6	c.s.		972	L978Fi

Statements:

11. A book that may be found in the shelving behind the Title Catalog.

12. A recording about the book "The Selling of the President."

13. A book on karate that must be asked for at Circulation Services.

MULTIPLE CHOICE: *Select the correct answer to complete each statement. Mark the appropriate letter-box on your answer sheet.*

14. The Bibliographic Indexes are in the study carrels located:

    A. in the Reference area.
    B. next to the microfilm cabinets.
    C. on the top floor of the library.
    D. next to the Hawaiian/Pacific collection.

15. Back Issue Periodicals are shelved next to the:

    A. Hawaiian/Pacific Collection.
    B. Current Periodicals Collection.
    C. Innovation Collection.
    D. Print Collection.

16. Recent issues of local newspapers may be found:

    A. with current periodicals.
    B. in hanging folders behind the print collection.
    C. on microfilm.
    D. in hanging folders in the Reference Area.

17. The Reference Desk is located:

    A. in the Reference Area.
    B. at the long counter next to the library exit.
    C. next to the Bibliographic Indexes.
    D. in the center of the Card Catalog area.

18. Which one of the following pieces of equipment is not available for your use in the Individualized Learning Center carrels:

    A. Computer terminal.
    B. Record player.
    C. Slide projector.
    D. Filmstrip projector.

19. To check out Reserve materials for use within the library you ask for the items from:

    A. Inter-Library Loan
    B. Reserve Collection Services
    C. Reference Desk
    D. Audio-Visual Services

20. The Map Collection is:

    A. in the gray cabinets next to the Xerox machine.
    B. in the large cabinet next to the atlas stand.
    C. filed in hanging folders next to the newspapers.
    D. filed in hanging folders behind the Print Collection.

Leeward Community College Library

LIBRARY UNIT TEST 781.Retest 2

INSTRUCTIONS: *Before beginning the test, please inspect this test card and the answer sheet. Each item number 1 through 20 on the answer sheet corresponds to a question on your test card. After each number are five choices. To mark your answer, make a heavy dark line through the letter of your choice with the special pencil provided with this test.*

If you change your mind about an answer, please erase it completely. We use a machine to score your answer sheet. The machine is sensitive to stray marks of any kind on your answer sheet and may interpret them as wrong answers.

Read each question carefully. Select the correct answer and mark the appropriate letter-box on your answer sheet. There is only one correct answer for each question. Guess if you must. You may take as much time as you want to work on this test. Return this test card with your answer sheet to the Reference Desk when you have finished.

True or False Statements: *Mark your answer sheet A for true statements or B for false statements.*

1. Circulation Services is located in the Reference area.

2. The Vocational Guidance Pamphlets are located in the gray cabinets next to the Xerox machine.

3. The Title Catalog is located between the Subject and Author Card Catalogs.

4. The Portrait Collection is kept in the yellow file cabinets in the Reference Area.

5. The Subject Card Catalog is on the main floor next to the brick wall.

6. Art prints checked out of the library may be renewed by simply telephoning Circulation Services.

7. When you are returning books to the library, you <u>must</u> take them to Circulation Services.

8. You may use your driver's license or other I.D. as a "library card" in this Library.

9. Books on the paperback exchange rack are for sale at ten cents each.

10. After filling out a charge card for an item you wish to borrow, you take the charge card and your I.D. to the Reference Desk.

MATCHING: *The choices given below are typical call numbers that may be found in the Leeward Library card catalog. Look at each call number carefully. Statements are given below the call numbers. Read each statement carefully. Assign a call number choice to each statement by marking the letter of the choice on the answer sheet.*

Choice A	Choice B	Choice C	Choice D	Choice E
PN2924.5	Doc.	Hawn./Pac.	Ref.	Rec.
K3G7813	J1.1417:	Ref.	Z1219	RM10
c.s.	974	TX945	C96	F7T8
		K36		

Statements:

11. A general reference book on book reviews.

12. Aretha Franklin's album "Two sides of love."

13. A book on Kabuki that must be asked for at Circulation Services.

True or False Statements: *Mark your answer sheet A for true statements or B for false statements.*

14. The Innovation Collection is in the left rear corner of the library next to the Print Collection.

15. Back Issue Periodicals are shelved next to the Hawaiian/Pacific Collection.

16. The *Hawaii Observer* newspaper is kept on microfilm only.

17. The Reference Desk is the tall white desk where the Reserve Notebooks are kept.

18. You may use the equipment in the Individualized Learning Center to tape record your own record album.

MULTIPLE CHOICE: *Select the correct answer to complete each statement. Mark the appropriate letter-box on your answer sheet.*

19. To check out general material you want to borrow, you should take the item to the:

A. Circulation Services
B. Reserve Collection Services
C. Reference Desk
D. Individualized Learning Center

20. The Periodical Indexes are in carrels:

    A. in the center of the Reference Area
    B. in the Reference Area next to the brick wall
    C. in back of the current issue periodicals
    D. in the center of the library behind the Author Catalog

Card Catalog

Leeward Community College Library

LIBRARY UNIT TEST 782.1

INSTRUCTIONS: *Read each question carefully. Select the correct answer and mark the appropriate letter-box on your answer sheet with the special pencil provided with this test. There is no time limit for this test. Guess if you must. There is only one correct answer for each question. Erase completely to change an answer. Return this test card with your answer sheet to the Reference Desk when you have finished.*

1. Which of the following groups is arranged in the correct order for filing in the card catalog?

A. Overall perspectives
    Over an underpass
    Overdeveloped land areas
    Overflowing thoughts
    Over the rainbow
    Over the whispers
    Overture to life
    Over twice as much
    Over Walton's Mountain
    Overweight problems

B. Over an underpass
    Over the rainbow
    Over the whispers
    Over twice as much
    Over Walton's Mountian
    Overall perspectives
    Overture to life
    Overweight problems
    Overflowing thoughts
    Overdeveloped land areas

C. Over the rainbow
    Over twice as much
    Over an underpass
    Over Walton's Mountain
    Over the whispers
    Overall perspectives
    Overdeveloped land areas
    Overflowing thoughts
    Overture to life
    Overweight problems

D. Over an underpass
    Over the rainbow
    Over the whispers
    Over twice as much
    Over Walton's Mountain
    Overall perspectives
    Overdeveloped land areas
    Overflowing thoughts
    Overture to life
    Overweight problems

E. Overall perspectives
    Overdeveloped land areas
    Overflowing thoughts
    Over the rainbow
    Overture to life
    Over twice as much
    Over an underpass
    Over Walton's Mountain
    Overweight problems
    Over the whispers

2. Which of the following groups is arranged in the correct order for filing in the card catalog?

A. She stoops to conquer
She will return
Shell and macrame ideas
She'll be a winner
Shell jewelry
She'll steal your heart

B. She stoops to conquer
She'll be a winner
She will return
She'll steal your heart
Shell and macrame ideas
Shell jewelry

C. Shell and macrame ideas
Shell jewelry
She stoops to conquer
She'll be a winner
She will return
She'll steal your heart

D. She'll be a winner
She'll steal your heart
She stoops to conquer
She will return
Shell and macrame ideas
Shell jewelry

E. Shell and macrame ideas
She'll be a winner
Shell jewelry
She'll steal your heart
She stoops to conquer
She will return

3. Which of the following would be filed first in the card catalog?

A. An angel in armor
B. Anatomy of suicide
C. And Abraham journeyed

D. Analytical geometry
E. A nail too rusty

4. Which of the following would be filed <u>last</u> in the card catalog?

A. Mr. Abrams
B. Miss Adkins
C. Mister Adams

D. Mrs. Abbott
E. Mistress Adele

5. The number 2,580 is filed as:

A. Two thousand five hundred and eighty
B. Twenty-five hundred and eighty
C. Two five eight zero

D. Two thousand five hundred eighty
E. Twenty-five eighty

```
M1629
L85F6Be    Lomax, John Avery, 1872-1948, comp.

              Best loved American folk songs.  4th ed.  New York,
           Grosset & Dunlap, 1954 [c1947]
              xvi, 407 p.  28 cm.

              First published in 1947 under title:  Folk song:  U.S.A.
           For voice and piano, with guitar symbols.


              1.  Folk-songs, American.  I.  Lomax, Alan, 1915-
           joint comp.  II.  Title
```

Refer to the catalog card reproduced above to answer questions 6-8.

6. The book that this card represents has been published in three previous editions.

        A. True   B. False

7. The book was copyrighted in 1954.

        A. True   B. False

8. Which of these four statements is the correct one?

    A.   John Avery Lomax wrote this book.
    B.   John Avery Lomax is the compiler of this book.
    C.   John Avery Lomax composed all the songs in this book.
    D.   John Avery Lomax is the editor of this book.

9. A bibliography may be defined as a list of material on a given subject, or the works of a given author.

        A. True   B. False

10. The number on the front of the card catalog drawer (in the lower left-hand corner) in which you should look to find out if this library has anything by Erwin Roy John is:

    A. 103   B. 61   C. 28   D. 51   E. 38

11. The call number of a book containing speeches, interviews and a letter by Malcolm X is:

    A. E185.97   B. E185.61   C. E185.97   D. E185.97   E. E185.61
        L5L6   L5A3   C57M9   L5A3   L577

12. A collection of essays written by many different authors is represented in the author card catalog by a card under the name of:

A. each author.
B. the editor.
C. the publisher.
D. the first author.
E. the author who wrote most of the essays.

13. The call number for a book this library has by the United States Lawn Tennis Association is:

A. Doc
   J1.1/2:

B. GV990
   U5
   1972

C. Doc.
   GV990
   U5
   1972

D. Ref.
   GV999
   T3

E. Ref.
   GV990
   U5
   1972

14. The total number of cards in the author card catalog to represent a phonograph record of *Love in Bath* is:

A. one card only, for the composer.
B. two cards: the composer and the conductor.
C. three cards: the composer, the conductor, the soprano.
D. four cards: the composer, the conductor, the soprano, the orchestra.
E. five cards: the composer, the conductor, the soprano, the orchestra, the pianist.

15. The call number for a book in this library about Louis Henry Sullivan is:

A. T1
   S5D44

B. NA737
   S9P3

C. PQ6388
   E2S8

D. NA737
   S9A3
   1956

E. Hawn./Pac.
   Ref
   AM101
   B47
   v.8
   no.2

16. The following five call numbers represent books which you are to arrange in the correct order in which they would be shelved. After arranging them in their correct shelving order, between which of these books should you place a book with the call number: DA19
   B22

DA28   DA235   DA2   DA170   DA3
B37   B42   B51   B13   B3

A. It would be between $\frac{DA2}{B51}$ and $\frac{DA235}{B42}$

B. It would be between $\frac{DA3}{B3}$ and $\frac{DA28}{B37}$

C. It would be between $\frac{DA170}{B13}$ and $\frac{DA2}{B51}$

D. It would be between $\frac{DA170}{B13}$ and $\frac{DA28}{B37}$

E. It would be between $\frac{D170}{B13}$ and $\frac{DA3}{B3}$

Arrange the following call numbers in the correct order in which they would be shelved and indicate that order by answering question 17.

(A)	(B)	(C)
C27	B73	BA31
D4	G5	A2

17. Which of the above call numbers should be shelved first, A, B, or C?

Arrange the following call numbers in the correct order in which they would be shelved and indicate that order by answering question 18.

(A)	(B)	(C)	(D)
ML62	ML62	ML62	ML62
C3	F18	D2	A24

18. Which of the above call numbers should be shelved last, A, B, C, or D?

19. Which of the following groups of call numbers is in the correct order for shelving?

Group A:

QA288	QA288	QA288	QA288	QA288
I2112M2	I212L2	I223L2	I22M4	I22N2

Group B:

QA288	QA288	QA288	QA288	QA288
I22M4	I22N2	I212L2	I223L2	I2112M2

Group C:

QA288	QA288	QA288	QA288	QA288
I2112M2	I212L2	I22N2	I223L2	I22M4

Group D:

QA288	QA288	QA288	QA288	QA288
I2112M2	I212L2	I22M4	I22N2	I223L2

20. On the shelves in the general book collection, locate a book about Karl Barth. Open the book to find the answer to this question and after you have done so, PLEASE REPLACE THE BOOK ON THE SHELF EXACTLY AS YOU FOUND IT FOR THE NEXT TEST TAKER TO FIND.

Question 20: What is the first word on page 32 of this book?

A. this   B. and   C. but   D. pointed   E. where

(alternate)

19. Which of the following groups of call numbers is in the correct order for shelving?

Group A:

QA288	QA288	QA288	QA288	QA288
I2112M2	I212L2	I223L2	I22M4	I22N2

Group B:

QA288	QA288	QA288	QA288	QA288
I22M4	I22N2	I212L2	I223L2	I2112M2

Group C:

QA288	QA288	QA288	QA288	QA288
I2112M2	I212L2	I22N2	I223L2	I22M4

Group D:

QA288	QA288	QA288	QA288	QA288
I2112M2	I212L2	I22M4	I22N2	I223L2

20. On the shelves in the general book collection, locate a book about Clyde Taylor Ellis. Open the book to find the answer to this question and after you have done so, PLEASE REPLACE THE BOOK ON THE SHELF EXACTLY AS YOU FOUND IT FOR THE NEXT TEST TAKER TO FIND.

Question 20: What is the first word on page 58 of this book?

A. that   B. though   C. the   D. men   E. why

Leeward Community College Library

LIBRARY UNIT TEST 782.Retest

INSTRUCTIONS: *Read each question carefully. Select the correct answer and mark the appropriate letter-box on your answer sheet with the special pencil provided with this test. There is no time limit for this test. Guess if you must. There is only one correct answer for each question. Erase completely to change an answer. Return this test card with your answer sheet to the Reference Desk when you have finished.*

1. Which of the following groups is arranged in the correct order for filing in the card catalog?

    A. Inadvertent conclusions
       I named the game
       In an old album
       Inca ruins
       Interception
       In their footsteps
       In the irreversible past
       In the thick of it
       Intimate moments
       I nullified the claim

    B. I named the game
       I nullified the claim
       In an old album
       In the irreversible past
       In the thick of it
       In their footsteps
       Inadvertent conclusions
       Inca ruins
       Interception
       Intimate moments

    C. I named the game
       I nullified the claim
       In an old album
       In the thick of it
       In the irreversible past
       In their footsteps
       Inca ruins
       Intimate moments
       Inadvertent conclusions
       Interception

    D. Inadvertent conclusions
       I named the game
       Inca ruins
       In the irreversible past
       In an old album
       Interception
       In their footsteps
       In the thick of it
       Intimate moments
       I nullified the claim

    E. I named the game
       I nullified the claim
       In the irreversible past
       In an old album
       In their footsteps
       In the thick of it
       Inadvertent conclusions
       Inca ruing
       Interception
       Intimate moments

2. Which of the following groups is arranged in the correct order for filing in the card catalog?

A. We'd love to see you
   We would plan carefully
   We'd quietly cry
   Wed on Sunday
   Wedding bells
   Wednesday is our day

B. We would plan carefully
   We'd love to see you
   Wed on Sunday
   We'd quietly cry
   Wedding bells
   Wednesday is our day

C. Wedding bells
   We'd love to see you
   Wednesday is our day
   Wed on Sunday
   We'd quietly cry
   We would plan carefully

D. We'd love to see you
   We'd quietly cry
   We would plan carefully
   Wed on Sunday
   Wedding bells
   Wednesday is our day

E. Wedding bells
   Wednesday is our day
   Wed on Sunday
   We'd love to see you
   We would plan carefully
   We'd quietly cry

3. Which of the following groups is arranged in the correct order for filing in the card catalog?

A. An analytic analysis
   An angel in disguise
   Analysis of costs
   Analytical art
   Anatomy of love
   And anarchy will prevail

B. Analysis of costs
   An analytic analysis
   Analytical art
   And anarchy will prevail
   Anatomy of love
   An angel in disguise

C. Analysis of costs
   An analytic analysis
   Analytical art
   Anatomy of love
   And ararchy will prevail
   An angel in disguise

D. Analysis of costs
   Analytical art
   An analytic analysis
   An angel in disguise
   Anatomy of love
   And anarchy will prevail

E. Analysis of costs
   An analytic analysis
   Analytical art
   And anarchy will prevail
   Anatomy of love
   An angel in disguise

4. The call number for a book this library has by David St. Clair is:

A. PZ4
   S132Ho3

B. Hawn./Pac.
   PZ9
   S35Ne

C. PZ7
   C525Be2

D. BF1261.2
   S25

E. G76.5
   A77G46

5. The <u>number</u> (not the date) 1930 is filed as:

   A. One nine three zero
   B. One thousand nine hundred and thirty[E.
   C. Nineteen thirty

   D. One thousand nine hundred thirty
   E. Nineteen hundred and thirty

```
GV1201
B345        Beard, Daniel Carter
1966            The American boys handy book:  What to do and how to do it.
            Rutland, Vt., C.E. Tuttle, 1966
                xxv, 391 p.  illus.

                First published in 1882 under title:  What to do and how to
            do it.


                1. Amusements.  2. Sports.  I. Title.
```

Refer to the catalog card reproduced above to answer questions 6-8. Mark your answer sheet "A" for True statements or "B" for False statements.

6. The book that this card represents was also published in an earlier edition.

7. The editor is C.E. Tuttle.

8. The book has pictures in it.

9. A bibliography may be defined as a list of material on a given subject, or the works of a given author.

                    A. True   B. False

10. The number on the front of the card catalog drawer (in the lower left-hand corner) in which you should look to find out if this library has anything by Oakley Ray is:

    A. 99   B. 81   C. 74   D. 84   E. 57

11. The number on the front of the card catalog drawer (in the lower left-hand corner) that you should look in to find the call numbers of books by J. J. Marric is:

    A. 71   B. 21   C. 64   D. 42   E. 50

12. The library has a book that is a collection of short stories by various authors which contains a story by Jack London that you wish to read. The book was compiled by Joseph Gores and illustrated by Robert Landis. What is the number on the front of the card catalog drawer (in the lower left-hand corner) in which you should look to find the call number for this book?

    A. 37   B. 69   C. 48   D. 61   E. 57

13. What is the number on the front of the card catalog drawer (in the lower left-hand corner) in which you should look to find out if this library has anything by the American College Testing Program?

    A. 2   B. 4   C. 19   D. 116   E. 3

14. The total number of cards in the author card catalog to represent a phonograph record of the original sound track recording of *West Side Story* is:

    A. one card only, for the person who wrote the music
    B. two cards: the person who wrote the music and the person who wrote the lyrics.
    C. three cards: the person who wrote the music, the person who wrote the lyrics, and the person who wrote the book.
    D. four cards: the person who wrote the music, the person who wrote the lyrics, the person who wrote the book, the female star.
    E. five cards: the person who wrote the music, the person who wrote the lyrics, the person who wrote the book, the female star, and the male star.

15. The call number for a book in this library about Marjorie Faith Barnard is:

    A. PS705   B. BL304   C. PR6011   D. LA205   E. PR6003
       F6   B3   R284   B36   A687Z9
                                   Z52

16. The following five call numbers represent books which you are to arrange in the correct order in which they would be shelved. After arranging them in their correct shelving order, between which of these books should you place a book with the call number: BF28
                                                                                        A21

    BF324   BF4   BF273   BF3   BF37
    A41   A3   A12   A51   A36

    A. It would be between BF273 and BF37
                          A12   A36

    B. It would be between BF273 and BF3
                          A12   A51

    C. It would be between BF273 and BF4
                          A12   A3

    D. It would be between BF4 and BF37
                          A3   A36

    E. It would be between BF3 and BF273
                          A51   A12

Arrange the following call numbers in the correct order in which they would be shelved and indicate that order by answering question 17.

    (A)   (B)   (C)
    DA22   E41   D63
    B4   B8   C9

17. Which of the above call numbers should be shelved first, A, B, or C?

Arrange the following call numbers in the correct order in which they would be shelved and indicate that order by answering question 18.

(A)	(B)	(C)	(D)
TX71	TX71	TX71	TX71
D3	G18	E2	B24

18. Which of the above call numbers should be shelved last, A, B, C, or D?

19. Which of the following groups of call numbers is in the correct order for shelving?

Group A:

HF978	HF978	HF978	HF978	HF978
J4334B3	J434A4	J44B5	J44C4	J443A4

Group B:

HF978	HF978	HF978	HF978	HF978
J4334B3	J434A4	J44C4	J443A4	J44B5

Group C:

HF978	HF978	HF978	HF978	HF978
J4334B3	J434A4	J443A4	J44B5	J44C4

Group D:

HF978	HF978	HF978	HF978	HF978
J44B5	J44C4	J434A4	J443A4	J4334B3

20. On the shelves in the general book collection, locate a book by Edmund Cooper. Open the book to find the answer to this question and after you have done so, PLEASE REPLACE THE BOOK ON THE SHELF EXACTLY AS YOU HAVE FOUND IT FOR THE NEXT TEST TAKER TO FIND.

Question 20: The first word on page 98 of Edmund Cooper's book is:

A. Three   B. I   C. Then   D. Self   E. Poised

Subject Headings

Leeward Community College Library

LIBRARY UNIT TEST 783.1

INSTRUCTIONS: *Each item number (1 through 20) on the answer sheet corresponds to the question of the same number below. Each question may have as many as five possible answers to choose from (A, B, C, D or E), and there are five spaces for each question on the answer sheet (the first space representing choice A, the second B, etc.) For True/False questions, mark "A" for True and "B" for False. Mark your answer like this:*

If the correct answer is C: === === ▬▬ === ===

Make a heavy dark line between the dotted lines with the special pencil provided. Because of computer scanning, it is essential to use this type of pencil. If you change your mind about an answer, be sure to erase completely. DO NOT MAKE ANY MARKS OTHER THAN ONE ANSWER FOR EACH QUESTION on your answer sheet. There is only one correct answer for each question. There is no time limit. Return this test to the Reference Desk with your answer sheet when you have finished.

1. The *Library of Congress Subject Headings* is best described as

    A. A catalog of unusable subject headings
    B. A complete guide to see references
    C. A guide to usable subject headings
    D. A list of cross references
    E. A list of "x" references

2. The *Library of Congress Subject Headings* is arranged

    A. Alphabetically by usable headings
    B. Alphabetically by cross references
    C. Alphabetically by lightface headings
    D. Alphabetically by lightface and boldface headings
    E. Alphabetically by boldface headings

3. In the *Library of Congress Subject Headings*, boldface type indicates

    A. Alternate headings   D. Related headings
    B. Usable headings   E. Unusable headings
    C. Additional headings

4. A see reference is best described as

    A. A reference from a subject heading to broader headings
    B. A reference from an unused heading to related headings
    C. A reference from a usable heading to a see also heading
    D. A reference from an unusable heading to a usable heading

5. What is the usable subject heading given by *Library of Congress Subject Headings* for "Exhaustion?"

    A. Weariness   B. Rest   C. Tiredness   D. Worn out   E. Fatigue

6. Select the correct call number from the subject card catalog for a book on the history of the comic strip.

    A. PN1922   B. PN1922   C. NC1355   D. NC1335   E. NC1333
        04   04   B28513   B28513   B28513
        1968

7. The heading, "Complexion," in the *Library of Congress Subject Headings* refers you to one of the following sets of usable headings.

    A. Cosmetics   C. Beauty   E. Color
        Color of man   Cosmetics   Cosmetics

    B. Beauty, Personal   D. Color
        Make-up   Beauty

8. Identify the usable subject heading on page 1910 of the *Library of Congress Subject Headings*.

    A. 5th Naval District   D. Univac programming
    B. Small Business Administration   E. United States. Navy Dept.
    C. UNITUTOR

9. A see also reference is best described as

    A. A reference from an unrelated subject heading
    B. A reference to usable and unusable headings
    C. A reference to related usually more specific headings
    D. A reference to an unusable heading
    E. A reference from a specific heading to a broad heading

10. Identify the related more specific reference for the heading, "Pottery," found in the *Library of Congress Subject Headings*.

    A. Chinaware   B. Vases   C. Ceramics   D. Archaeology   E. Glazing

11. Select from the following a related more specific reference of "Poisons" in the *Library of Congress Subject Headings*. Then find it in the subject card catalog.

    A. Synthetic poisons   D. Pesticides
    B. Toxic substances   E. None of the above
    C. Drugs

12. An xx reference is best described as

    A. A more specific subject heading   D. A related see reference
    B. A broader subject heading   E. A broader "x" reference
    C. An unrelated subject heading

13. Select from the following choices the related broader heading for "Costume" in the *Library of Congress Subject Headings*.

    A. Academic costume
    B. Fancy dress
    C. Wigs
    D. Uniforms
    E. Disco wear

14. Select a related broader heading of "Extremities (Anatomy)" in the *Library of Congress Subject Headings*. Then find it in the subject card catalog.

    A. Arm
    B. Anatomy, Human
    C. Leg
    D. Limbs (Anatomy)
    E. Skeleton

15. In *Library of Congress Subject Headings,* the dash (—) is used to indicate:

    A. A compound heading
    B. A subtopic
    C. A related heading
    D. An alternate heading
    E. An unusable heading

16. Which of the following is a usable subdivision of the heading, "Moving pictures," in the *Library of Congress Subject Headings?*

    A. Cinema
    B. Costume
    C. Academy awards
    D. Evaluation
    E. Newsreel

17. Which of the following is a subdivision of the subject, "GEOGRAPHY," to be found in the subject card catalog?

    A. ANCIENT   B. ECONOMIC   C. PHILOSOPHY   D. POLITICAL   E. HISTORICAL

18. How many place subdivisions can you find in the subject card catalog from "COOKERY (EGG)" through "COOKERY, HUNGARIAN?"

    A. 1   B. None   C. 2   D. 3   E. 4

19. What is the proper heading in the subject card catalog under which you will find materials on Central Park, New York City?

    A. CENTRAL PARK, NEW YORK
    B. NEW YORK - CENTRAL PARK
    C. NEW YORK (CITY) - PARKS - CENTRAL PARK
    D. PARK, CENTRAL
    E. NEW YORK (CITY) - CENTRAL PARK

20. What is the proper heading in the subject card catalog for materials on Hawaiian cookery?

    A. HAWAIIAN COOKING
    B. COOKING, HAWAIIAN
    C. COOKING - HAWAII
    D. COOKERY - HAWAII
    E. COOKERY, HAWAIIAN

Leeward Community College Library

LIBRARY UNIT TEST 783.Retest

INSTRUCTIONS: *Each item number (1 through 20) on the answer sheet corresponds to the question of the same number below. Each question may have as many as five possible answers to choose from (A, B, C, D or E), and there are five spaces for each question on the answer sheet (the first space representing choice A, the second B, etc.) For True/False questions, mark "A" for True and "B" for False. Mark your answer like this:*

If the correct answer is C: === === ▬▬ === ===

Make a heavy dark line between the dotted lines with the special pencil provided. Because of computer scanning, it is essential to use this type of pencil. If you change your mind about an answer, be sure to erase completely. DO NOT MAKE ANY MARKS OTHER THAN ONE ANSWER FOR EACH QUESTION on your answer sheet. There is only one correct answer for each question. There is no time limit. Return this test to the Reference Desk with your answer sheet when you have finished.

1. The *Library of Congress Subject Headings* is best described as

    A. A guide to the usable subject headings
    B. A complete guide to alternate subject headings
    C. A catalog of unusable subject headings
    D. A guide to see and see also references
    E. A guide to all cross references

2. The *Library of Congress Subject Headings* is arranged

    A. Alphabetically by boldface headings
    B. Alphabetically by see also references
    C. Alphabetically by cross references
    D. Alphabetically by usable and unusable headings
    E. Numerically by usable subject headings

3. In the *Library of Congress Subject Headings,* boldface type indicates

    A. Alternate headings   D. Related headings
    B. Additional headings   E. Unused headings
    C. Usable headings

4. A see reference is best described as

    A. A reference from a usable to an unusable heading
    B. A reference from a heading to additional headings
    C. A reference from unused headings to x references
    D. A reference from a usable heading to see also heading
    E. A reference from an unusable heading to a usable heading

5. What is the usable subject heading given by *Library of Congress Subject Headings* for "Ices?"

   A. Frozen ices
   B. Italian ices
   C. Ice cream, ices, etc.
   D. Shave ice
   E. Sherbets

6. Select the correct call number from the subject card catalog for a book on Japanese wrestling.

   A. GV1197
      K4
      c.s.
   B. GV1192
      H4
   C. GV1197
      X44
   D. GV1197
      H44
   E. GV1197
      K4

7. The heading, "Beauty," in the *Library of Congress Subject Headings* refers you to which of the following sets of usable subject headings?

   A. Complexion
      Beauty, Personal
   B. Aesthetics
      Beauty, Personal
   C. Charm
      Complexion
   D. Prettiness
      Chique
   E. Beauty, Personal
      Prettiness

8. Identify the usable subject heading on page 789 of the *Library of Congress Subject Headings*.

   A. House of Commons
   B. Great Britain. Parliament House
   C. Chremonidean War
   D. Greece
   E. Grebo folk-lore

9. A see also reference is best described as

   A. A reference to other subject headings
   B. A reference to alternate cross references
   C. A reference to related, usually more specific headings
   D. A reference to broader subject headings
   E. A reference to additional see also headings

10. Identify the related more specific reference for the heading, "Dinners and dining," in the *Library of Congress Subject Headings*.

    A. Eating   B. Carving   C. Desserts   D. Entertaining   E. Banquets

11. Select from the following a related more specific heading of "Color" in the *Library of Congress ·Subject Headings*. Then find it in the subject card catalog.

    A. Colors
    B. Dyes and dyeing
    C. Chromatics
    D. Painting
    E. None of the above

12. A xx reference is best described as

    A. A broader subject heading
    B. A more specific subject heading
    C. A related subject heading
    D. A usable cross reference
    E. An additional subject heading

13. Identify the related broader heading for "Flower arrangement" in the
    Library of Congress Subject Headings.

    A. Corsages   D. Cut flowers
    B. Floral decoration   E. Dried flower
    C. Decoration

14. Select a related broader heading for "Discrimination in employment" in the
    Library of Congress Subject Headings. Then find it in the subject card catalog.

    A. Age and employment   D. Fair employment practice
    B. Labor and laboring classes   E. Job discrimination
    C. Right to labor

15. In the *Library of Congress Subject Headings,* the dash (—) is used to indicate

    A. A subheading   D. A broader heading
    B. A subtopic   E. Alternate heading
    C. A more specific heading

16. Select a usable subdivision of the heading, "Fruit," in the *Library of Congress
    Subject Headings.*

    A. Canning   B. Fruit-culture   C. Drying   D. Color of fruit   E. Food

17. Which one of the following is a subdivision of the subject heading, "BIRDS"
    which is found in the subject card catalog?

    A. HAWAIIAN   B. MIGRATION   C. EXTINCT   D. AMERICAN   E. IN LITERATURE

18. How many place subdivisions can you find in the subject card catalog under
    the group of subject headings starting with "TALES" through "TALES, JAPANESE?"

    A. 2   B. 4   C. 1   D. 3   E. None

19. What is the proper heading in the subject card catalog under which you will
    find materials on Mount Fuji in Japan?

    A. MOUNTAINS - JAPAN   C. FUJI   E. FUJIYAMA
    B. JAPAN - MOUNT FUJI   D. JAPAN - FUJI

20. What is the proper heading in the subject card catalog under which to look for
    materials on the Bishop Museum?

    A. MUSEUMS - HAWAII   D. BERNICE BISHOP MUSEUM
    B. BERNICE PAUAHI BISHOP MUSEUM, HONOLULU[E. PAUAHI BISHOP MUSEUM
    C. HONOLULU'S BISHOP MUSEUM

Periodical Indexes

Leeward Community College Library

LIBRARY UNIT TEST 784.1

INSTRUCTIONS: *Read each question carefully. Select the correct answer and mark the appropriate letter-box on your answer sheet with the special pencil provided with this test. There is no time limit for this test. Guess if you must. There is only one correct answer for each question. Erase completely to change an answer. Return this test card with your answer sheet to the Reference Desk when you have finished.* DO NOT MAKE ANY MARKS IN THE INDEXES.

MULTIPLE CHOICE: *Select the correct answer and mark the appropriate letter-box on your answer sheet.*

1. How many citations are there about transit systems in both France and West Germany in the *New York Times Index* for 1973?

   A. 6   B. 5   C. 2   D. 7

2. How many citations are there about military bases of the North Atlantic Treaty Organization in Malta in the same 1973 *New York Times Index*?

   A. 4   B. 5   C. 2   D. 3

3. How many articles are there on gliders and subjects related to gliders in the *Honolulu Star-Bulletin* for 1970?

   A. 1   B. 2   C. 4   D. 3

4. In the following citation from the *Index to the Honolulu Advertiser* and *Honolulu Star Bulletin* what does the letter "A" in front of the "8" stand for?

   Lack of spare part halts interisland service S6/25/75 A8:2

   A. Advertiser B. August   C. Hawaii Observer D. Section A

5. The index to the *Honolulu Advertiser* and *Honolulu Star Bulletin* for this year is located

   A. at the University of Hawaii Library.
   B. in periodical index carrels 11 and 12.
   C. at the Hawaii State Library.
   D. at the Reference Librarian's desk.

6. What does 2:3 stand for in a newspaper index citation?

   A. Volume and page   C. Pages
   B. Page and column   D. Month and date

7. Leeward Community College Library

    A. has the *Journal of Modern History* on microfilm only.
    B. has the *Journal of Modern History* back issues in paper form until replaced by microfilm copy.
    C. does not have the *Journal of Modern History*.
    D. has the *Journal of Modern History* in paper form only.

8. What does 12:2 stand for in a periodical index citation?

    A. Month and date   C. Pages
    B. Page and column   D. Volume and page.

For questions nine to thirteen use the Readers' Guide to Periodical Literature *for March 1974 - February 1975.* (DO NOT MAKE ANY MARKS IN THE INDEX BOOK)

9. How many citations are there for articles about the testing of guided missiles?

    A. 4   B. 3   C. 6   D. 5

10. How many usable subdivisions are there under the subject heading, "Coal mines and mining?"

    A. 10   B. 9   C. 8   D. 7

11. How many citations are there under the heading for Lightning and its related headings?

    A. 1   B. 4   C. 3   D. 6

12. How many citations are there for articles about the prevention of heart disease?

    A. 11   B. 8   C. 12   D. 6

13. What does the magazine title abbreviation, "Sch Arts" stand for?

    A. *Scholarship & Arts*   C. *School Artists*
    B. *Scholastic Arts*   D. *School Arts*

For questions 14 and 15 use the Business Periodicals Index *for August 1973 - July 1974.*

14. What is the subject heading that is used in this index for material about unions of newspaper employees?

    A. Employees - Newspapers - Unions
    B. Unions - Employees - Newspapers
    C. Newspapers - Employees - Unions
    D. Newspapers - Unions - Employees

15. Find an article about the regulation of foreign exchange in Japan in this index. What is the title of the article?

    A. No yen for a devaluation of yen.
    B. Sazaki san says devalue yen.
    C. Regulating Japan's foreign commerce.
    D. New regulations for foreign exchange in Japan.

For items sixteen and seventeen mark your answer sheet (a) True or (b) False.

16. The *Readers' Guide to Periodical Literature* is a subject and author index to many general interest American magazines.

17. Playboy magazine is indexed in the *Readers' Guide to Periodical Literature.*

The column on the left is a list of subjects. The column on the right is a list of specialized periodical indexes. Select the index that would be best to use to find articles on each of the topics on the left and mark the appropriate letter for that index on your answer sheet.

18. Home mortgage interest rates.   A. *Applied Science and Technology Index.*
                                         B. *Education Index.*
19. Metabolism of plants.   C. *Business Periodicals Index.*
                                       D. *Biological and Agricultural Index.*
                                       E. *Biography Index.*

20. The following four magazines contain articles on solar energy. Which one of the articles should be available for you to read in this library?

    A. *Clearing House,* September, 1971
    B. *Geological Review,* Fall, 1971
    C. *Journal of Soil and Water Conservation,* September, 1971
    D. *Environment,* August, 1971.

Leeward Community College Library

LIBRARY UNIT TEST 784 Retest

INSTRUCTIONS: *Read each question carefully. Select the correct answer and mark the appropriate letter-box on your answer sheet with the special pencil provided with this test. There is no time limit for this test. Guess if you must. There is only one correct answer for each question. Erase completely to change an answer. Return this test card with your answer sheet to the Reference Desk when you have finished.*

MULTIPLE CHOICE: *Select the correct answer and mark the appropriate letter-box on your answer sheet. (DO NOT MARK THE INDEXES!)*

1. How many citations are there relating to robberies and thefts in both Colorado and Illinois in the *New York Times Index* for 1968?

   A. 7   B. 5   C. 4   D. 6

2. How many citations are there about the expansion of production facilities in the steel and iron industry in the United States in this same 1968 *New York Times Index*?

   A. 7   B. 9   C. 6   D. 8

3. How many articles are there on hang gliding and subjects related to it in both the *Honolulu Advertiser* and the *Honolulu Star-Bulletin* for 1975?

   A. 4   B. 3   C. 5   D. 1

4. In the following citation from the *Index to the Honolulu Advertixer and Honolulu Star-Bulletin* what does the letter, "A," in front of the "4" stand for?

   Isle flights run late survey shows S11/11/75 A4:2

   A. April   B. Advertiser   C. Section A   D. August

5. The index to the *Hawaii Observer* for this year is located

   A. at the University of Hawaii Library.
   B. in the Hawaiian Room of the Hawaii State Library.
   C. in periodical index carrels 11 and 12.
   D. on top of the Title Catalog.

6. In the following citation from the *New York Times Index*, what does "9:1" stand for?

   Party's Natl Cong elects Prime Min Chiang Ching-Kuo chmn (s), N 17, I, 9:1

   A. Volume and page B. Page and column C. Pages   D. Month and date

7. What does "(s)" stand for in the above citation?

   A. Short   B. Section   C. Sunday   D. September

8. Leeward Community College Library

   A. has the magazine, *Popular Photography*, in paper form only.
   B. does not have the magazine, *Popular Photography*.
   C. has the magazine, *Popular Photography*, in paper form until replaced by microfilm.
   D. has the magazine, *Popular Photography*, on microfilm only.

For questions nine through eleven, use the Readers' Guide to Periodical Literature *for March, 1969-February, 1970.*

9. How many citations are there under the heading for "Holy Spirit" and its related headings?

   A. 6   B. 5   C. 2   D. 4

10. How many usable subdivisions are there under the subject heading, "Guided Missiles?"

   A. 1   B. 14   C. 12   D. 2

11. How many citations are there for articles about the specifications, testing, and maintenance and repair of the propulsion systems of space vehicles?

   A. 2   B. 3   C. 1   D. 4

For questions twelve through fourteen, use the Education Index *for July, 1972-June, 1973.*

12. What is the subject heading that is used in this index for material about the education of emotionally disturbed children in Hawaii?

   A. Education - Emotionally disturbed children - Hawaii
   B. Hawaii - Emotionally disturbed children - Education
   C. Emotionally disturbed children - Hawaii - Education
   D. Emotionally disturbed children - Education - Hawaii

13. Find an article about the personnel records of students in high schools. What is the title of the article?

   A. High school transcript, who needs it?
   B. Student personnel records; open or closed?
   C. Federal law on student personnel files; a guide for administrators.
   D. Student transcripts and the need to know.

14. What does the magazine title abbreviation, "Ind Sch Bull," stand for?

   A. Indiana School Bulletin   C. Independent School Bulletin
   B. Industrial School Bulletin   D. Indian Schools Bulletin

For items fifteen through seventeen, mark your answer sheet (A) True or (B) False.

15. *Scientific American* magazine is indexed in the *Education Index*.

16. The *Index to the Honolulu Advertiser and Honolulu Star-Bulletin* includes indexing for the *Hawaii Observer*.

17. The numbers, 42:4 in a periodical index stand for volume and page.

The column on the left is a list of subjects. The column on the right is a list of specialized periodical indexes. Select the index that would be best to use to find articles on each of the topics on the left, then mark the appropriate letter for that index on your answer sheet.

18. Excavating machinery   A. *Business Periodicals Index*
                                    B. *Art Index*
                                    C. *Social Sciences Index*
19. Raku pottery   D. *Applied Science and Technology Index*
                                    E. *Public Affairs Information Service*

20. The following four magazines contain articles on the use of Vitamin C in the prevention of colds. Which one of the articles should be available for you to read in this library?

A. *Redbook*, February, 1972
B. *Prevention,* March, 1972
C. *Natural Gardening,* February, 1972
D. *Child Development,* March, 1972

Appendix I

LEEWARD COMMUNITY COLLEGE LIBRARY
Basic Library Instruction Unit

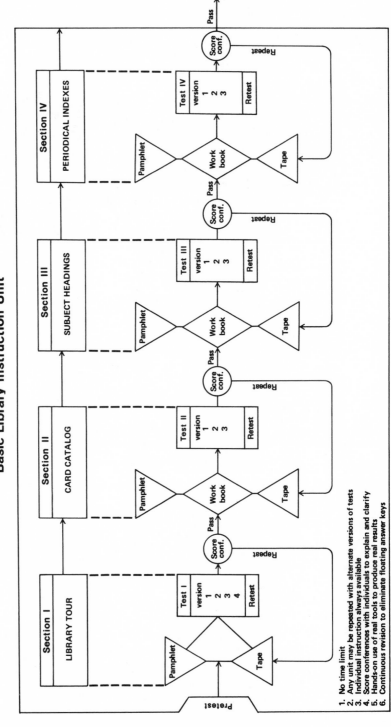

1. No time limit
2. Any unit may be repeated with alternate versions of tests
3. Individual instruction always available
4. Score conferences with individuals to explain and clarify
5. Hands-on use of real tools to produce real results
6. Continuous revision to eliminate floating answer keys

APPENDIX I

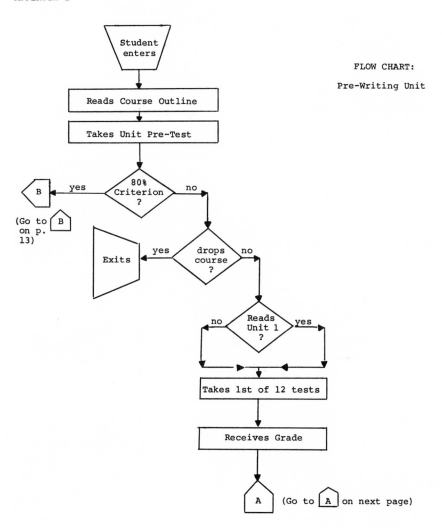

FLOW CHART:

Pre-Writing Unit

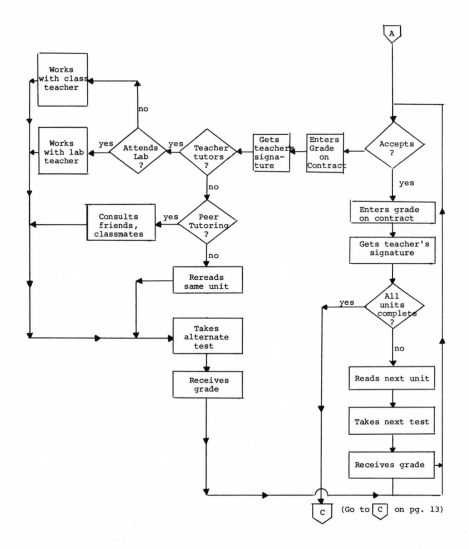

(Go to C on pg. 13)

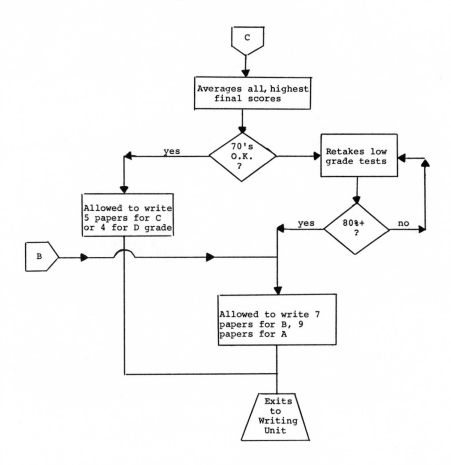

ENGLISH 100

STUDENT/INSTRUCTOR PERFORMANCE CONTRACT

NAME_____Fall_____Spring_____197____

SECTION_____DAYS_____TIME_____BLDG./ROOM___

SOCIAL SECURITY NUMBER_____MAJOR_____

ADDRESS_____PHONE NO._____

HIGH SCHOOL_____PRE-TEST SCORE_____

Not Excused /‾‾/
Excused /‾‾/

I have read the course outline, understand the requirements of English 22/
English 100 and have completed the preliminary steps of the course. I
agree to complete the assignments. I understand that I can take the tests
as many times as I wish, until I am satisfied with my score (except the halfway and post-tests, which may only be retaken once), and that I will redo
my writing assignments until they are "acceptable" according to the
criteria in the course outline.

Student's Signature/Date

I have completed:

Unit I--English 3200 test average _____

Unit II--Essays /‾‾/ 1; /‾‾/ 2 and /‾‾/ 3 (and/or /‾‾/ 3a); /‾‾/ 4.

Unit III--Library test average _____

Unit IV--Essays /‾‾/ 5; /‾‾/ 6; /‾‾/ 7; /‾‾/ 8a; /‾‾/ 8.

and I want to receive this grade.

Student's Signature/Date

Instructor's Signature/Date

Name _____

UNIT I: LANGUAGE USAGE

Test No.	Date / Score	Instr.'s Initials	Date / Score	Instr.'s Initials	Date / Score	Instr.'s Initials	Final Score	Student/Instructor Signatures Date
1								
2								
3								
4								
5								
6								
Half Way Test					(Halfway Test may only be retaken once)			
7								
8								
9								
10/11								
12								
Post Test					(Post-test may only be retaken once)			
70% = C 80% = B 90% = A					Average Score on all Tests			

Name _____.

UNIT II: WRITING I

Assign. No.	Dates Due				Accepted	Student/Instructor Signatures	Date
	1st Draft	Revis. 1	Revis. 2	Revis. 3			
1 Enumeration							
2 Comparative							
3 Contrast							
3a Comparison/ Contrast							
4 Cause-Effect							

I have completed writing assignments ⟋⟍ 1; ⟋⟍ 2 and ⟋⟍ 3 (or ⟋⟍ 3a); ⟋⟍ 4, and I have completed the <u>English 3200</u> tests to an average of _____.

_____
Student's Signature/Date

_____
Instructor's Signature/Date

Name _____

PART III: LIBRARY USE

Library Tests	Date / Score	Instr.'s Initials	Date / Score	Instr.'s Initials	Date / Score	Instr.'s Initials	Final	Student/Instructor Signatures Date
1								
2								
3								
4								
					Average Score on Library Tests			

Name _____

UNIT IV: WRITING II

C-Level

Assign. No.	Dates Due				Accepted	Student/Instructor Signatures	Date
	1st Draft	Revis. 1	Revis. 2	Revis. 3			
5 Defini- tion							

I have now completed the English 3200 Tests, the library exercises, and the writing assignments for a C in English 100. I wish to /‾‾/ receive a C for the
course, /‾‾/ continue and begin working on the B-level assignment.

Student's Signature   Date

Instructor's Signature   Date

B-Level

Assign. No.	Dates Due				Accepted	Student/Instructor Signatures	Date
	1st Draft	Revis. 1	Revis. 2	Revis. 3			
6 Argu- ment							
7 Critical Writing							

I have now completed English 100 to the B level and wish to /‾‾/ receive a B
for the course, /‾‾/ continue and begin working on the A-level assignments.

Student's Signature   Date

Instructor's Signature   Date

Name _____

A-Level

Assign. No.	Dates Due				Accepted	Student/Instructor Signatures	Date
	1st Draft	Revis. 1	Revis. 2	Revis. 3			
8a Research Proposal							
8 Research Paper							

I have now completed English 100 to the A level and wish to receive an A for the course /__/.

_____
Student's Signature   Date

_____
Instructor's Signature   Date

Appendix 2

UNIVERSITY OF HAWAII

LEEWARD COMMUNITY COLLEGE
LIBRARY

MEMORANDUM

TO: Language Arts Faculty

FROM: Floyd M. Cammack, Library

SUBJECT: Revised Library Instructional Unit

Again a newly revised version of the library instructional unit is available in four sections for use as an integrated part of language arts courses. For those requesting the service, the library staff will administer all instructional and test material, reporting scores to instructors and to each student as individual sections are completed. Faculty may elect to use the Unit as a whole or to select separate sections covering (1) Library Tour, (2) The Card Catalog, (3) Library Subject Headings and (4) Periodical and Newspaper Indexes.

A new pretest is available this semester. Suggestions concerning its use have been provided in a separate memorandum.

Faculty members wishing to include the Library Unit as part of their course requirements are requested to complete the attached form and return it to me at L302C. Librarians are available for consultation on any aspect of the materials or their potential use. The Library Unit has become a central part of daily library service to LCC students. All instructional faculty are invited to avail themselves of the service where they feel it to be appropriate.

A form is attached for your convenience in letting us know if you are interested in utilizing the service during this semester.

Enc: Unit Diagram
      Sample student comments
      Application form

96-045 Ala Ike · Pearl City, Hawaii 96782 / Cable Address: UNIHAW
An Equal Opportunity Employer

Sample of Library Instruction Unit Student Evaluation Comments

Comment 1 - I worked in the library when I was in intermediate school, but Leeward Community College library was different. I'm glad that there is a Library Use Unit because I don't ask for help.

Comment 2 - I feel this unit is a <u>must</u> for all courses which deals with research papers or similarities.

Comment 3 - I was most impressed by the wealth of information readily available through periodicals and their indexes. Until now, I gave little attention to that part of the library.

Comment 4 - Library Use Unit should be made compulsory for Fall Term students who are taking any courses where "writing papers" are concerned. So by the time they start the Spring Semester, they will already have been familiarized with the different uses of the library.

Comment 5 - The knowledge gained through this study and test will make college life much easier now. I am grateful for this opportunity.

Comment 6 - I feel that taking these various library tests have helped me a lot in getting the things that I need in my school assignments. If not for these tests, I think I'd think I'd be like a chicken without a head not knowing where to go!

Comment 7 - A very useful and worthwhile unit. Should be required of every new student in Leeward Community College; not just English students.

Comment 8 - Library use instructional materials availability is a good idea. Such materials are especially valuable to those inexperienced in using a library. Leeward Community College has a very well-organized library.

Comment 9 - A program should be started to make students become aware of the tremendous information a library has to assist them in relation to their enrolled courses.

Comment 10 - Excellent methods! It was a good experience and I profited much from the tests and workbook exercises. Some of the tests were difficult but it was worth it.

Comment 11 - Excellent; <u>a must</u>!

Comment 12 - It's about time somebody put together a course on how to use the library to its fullest extent rather than let all the material go to waste or to the use of those intelligent people who "live" in the library.

MEMORANDUM

FROM:

TO: Floyd M. Cammack, Library 302C

SUBJECT: Use of Library Unit, Fall Semester

          am
I. I   interested in using the Library Unit for my course(s) no.
    am not

    _____.

II. I will need _____ copies of the Library Unit outline for distribution.

III. I would like to have a library staff member explain the Library Unit to
my class(es) in about ten minutes of class time according to the following
schedule:

Course Title	Date	Room Number	Time

IV. I would like to have the Library Unit Pretest administered in addition
to the ten-minute orientation.

THE LIBRARY UNIT   COURSE OUTLINE

This unit offers you a "tool-kit" for finding information in a library. Finding it at any time you want to know it, without having to stand in line or ask someone else to do it for you. It's a do-it-yourself learning kit which works not only on the Leeward campus, but just about any place in the world. Once through the unit, you automatically become a member of the club of "insiders" who have the key to good grades and easy access to all the kinds of information which a college student is expected to be able to handle.

Anywhere you go, college English courses all have one thing in common; they are concerned with the organization of ideas on paper, with the giving and getting of information by means of the printed or handwritten page. Over the years, a system of organizing written information has developed, and librarians are the people who make a profession of collecting it, storing it, and being able to get at any chunk of it whenever it is needed.

As a college student, you are expected to know your way around this world of printed information and to be able to dip into it and use it when you need it,--not just for English courses, but for ordinary, everyday needs as well. By completing this unit on information handling, you will have acquired something very much like an academic "drivers' license". Nobody expects you to become a professional "driver", but to succeed in college (and in many other aspects of everyday life) you must be competent to handle your-self on the "road".

In the following course outline you will find step-by-step procedures for completing the library unit.

GOAL: The student will learn how to use basic library resources effec-tively and become familiar with the resources of this particular library.

OBJECTIVES: The student will:

1. locate the various resources and services of LCCL and learn their potential uses.

2. learn the uses of a library card catalog.

3. efficiently use the card catalog to locate library material.

4. demonstrate an understanding of the arrangement, by Library of Congress classification call numbers, of material in the library by arranging groups of call numbers in correct shelf order.

5. interpret the Library of Congress Subject Heading List.

6. find material on a given subject by using the card catalog and the Library of Congress Subject Heading List and retrieve the material from the library shelves.

7. compare the various magazine indexes available in LCCL.

COURSE OUTLINE   page 2

8. interpret magazine index citations.

9. interpret newspaper index citations.

10. find material on a given subject by using magazine and newspaper indexes
    and retrieve the material from the magazine and newspaper collection.

The Library Use Unit is composed of four sections:

1. Library Tour
2. The Card Catalog
3. Library Subject Headings
4. Periodicals and Periodical Indexes

Follow the procedures below in the order listed to complete the Unit.

PROCEDURES:

Section One

1. Prepare for this section by doing one (or both) of the following (a, b):

    a. listen to Tape TC16 (on reserve; available with cassette player at
        the Circulation Desk)

                OR in place of or in addition to the tape

    b. read the pamphlet, "Library Tour" (on reserve at the Circulation
        Desk)

2. Take Test I in the Library (available from a librarian). Obtain test
    results from a librarian.

Section Two

3. Pick up a workbook for this section from a librarian. For instruction
    to complete the workbook do one (or both) of the following (a, b):

    a. listen to Tape TC17a (on reserve; available with cassette player at
        the Circulation Desk) and complete the workbook as directed while
        listening to the tape.

                OR in place of or in addition to the tape

    b. read the pamphlet, "The Card Catalog" (on reserve at the Circulation
        Desk) and complete the workbook as directed while reading the pamphlet.

4. Take Test II in the Library (available from a librarian). Obtain test
    results from a librarian.

Section Three

5. Pick up the workbook for Section Three/Four from a librarian. For instruction to complete the first half of the workbook do one (or both) of the following (a, b):

    a. listen to Tape TC17b (on reserve; available with cassette player at the Circulation Desk) and complete the first portion of the workbook (Exercises 1 through 4) as directed while listening to the tape.

    OR in place of or in addition to the tape

    b. read the pamphlet, "Library Subject Headings" (on reserve at the Circulation Desk) and complete the first portion of the workbook (Exercises 1 through 4) as directed while reading the pamphlet.

6. Take Test III in the Library (available from a Librarian). Obtain test results from a librarian.

Section Four

7. Prepare for this section by doing one (or both) of the following (a, b):

    a. listen to Tape TC18 (on reserve; available with cassette player at the Circulation Desk) and complete the last section of the workbook (Exercises 5 through 8) as directed while listening to the tape.

    OR in place of or in addition to the tape

    b. read the pamphlet, "Periodicals and Periodical Indexes" (on reserve at the Circulation Desk) and complete the last section of the workbook (Exercises 5 through 8) as directed while reading the pamphlet.

8. Take Test IV in the Library (available from a librarian). Obtain test results from a librarian.

GRADING:

90% – 100% = A	70% – 79% = C	Below 60% = Not passing
80% – 89% = B	60% – 69% = D	

Leeward Community College Library Unit Answer Sheet

Instructor use only

TEST #

2nd RETEST

SCORE

NAME (Please Print)

Last Name   First Name   DATE

INSTRUCTOR   COURSE   SECTION

INSTRUCTIONS

1. Print clearly all information requested above.

2. Fill in your ID (Social Security) Number, starting at the top as indicated by the red arrow and code each digit as shown in the sample provided.

3. Each item (1 - 20) corresponds to the question of the same number on your test form. When you have selected the correct answer (A, B, C, D, or E) mark your answer as shown, the first space for A, the second for B, etc.

   EXAMPLE: Correct answer, C   :::   :::   ▆   :::   :::

4. Use a number-two (or provided) pencil only, making no stray marks and erasing completely should you wish to change an answer. ANY STRAY MARKS BELOW THE DOUBLE LINE WILL REGISTER AS WRONG ANSWERS ON COMPUTER SCANNER.

IBM 507   PRINTED IN U. S. A.

IDENTIFICATION NUMBER

GENERAL PURPOSE — NCS — ANSWER SHEET

SIDE 1

SEE IMPORTANT MARKING INSTRUCTIONS ON SIDE 2

SEX

GRADE OR EDUC.

NAME (Last, First, M.I.)

791.5

BIRTH DATE

IDENTIFICATION NUMBER

SPECIAL CODES

MO. DAY YR.

Jan. Feb. Mar. Apr. May Jun. Jul. Aug. Sep. Oct. Nov. Dec.

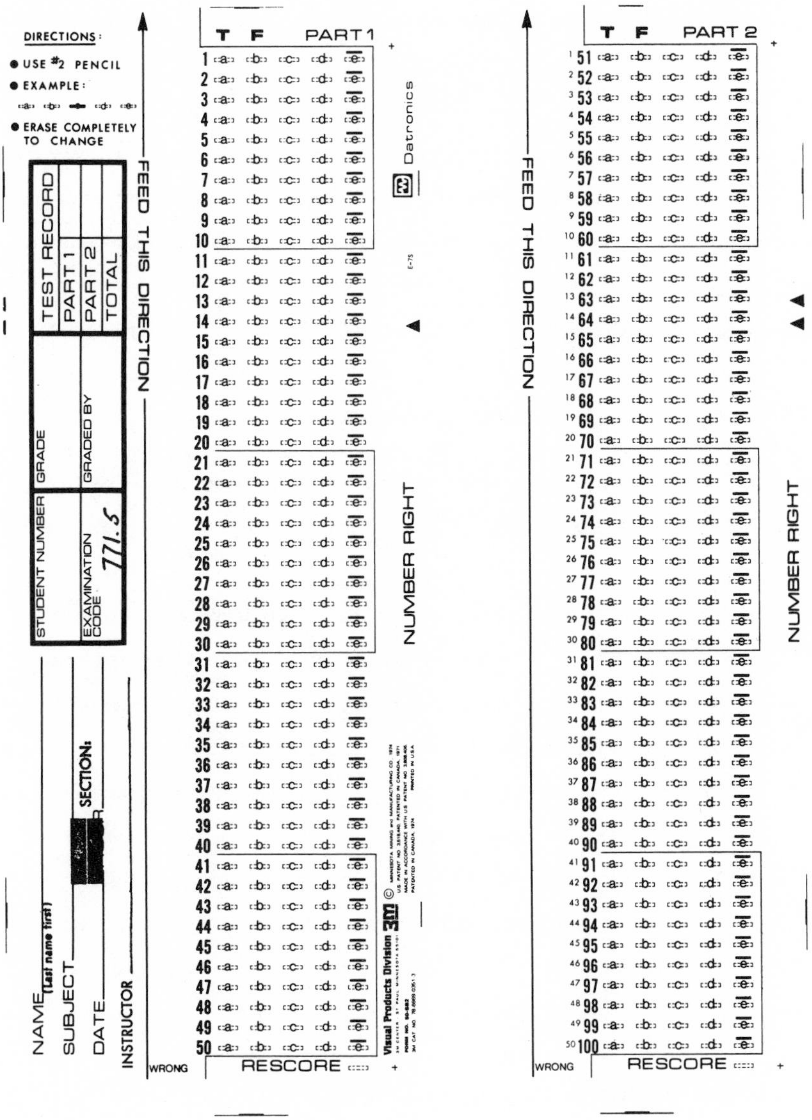

LEEWARD COMMUNITY COLLEGE LIBRARY   Library Instruction Unit

Inventory and Operating Procedures

The materials listed and procedures outlined constitute the library instruction unit for the Fall Semester, 1978. Personnel undertaking each function vary, but, in general, any professional staff member should be able to
handle any aspect of the daily operating procedure. Regular reference duties
are maintained by the same personnel handling library instruction duties.

Materials Inventory

The following materials, prepared in large part prior to the beginning of
each fall semester, are produced on campus and are subject to replenishment as
required.

    (1) Memorandum of explanation and invitation to faculty to employ the
        Library Unit as part of their course materials and requirements.

    (2) Memorandum of explanation to Language Arts faculty with schedule
        form for classroom introductions by library staff.

    (3) Memorandum to faculty introducing Library Unit Pretest, available for
        administration in classrooms at the beginning of each semester.

    (4) Course Outlines for the Library Unit, (mimeographed) with an
        introductory statement for students. (These are primarily for
        distribution in classrooms during orientation talks by librarians.)

    (5) Four instructional pamphlets (mimeographed), each for a single section
        of the unit, obtained by students from the Reserve Desk and for use
        only in the library. From 8 to 20 copies available.

(6) Four instructional cassette tapes (recorded from prepared scripts), each for a single section of the unit, obtained by students from the Reserve Desk with a small battery-operated portable player and for use only in the library. From 6 to 12 copies available.

(7) Three workbooks (mimeographed) and distributed at the reference desk free of charge to each student as he completes successive sections of the instructional program. These contain sample questions and exercises, designed to be used in conjunction with instructional pamphlets mentioned above. Workbooks cover sections 2, 3, and 4.

(8) A number of "dummy" volumes on main collection shelves both for workbook exercises and for certain test questions requiring stack searches.

(9) Sign-up sheet kept at reference desk for daily log of student test activity.

(10) Thirteen new tests on laminated 8 1/2 x 14" sheets, numbered 781.1—784.Retest. The first two digits stand for the current year. The remaining numbers stand for individual sections (1-4) and (following the decimal) individual versions of each test as follows: (Two copies of each test are adequate.)

781.1, .2, .3, .4	Library Tour — 4 versions
781.Re1, Re2	Library Tour — 1st and 2nd retests
782.1, .2, .3	Card Catalog — 3 versions
782.Re	Card Catalog — Retest
783.1, .2, .3	Subject Headings — 3 versions
783.Re	Subject Headings — Retest
784.1, .2, .3	Periodicals and Indexes — 3 versions
784.Re	Periodicals and Indexes — Retest

These tests represent a bank of 360 items (some overlapping) from which each student taking the unit is asked to answer 80. (For a "passing" grade of 80, the student should answer correctly 64 questions.)

(11) IBM 507 answer sheets for individual tests capable of being optically scanned for final tabulation at the university's computer service center, also gradable in-house with a scoring pattern (template) so each day's scores are available within less than 24 hours.

(12) Answer key templates for each test.

(13) Student score report form submitted regularly to each faculty member with record of student performance.

(14) Two "conference copies" of each test kept at reference desk and marked with correct answers and brief explanations of points missed.

(15) Evaluation sheet issued to each student completing section 4.

(16) Faculty evaluation form for faculty, distributed at end of each semester.

Outline of Operating Procedures

1. Test cards (laminated for repeated use) are signed out to students on request, after staff ascertain that the student has completed the instructional material, submitted workbook (where applicable) or is prepared for a retest. Answer sheet (prenumbered) and special scoring pencil are issued at the same time. Sign-out sheet information completed as required.

2. When completed tests are returned, staff mark off student's name on sign-out sheet, file answer sheet with those to be graded, and refile test form. Staff instruct student on next stage of the unit and when he can expect to return for grade information.

3. Tests are corrected, scores reported to appropriate instructor and tests are filed in a "For Student Conference" file at the Reference Desk.

4. When student returns for results of test, staff retrieve answer sheet and go over any errors with conference copy, answering questions as required and informing student of retest possibilities as applicable. When complete, staff refile conference copy and file answer sheet (checked as having been seen by student) in "Conference Completed" file.

5. Scoring and reporting of grades to instructors are usually assigned on a rotation basis, with each librarian undertaking this duty approximately once a week.

6. Classroom visits to introduce the library unit and/or to administer pretests are usually restricted to the first weeks of the semester and are assigned among professional staff as schedules allow.

7. Maintaining inventory (of answer sheets, workbooks, etc.) is usually assigned to one member of the operating team.

8. One librarian is responsible for each of the four sections, requiring usually some revisions at the mid-term break, and major revision during the summer months.

9. Collecting statistics and reporting data is assigned to a library instruction coordinator as part of his regular duties.

Bibliography

This bibliography is confined to literature in the English language appearing from 1965–1978 pertinent to library instruction at the college and university level. (The beginning date was determined by the existence of several bibliographies on the subject covering material up to 1965.) Most of the material is specifically directed to the academic situation, but a few references relating to high schools, special adult groups, and special libraries have been included because of their value and adaptive applicability to college and university libraries.

The following types of material have generally·been excluded: literature specifically directed to the graduate library school and training of the professional librarian; directories of programs; course materials such as manuals, handbooks, and texts; bibliographies of course materials; other bibliographies on the subject of library instruction.

"Academic Libraries Teach Library Skills to High School Students." (Action Exchange Column) *American Libraries* 9 (April 1978): 200.

Adams, Roy J. "Teaching Packages for Library User Education." *Audiovisual Librarian* 3 (Winter 1976–77): 100–106.

Adkins, Elizabeth F. "Library Orientation for Student Nurses; a New Approach." *Special Libraries* 61 (Jan. 1970): 21–25.

Alexander, Malcolm D. *A Measure of the Library Skills of High School Graduates of Washington State as Demonstrated by Freshmen of Central Washington State College.* Master of Education thesis. Ellensburg, Wash.: Central Washington State College, Graduate School, 1972. 96 pp. (ERIC Doc. #: ED 081 441).

Allard, M. Kay, et al. "An AV Workshop Approach to Teaching the Use of CA Indexes." *Special Libraries* 62 (Oct. 1971): 435–437.

Allen, Kenneth W. "The Use of Slides for Teaching Reference." *Journal of Education for Librarianship* 6 (Fall 1965): 137–139.

Allen, Marian M. "Spacious Closet of Reading." In Conference on the Present Status and Future Prospects of Reference/Information Service, 1966, Columbia University. *Present Status and Future Prospects of Reference/Information Service.* Chicago: American Library Association, 1967, pp. 34–47.

Aluri, Rao. *Library-Use Instruction for Engineering Students.* Buffalo, N.Y.: State University of New York, 1977. 11 pp. (ERIC Doc. #: ED 143 367).

Anderson, A. "Review: 'Seminar on Human Aspects of Library Instruction, Reading, 9 December 1969. Proceedings.' Cardiff, SCONUL, 1970." *Journal of Documentation* 26 (Dec. 1970): 381–383.

Anderson, David. "Graduate Research in English: A Foreign Point of View." *Literary Research Newsletter* 3 (Winter 1978): 15–21.

Anderson, L. "Training in the Use of Libraries." In Library Association of Australia. 14th Biennial Conference, Brisbane, 1967. *Changing Concepts of Librarianship: Proceedings of the Conference.* Brisbane: The Conference Committee, 1968, pp. 13–25.

Arciprete, Giovanni. "Need to Provide Special Instruction for Information Clients to Enable Them to Take Part Intelligently in Information Systems." In: International Conference on Training for Information Work, Rome, 15–19 November, 1971. *Proceedings.* Rome: Italian National Information Institute; The Hague: International Federation for Documentation, 1972, pp. 409–413.

Ardagh, J. "Leeds Shows How TV Can Help." *The Observer,* Jan. 16, 1966.

Ardhanareeswaran, B. "Reference Skills and Education for Development." *Journal of Reading* 20 (May 1977): 674–676.

Association of College and Research Libraries. *Library Orientation Kit.* Chicago: author, 1967. 28 pp.

———. Bibliographic Instruction Task Force. "Draft Guidelines for Bibliographic Instruction in Academic Libraries." *College and Research Libraries News,* no. 11 (Dec. 1976), p. 301.

———. Bibliographic Instruction Task Force. "Guidelines for Bibliographic Instruction in Academic Libraries." *College and Research Libraries News,* no. 4 (April 1977), p. 92.

———. Bibliographic Instruction Task Force. "Toward Guidelines for Bibliographic Instruction in Academic Libraries." *College and Research Libraries News,* no. 5 (May 1975), pp. 137–139, 169–171.

Association of Research Libraries. University Library Management Studies Office. *Library Instruction.* Washington, D.C.: author, 1975. 150 pp.

———. University Library Management Studies Office. *Library Use Instruction in Academic and Research Libraries.* (Management Supplement, vol. 5, #1) Washington, D.C.: author, 1977.

Atkins, Thomas V. "Libraries and Academic Instruction." *LACUNY Journal* 3 (Fall 1974): 13–16.

Aull, Sara. " 'Your Library' an Orientation Film-Tour of the University of Houston Library." M.A. thesis. Houston, Texas: University of Houston, 1965.

Axeen, Marina Esther. *Teaching Library Use to Undergraduates—Comparison of Computer-Based Instruction and the Conventional Lecture.* Urbana: University of Illinois, Coordinated Science Laboratory, 1967. 113 pp. (ERIC Doc. #: ED 014 316).

———. "Teaching the Use of the Library to Undergraduates: An Experimental Comparison of Computer-Based Instruction and the Conventional Lecture Method." Ph.D. dissertation. Urbana: University of Illinois, 1967. 208 pp.

Aylward, G. H., et al. "Education in the Retrieval and Interpretation of Chemical Data." *Journal of College Science Teaching* 4 (Sept. 1974): 31–33.

Bailey, Lucille E., et al. "Library Instruction in the City University of New

York." *LACUNY Journal* 3 (Spring 1974): 2–6.

Bailey, Martha J. "Bibliography and Reference Aids in the Physics Library." *Special Libraries* 67 (April 1976): 202–207.

Baillie, J. "Reader Education, (2): Student Instruction in Biomedical Bibliography." *Australian Academic and Research Libraries* 1 (Autumn 1970): 21–27.

Barr, K. P. "SCONUL Tape/Slide Presentations for Library Instruction." In *Exploitation of Library Resources: A Systems Approach; A Workshop at the Hatfield Polytechnic, April 22nd, 1972.* Hatfield, England: Hatfield Polytechnic, 1972, pp. 18–19.

Bate, John. "An L-Test for Library Users." *Scottish Library Association News* 122 (July/Aug. 1974): 103–105.

    Comment by A. J. Mullary. *Scottish Library News* 124 (Nov. 1974): 191–192.

    Comment by J. A. Howe. *Scottish Library News* 125 (Jan. 1975): 220.

Bath University. *See* University of Bath.

Beck, Richard J., and Norris, Lynn. "Communication Graphics in Library Orientation." *Catholic Library World* 47 (Dec. 1975): 218–219.

Beede, Benjamin R., and Sadow, Sandra. "Reference Service: From Zero to Total Commitment." *RQ* 13 (Winter 1973): 147–148.

Beeler, Richard J. "Library Orientation and Instruction at the University of Denver." *Colorado Academic Library* 8 (Spring 1972): 20–24.

Beeler, Richard J., ed. *See also* University of Denver Conference on the Evaluation of Library Instruction, 1973.

Beltran, Alfred A. "Information Retrieval Courses in an Industrial Organization." In American Documentation Institute. *Proceedings of the Annual Meeting, Santa Monica, California, October 3–7, 1966.* Woodland Hills, Calif. Adrianne Press, 1966, pp. 9–16.

Berry, John. "The Two Professions." *Library Journal* 102 (Sept. 1, 1977): 1699.

Beswick, Norman W. "Librarians and Tutor-Librarians: Library Use in Higher Education." *Library-College Journal* 2 (Spring 1969): 12–23.

Bhattacharjea, S. "Orientation of Staff and Students for Better Use of the Libraries." *New Frontiers in Education* 8 (July –Sept.) 1978): 15–19.

"Bibliographic Instruction at Harvard: Team Named." *Library Journal* 103 (March 15, 1978): 604.

Biermann, June A. "Technological Tools and Toys." Comment on an article by R. Vuturo. *Wilson Library Bulletin* 52 (Sept. 1977): 26.

Blum, Mark E., and Spangehl, Stephen. *Introducing the College Student to Academic Inquiry: An Individualized Course in Library Research Skills.* LaFayette, Ind.: International Congress for Individualized Instruction, 1977. 35 pp. (ERIC Doc. #: ED 152 315).

Blume, Julie. "Instruction in Catalog Use." M.A. thesis. Chicago: University of Chicago, 1975. 99 pp.

Boehm, Eric H. "On the Second Knowledge: A Manifesto for the Humanities." *Libri* 22, no. 4 (1972): 312–323.

Bolner, Mary. *See* Butterfield, Mary Bolner.

Boone, Morell D. "Experiment in Library Instruction: The Initial Step in the

Identification of Library Users' Needs at a Liberal Arts College." In New York Library Association, College and University Libraries Section. *Use, Mis-use and Non-use of Academic Libraries.* Woodside, N.Y.: author, 1970, pp. 31–41. (ERIC Doc. #: ED 046 419).

Borda, Eva, and Murray, Mary E. "Introduction to Library Services for Allied Health Personnel." *Bulletin of the Medical Library Association* 62 (Oct. 1974): 363–366.

Bottle, Robert T. *Courses in the Use of Scientific and Technical Literature in Central and Eastern Europe.* Bradford, England: University of Bradford, 1967. 18 pp.

———. "Training Students to Use Scientific and Technical Information." In *Progress in Library Science, 1967.* London: Butterworth & Co. (Archon Books), 1967, pp. 97–115.

———. "University Instruction in the Structure and Use of Chemical Literature in Central Europe." *Journal of Chemical Documentation* 6 (Feb. 1966): 3–6.

Bottle, Robert T., and Schur, H. "Is British Chemical Education Keeping Pace with the Chemical Literature?" *Education in Chemistry* 5 (March 1968): 68–70.

Bowen, Ada M. "On-line Literature Retrieval as a Continuing Medical Education Course." *Bulletin of the Medical Library Association* 65 (July 1977) 384–386.

Bowers, Dorothy. "Maximizing Learning by Minicourse Instruction." *Learning Today* 6 (Spring 1973): 50–60.

Bradfield, Valery; Houghton, Beth; and Siddall, Patricia M. "Librarians or Academics? User Education at Leicester Polytechnic." *Aslib Proceedings* 29 (March 1977): 133–142.

Brand, Marvine. "Using the Chemistry Library: Questions Students Ask." *Journal of College Science Teaching* 6 (Jan. 1977): 192.

Brearley, Ann. "Library Handbook for Metallurgy Students." *Special Libraries* 56 (March 1965): 192.

Breem, Wallace Wilfred Swinburne. "Educating the Library User: One-Day Seminar for Law Librarians and Law Teachers." *Law Librarian* 3 (Aug./ Nov. 1972): 17.

———. "Reader Instruction and the Law at Buckingham." *Law Librarian* 8 (Aug. 1977): 28.

Breivik, Patricia Senn. "Effects of Library-Based Instruction in the Academic Success of Disadvantaged College Freshman." D.L.S. dissertation. New York: Columbia University, 1974. 176 pp.

———. "Leadership, Management, and the Teaching Library." *Library Journal* 103 (Oct. 15, 1978): 2045–2048.

———. *Open Admissions and the Academic Library.* Chicago: American Library Association, 1977. 131 pp.

———. "Resources: The Fourth R." *Community College Frontiers* 5 (Winter 1977): 46–50.

Brewer, James Gordon. "Algorithms in Library Instruction: A Systems Approach to Information Retrieval." *Libri* 21, no. 4 (1971): 328–335.

Brewer, James Gordon, and Hills, P. J. "Evaluation of Reader Instruction."

Libri 26 (March 1976): 55–66.

Bristow, Thelma. "Instruction or Induction: The Human Approach to Student Involvement in Library Materials" (with discussion). In Seminar on Human Aspects of Library Instruction, University of Reading, Dec. 9, 1969. *Proceedings*. Cardiff, Wales: Standing Conference on National and University Libraries, 1970, pp. 8–23.

————. *Library Learning: The Way to Self-Help in Education. Education Libraries Bulletin*, Supplement 20. London: University of London. Institute of Education Library, 1977. 96 pp.

————. "A Reading Seminar." *Library-College Journal* 3 (Summer 1970): 13–22.

Brittain, Michael, and Irving, Ann. *Trends in the Education of Users of Libraries and Information Services in the USA*. Loughborough, Leicestershire, England: Loughborough University of Technology Library, April 1976.

Brody, C. "Profile of a Librarian: Dorothy Simon." *LACUNY Journal* 1 (Winter 1972): 8–11.

Brooke, Ann, et al. *Academic Library Instruction in the Southwest*. Stillwater, Okla.: Southwestern Library Association, 1976. 111 pp. (ERIC Doc. #: ED 140 778).

Brown, Clayton M. "TV or the Herded Tour." *Library Journal* 90 (May 15, 1965): 2214–2218.

Brown, Helen M. "ALA Activities to Promote Better Instruction in the Use of Academic Libraries." *Drexel Library Quarterly* 7 (July/Oct. 1971): 323–326.

Brown, J. "Assignment in Learning Analysis of Results of a Questionnaire: Library Related Content Included in Teacher Training in Canada." *Moccasin Telegraph* 17 (Autumn 1974): 50–55.

Brown, Jeanne Y., and Carter, Robert R. "Mix well with Media; Individualization of a Course on Basic Library Procedures." *California School Libraries* 41 (Jan. 1970): 92–93, 95.

Bruner, John M., and Lee, John W. "Fact, Fallacy and the Business Library." *Improving College and University Teaching* 18 (Autumn 1970): 292–293.

Bryson, JoAnn. "Library Orientation and Instruction in North Carolina Academic Libraries." *North Carolina Libraries* 33 (Summer/Fall 1975): 19–23.

Bryson, Montez. "Libraries Lend Friendship." *International Educational and Cultural Exchange* 10 (Feb. 1974): 29–30.

Bunge, Charles A. "Library Instruction Studies." *RQ* 8 (Winter 1969): 129–130.

Burchinal, Lee G. "Preparing Users for Effective Utilization of Information Systems." In International Federation for Documentation. *Proceedings of the 33rd Conference of FID and International Congress on Documentation, Tokyo, Sept. 12–22, 1967*. The Hague: author, 1967, Paper II.3, 10 pp.

Burke, Redmond A. "The Separately Housed Undergraduate Library Versus the University Library." *College and Research Libraries* 31 (Nov. 1970): 399–402.

Burton, Hilary D. "Techniques for Educating SDI Users." *Special Libraries* 66 (May/June 1975): 252–255.

Butterfield, Mary Bolner. "Project LOEX (Library Orientation–Instruction

Exchange) and Continuing Education." *Michigan Librarian* 41 (Fall 1974): 11–12.

Butterfield, Mary Bolner. "Project LOEX Means Library Orientation Exchange." *RQ* 13 (Fall 1973): 39–42.

Butterfield, May Bolner, ed. *See* Conference on Library Orientation for Academic Libraries, Third, 1973.

Cain, Melissa. *Institutional Support for Library Instruction Programs.* Urbana, Ill.: Illinois Clearinghouse on Academic Library Instruction, 1976.

Cain, Melissa, and Allen, Nancy. "Library and Bibliographic Instruction." *American Libraries* 9 (March 1978): 159–160.

Cain, Melissa, and Pausch, Lois. *Library Instruction Programs in Illinois Academic Libraries: A Directory and Survey Report.* Chicago: Illinois Library Association and the Illinois Association for College and Research Libraries, 1978.

Cameron, Kenneth J. "Open University Summer School at Stirling, 1973; Some Reflections on Library Usage." *Scottish Library Association News* 177 (Sept. 1973): 325 +.

　　Comment by E. Edward (letter), with rejoinder. *Scottish Library Association News* 118 (Nov. 1973): 362–363 +.

Cameron, Samuel H., and Messinger, Karlyn W. "Face the Faculty: Prevalent Attitudes Regarding Librarian-Faculty Relationship." *Pennsylvania Library Association Bulletin* 30 (March 1975): 23–26. Part 2: 30 (May 1975): 48–51.

Cammack, Floyd M. "Radio Active Library." *Library Journal* 90 (Oct. 15, 1965): 4300–4302.

Cammack, Floyd M., and DeCosin, Marri. "A Community College Instruction System." *HLA Journal* 34 (1977): 11–21.

Canadian Association of College and University Libraries. Orientation Programmes Committee. *Summary of Library Orientation Programmes in Eight Canadian University Libraries.* Waterloo, Ontario, Canada: University of Waterloo Press, 1967. 15 pp.

Canfield, Marie P. "Library Pathfinders." *Drexel Library Quarterly* 8 (July 1972): 287–300.

Carey, Robert John Pearce. "Experiment in Cooperative Library Instruction." *Library Association Record* 70 (April 1968): 98–99.

―――. "Handling Information; a Tape/Chart Course, an Aid for Teachers and Librarians." *Education Libraries Bulletin* 46 (Spring 1973): 12–15.

―――. *Library Guiding; a Program for Exploiting Library Resources.* Hamden, Conn.: Shoe String Press (Linnet Books), 1974. 186 pp.

―――. "Library Instruction in Colleges and Universities of Britain." *Library Association Record* 70 (March 1968): 66–70.

　　Comment by F. Hatt and H. A. Chesshyre. *Library Association Record* 70 (May 1968): 134.

　　Comment by G. Dixon, with rejoinder. *Library Association Record* 70 (July 1968): 187–188.

―――. "Making Libraries Easy to Use: A Systems Approach." *Library Association Record* 73 (July 1971): 132–135.

―――. "A Systems Approach to Exploitation." *New Library World* 73 (July 1972): 347–349.

———. "A Systems Approach to Exploiting Library Resources: Some Experimental Factors and Problems." In *Exploitation of Library Resources: A Systems Approach; A Workshop at the Hatfield Polytechnic, April 22nd, 1972.* Hatfield, England: Hatfield Polytechnic, 1972, pp. 11–17.

———. *The Teaching and Tutorial Activities of Librarians with Students Not Training for the Library Profession.* Thesis for Fellowship of the Library Association. London: The Library Association, 1966.

———. "Thinking around the Cooperative Library Instruction Experiment." *CTFE Bulletin* 1 (March 1969): 8–10.

Carpenter, Eric J. "The Literary Scholar, the Librarian, and the Future of Literary Research." *Literary Research Newsletter* 2 (Oct. 1977): 143–155.

Carter, Robert R. "Learning to Look It Up." *California Librarian* 30 (Jan. 1969): 53–55.

Cassata, Mary B. *Library Instruction Program Proposal.* Buffalo: State University of New York Libraries, 1973. 9 pp. (ERIC Doc. #: ED 077 541).

Chapman, Edward A. "Non-use of an Academic Library." In New York Library Association. College and University Libraries Section. *Use, Misuse and Non-use of Academic Libraries.* Woodside, N.Y.: author, 1970, pp. 83–88. (ERIC Doc. #: ED 046 419).

Chapman, Geoffrey. *Prospective Manitoba Teachers and the Library.* (Occasional Paper #84) Ottawa, Ontario: Canadian Library Association, 1975. 16 pp.

Chesshyre, H. A., and Hills, P. J. "Evaluation of Student Response to a Library Instruction Trials Programme Using Audiovisual Aids." In International Association of Technological University Libraries. Conference, 1970, Loughborough. *Educating the Library User; Proceedings of the Fourth Triennial Meeting, April 1–3, 1970.* Loughborough, England: Loughborough University of Technology Library, 1970, pp. KI–II.

Christensen, Terje B. "Information Search in Biochemistry—A Short Course for Students." *Biochemical Education* 5 (1977): 31.

Christie, David. "Tutor-Librarianship—A Personal View." *Scottish Library Association News* 94 (Nov./Dec. 1969): 414–416.

    Comment by S. McCrae. *Scottish Library Association News* 95 (Jan. 1970): 18–19.

Christine, Emma Ruth. "Mini-units for Maxi Utilization." *California School Libraries* 43 (Fall 1971): 14–18.

Clark, Alice S. "Slide/Tape Instruction to a Research Library: Ohio State University." *Ohio Library Association Bulletin* 45 (Jan. 1975): 33.

Clark, Daphne, and Harris, Colin. "Can Users be Instructed by Package?" *Library Association Record* 80 (June 1978): 279–281.

Cliffe, G. R. "Education and Training: For Staff and Users." *Aslib Proceedings* 25 (Oct. 1973): 381–384.

    Comment by A. E. Standley. *Aslib Proceedings* 26 (Feb. 1974): 90–91.

    Comment by John L. Bate. *Aslib Proceedings* 26 (June 1974): 261–262.

Closurdo, Janette S. "Teaching Library Skills." *Hospital Progress* 55 (Sept. 1974): 36, 40, 42.

Conference on Library Orientation, First, Eastern Michigan University, 1971.

Library Orientation. Ann Arbor, Mich.: Pierian Press, 1972. 45 pp.

Conference on Library Orientation for Academic Libraries, Second, Eastern Michigan University, 1972. *A Challenge for Academic Libraries: How to Motivate Students to Use the Library.* Ann Arbor, Mich.: Pierian Press, 1973. 98 pp.

Conference on Library Orientation for Academic Libraries, Third, Eastern Michigan University, 1973. *Planning and Developing a Library Orientation Program.* Ann Arbor, Mich.: Pierian Press, 1975. 72 pp.

Conference on Library Orientation for Academic Libraries, Fourth, Eastern Michigan University, 1974. *Academic Library Instruction; Objectives, Programs, and Faculty Involvement.* Ann Arbor, Mich.: Pierian Press, 1975, 84 pp.

Conference on Library Orientation for Academic Libraries, Fifth, Eastern Michigan University, 1975. *Faculty Involvement in Library Instruction: Their Views on Participation in and Support of Academic Library Use Instruction.* Ann Arbor, Mich.: Pierian Press, 1976. 119 pp.

Conference on Library Orientation for Academic Libraries, Sixth, Eastern Michigan University, 1976. *Library Instruction in the Seventies: State of the Art.* Ann Arbor, Mich.: Pierian Press, 1977. 130 pp.

Conference on Library Orientation for Academic Libraries, Seventh, Eastern Michigan University, 1977. *Putting Library Instruction in Its Place: In the Library and in the Library School.* Ann Arbor, Mich.: Pierian Press, 1978.

Cook, James. "The Science Information Problem." *The Advancement of Science* 23 (Oct. 1966): 305–309.

Cook, Lynn, et al. *Documents Education Project.* Toledo, Ohio: University of Toledo. Dept. of Library and Information Services, 1975. 34 pp. (ERIC Doc #: ED 121 247).

Cooper, Noelle P. "Library Instruction at a University-Based Information Center: The Informative Interview." *RQ* 15 (Spring 1976): 233–240.

Corey, James F., and Bellomy, Fred. "Determining Requirements for a a New System." *Library Trends* 21 (April 1973): 533–552.

Corlett, Donna. "Library Skills, Study Habits and Attitudes, and Sex as Related to Academic Achievement." *Educational and Psychological Measurement* 34 (Winter 1974): 967–969.

Corrigan, John T. "Library Instruction." *Catholic Library World* 49 (Feb. 1978): 272.

Cottam, Keith M. "Library Use Instruction in Tennessee's Academic Libraries: An Analysis and Directory." *Tennessee Librarian* 26 (Summer–Fall 1974): 73–79.

    Erratum. *Tennessee Librarian* 27 (Winter 1975): 11.

"Council on Library Resources Has Awarded a Three-Year Grant of $42,771 to the Library Orientation-Instruction Exchange (LOEX) at Eastern Michigan University." *Library of Congress Information Bulletin* 34 (Feb. 7, 1975): 57.

Cravey, Pamela. "Library Orientation and Bibliographic Instruction Committee." *Southeastern Librarian* 28 (Spring 1978): 52–53.

Crawford, Richard. "The Place of the Library in Open University Preparation Courses." *Assistant Librarian* 67 (Sept. 1974): 143–144.

Comment by B. L. Pearce. *Assistant Librarian* 70 (June 1977): 110.

Crittenden, Sara N. "Use of Closed Circuit Television in Library Orientation." Unpublished paper. St. Petersburg, Fla.: St. Petersburg Junior College, May 12, 1967.

Crossley, Charles A. "Education in Literature and Library Use." *Library World* 71 (May 1970): 340–341, 344–347.

———. "Tuition in the Use of the Library and of Subject Literature in the University of Bradford." *Journal of Documentation* 24 (June 1968): 91–97.

Culkin, Patricia B. "CAI Experiment." *American Libraries*, 3 (June 1972): 643–645.

———. "Computer Assisted Instruction in Library Use." *Drexel Library Quarterly* 8 (July 1972): 301–311.

Cully, James D.; Healy, Denis F.; and Cudd, Kermit G. "Business Students and the University Library: An Overlooked Element in the Business Curriculum." *Journal of Academic Librarianship* 2 (Jan. 1977): 293–296.

Dale, Doris Cruger. "The Community College Library in the Mid-1970's." *College and Research Libraries* 38 (Sept. 1977): 404–411.

———. "Mastering Library Research Techniques through Self-Instruction." *Technological Horizons in Education Journal* (Nov.–Dec. 1977): 44–46.

———. "Questions of Concern: Library Services to Community College Students." *Journal of Academic Librarianship* 3 (May 1977): 81–84.

Dannenberg, Dena. "A Course in Information Techniques for Dental Students." *Bulletin of the Medical Library Association* 60 (Jan. 1972): 111–114.

Dash, Ursula. "Equipping Students to Find Out for Themselves." *Vestes* 20, no. 1 (1977): 37–38.

———. "Self-Guided Library Tour." *Australian Academic and Research Libraries* 8 (March 1977): 33–38.

Daum, Josef. "Library User Education by Means of a Tape-Slide Program at the Technological University of Brunswick." [Text in German; abstract in English] *IATUL Proceedings* 9 (1977): 30–36.

Davies, I. R. "The Dual Role of the Tutor-Librarian." *Teacher in Wales* 5 (1965): 1–3.

Davis, Elisabeth B., et al. "A Two-Phased Model for Library Instruction." *Bulletin of the Medical Library Association* 65 (Jan. 1977): 40–45.

Davis, Elmyra. "The Unchanging Profile—A Review of Literature." *Library College Journal* 3 (Fall 1970): 11–19.

Dean, E. Barbara. "Television in the Service of the Library." *Library Association Record* 71 (Feb. 1969): 36–38.

Delgado, Hannelore B. *See* Rader, Hannelore B.

De Long, Edward James. *An Evaluative Report of the Richmond College Freshman Library Instruction Program*. Richmond, Va.: Richmond University. Richmond College Library, 1978. 30 pp. (ERIC Doc. #: ED 157 547).

Dermon, Edward S. "Getting to Know the Library." (High school) *Media and Methods* 13 (April 1977): 54.

Dhyani, P. "Need for Library Instruction to Readers in Rajasthan University (India): A Survey." *Unesco Bulletin for Libraries* 28 (May/June 1974): 156–159.

Dillon, Howard W. "Organizing the Academic Library for Instruction." *Journal of Academic Librarianship* 1 (Sept. 1975): 4–7.
> Comment by R. Horn. *Journal of Academic Librarianship* 1 (Jan. 1976): 53.
> Comment by L. N. DiPietro. *Journal of Academic Librarianship* 2 (March 1976): 26.
Dinnan, James A. "Library Skill—Whose Responsibility?" *Journal of Reading Behavior* 1 (Fall 1969): 31–37.
Dittmar, Jeanne. *Library Service Enhancement Program, F. W. Crumb Memorial Library, State University College, Potsdam, New York. Final Report.* Potsdam, N.Y.: State University of New York. F. W. Crumb Memorial Library, 1977. 34 pp. (ERIC Doc. #: ED 157 554).
"Division of Library Services and the Department of Library Science at Western Kentucky University has offered for one academic year a formal course of instruction to all freshmen." *College and Research Libraries News*, no. 5 (May 1974), pp. 105–106.
"Dr. Peter Mann's Survey of Reading Habits among 763 Undergraduates at Sheffield University." *New Library World* 74 (July 1973): 157.
Doig, Judith. "CCTV: the Second Year at Windsor." *Canadian Library* 25 (July 1968): 44–46.
Dougherty, Richard Martin, and Webb, William Henry. "Editorial: Library Instruction." *Journal of Academic Librarianship* 2 (Sept. 1976): 171.
Douglas, John R. "Librarian-Tutor in an Innovative College Experiment." *Learning Today* 4 (Fall 1971): 44–53.
Drake, Miriam M. "Librarian's Role in Interdisciplinary Studies." *Special Libraries* 66 (March 1975): 116–120.
Droog, Jan. "The Education of the Information User." *International Forum on Information and Documentation* (FID) 1, no. 4 (1976): 26–32.
Dubin, Eileen; Hurych, Jitka; and McMillan, Patricia. "An In-Depth Analysis of a Term Paper Clinic." *Illinois Libraries* 60 (March 1978): 324–333.
Dudley, Miriam Sue. *Chicano Library Program, Based on the "Research Skills in the Library Context" Program Developed for Chicano High Potential Students in the Department of Special Educational Programs.* Los Angeles: University of California Libraries, 1970. 87 pp. (ERIC Doc. #: ED 045 105).
———. "Teaching Library Skills to College Students." In *Advances in Librarianship*, vol. 3. New York: Seminar Press, 1972, pp. 83–105.
Dunkley, M. E. "Developing Library Skills in Mathematics." *Australian Mathematics Teacher* 27 (June 1971): 49–52.
Dunlap, Connie R. "Library Services to the Graduate Community: The University of Michigan." *College and Research Libraries* 37 (May 1976): 247–251.
Durey, Peter B. "University Library Service to Undergraduates." *International Library Review* 5 (July 1973): 321–327.
Dusenbury, Carolyn. "Education for Bibliographic Instruction Committee at Midwinter." *College and Research Libraries News*, no. 5 (May 1978), pp. 131–132.
Duvall, Scott H. *Library Instruction: Two Teaching Methods.* Provo, Utah: Brigham Young University. Graduate Department of Library and Information Sciences, 1975. 52 pp. (ERIC Doc. #: ED 112 898).

Dyson, Allan J. *Organizing Undergraduate Library Instruction: The English and American Experience.* Washington, D.C.: Council on Library Resources, 1974. 29p. (ERIC Doc. #: ED 152 309). Also in *Journal of Academic Librarianship* 1 (March 1975): 9–13.
  Erratum. *Journal of Academic Librarianship* 1 (May 1975): 47. Comment by F. D. Doble. *Journal of Academic Librarianship* 1 (Sept. 1975): 19.
Earnshaw, F. "Cooperative Production of Tape/Slide Guides to Library Services." *Library Association Record* 73 (Oct. 1971): 192–193.
Eaton, Elizabeth S. "Library Orientation Methods: J. Hillis Miller Health Center Library Program." *Medical Library Association Bulletin* 60 (Jan. 1972): 133–137.
"Educating the User; New Approaches Tried." *Library Journal* 103 (Feb. 15, 1978): 424, 427.
  Comment. *Learning Today* (Spring 1978): 28–29.
The Education of Users of Scientific and Technical Information; Report from a Workshop Held at the University of Bath, 14–16 September 1973. Bath, England: University of Bath Library, 1973. 34 pp.
Eisenbach, Elizabeth. "Bibliographic Instruction from the Other Side of the Desk." *RQ* 17 (Summer 1978): 312–316.
Elkins, Elizabeth, and Byman, Judith A. *Developing Printed Material for Library Instruction.* [Workshop] sponsored by College and University Section of NYLA and New York Library Instruction Clearinghouse. Syracuse, N.Y.: New York Library Instruction Clearinghouse, 1976. 23 pp.
Ellsworth, Ralph E. "The Contribution of the Library to Improving Instruction." *Colorado Academic Library* 4 (Summer 1968): 15–19. Also in *Library Journal* 94 (May 15, 1969): 1955–1957.
Elza, Betty, and Maslar, Isobel. "REFECOL." *Science Teacher* 42 (Nov. 1975): 31–32.
Enright, Brian J. *New Media and the Library in Education.* Hamden, Conn.: Shoe Sting Press (Linnet Books), 1972. 162 pp.
Essary, Kathy, and Parker, Steve. "Educating Your Patrons." *Arkansas Libraries* 32 (1975): 16–29.
Ettelt, H. J. "Research Guides for Students." *Wilson Library Bulletin* 47 (Oct. 1972): 140, 142.
Evans, A. J. "The Library as an Academic Department." In International Association of Technological University Libraries. Conference, 1970, Loughborough. *Educating the Library User; Proceedings of the Fourth Triennial Meeting, April 1–3, 1970.* Loughborough, Leicestershire, England: Loughborough University of Technology Library, 1970.
Evans, A. J.; Rhodes, R. G.; and Kenan, S. *Education and Training of Users of Scientific and Technical Information; UNISIST Guide for Teachers.* Paris: UNESCO, 1977. 155 pp. (ERIC Doc. #: ED 146 926).
Evans, Al. "From A to V: Audio Tour of the Library." *Kentucky Library Association Bulletin* 38 (Fall 1974): 18–21.
Evans, Carol. "Research without Result" (comment on article by A. R. Schiller). *Catholic Library World* 36 (May 1965): 629–631.
Evans, Roy W. "Using Slides for Library Orientation." *Illinois Libraries* 51 (April 1969): 300–303.

Everts, Evelyn. "Try It, You'll Like It: Library Orientation." *Idaho Librarian* 26 (April 1974): 55–56.

Eyman, David H., and Nunley, Alven C., Jr. *The Effectiveness of Library Science 1011 in Teaching Bibliographical Skills.* Tahlequah, Okla.: Northeastern Oklahoma State University, 1977. 30 pp. (ERIC Doc. #: ED 150 962).

Farber, Evan I., and Kirk, Thomas. "Instruction in Library Use." In *The ALA Yearbook.* Chicago: American Library Association 1976, p. 59.

Fast, Betty. "Mediacentric." *Wilson Library Bulletin* 51 (May 1977): 732–733.

Fitzgerald, Sylvia. "An Effective Approach to Library Instruction in Departmental Training Courses." *State Librarian* 25 (July 1977): 25.

Fjällbrant, Nancy. "Courses in Library Techniques for University Students in Britain." *Tidskrift för Dokumentation* 28, no. 3 (1972): 75–79.

———. "The Design and Development of a Course of Information Retrieval for Engineering Students." *European Journal of Engineering Education* 2 (1977): 213–222.

———. "Evaluation in a User Education Programme." *Journal of Librarianship* 9 (April 1977): 83–95.

———. "Library Instruction for Students in Universities in Britain." In *Transactions of the Chalmers University of Technology, Gothenburg, Sweden,* no. 335 (1974), p. 19.

———. "Library Instruction in Academic Libraries in Sweden." In *Transactions of the Chalmers University of Technology, Gothenburg, Sweden,* no. 336 (1974).

———. "The Need for Library User Orientation and the Design and Development of Material and Methods to Meet this Need." In *Aspects of Educational Technology.* Vol. 11: *The Spread of Educational Technology.* London: Kogan Page, 1977, pp. 98–108.

———. "Planning a Programme of Library User Education." *Journal of Librarianship* 9 (July 1977): 199–211.

———. "Teaching Methods for the Education of the Library User." *Libri* 26 (Dec. 1976): 252–267.

———. "The Use of Slide/Tape Guides in Library Instruction." *Tidskrift för Dokumentation* 29, no. 5 (1973): 116–121, 125.

Fjällbrant, Nancy, ed. "User Education at University of Technology Libraries" (title of entire issue). *IATUL Proceedings* 9 (1977): 2–4.

———. "User Instruction in the Libraries of the Technological Universities in Scandinavia; Some Recent Developments." *IATUL Proceedings* 7 (Dec. 1974): 54–59.

———. *See also* NVBF Anglo-Scandinavian Seminar on Library User Education, November 2–4, 1976, Gothenburg, Sweden. *Proceedings.*

Fjällbrant, Nancy, and Stevenson, Malcolm B. *User Education in Libraries: Problems and Practice.* Hamden, Conn.: Shoe String Press (Linnet Books), 1978. 173 pp.

Ford, Geoffrey, "Research in User Behavior in University Libraries." *Journal of Documentation* 29 (March 1973): 85–106.

Foss, Valerie M. "Reader Instruction at Faurah Bay College Library, University of Sierra Leone." *Sierra Leone Library Journal* 1 (Jan. 1974): 36–39.

Foster, Barbara. "Do-It-Yourself Videotape for Library Orientation Based on a Term Paper Project." *Wilson Library Bulletin* 48 (Feb. 1974): 476–481. Also in *Expanding Media*. Phoenix, Ariz.: Oryx Press, 1977, pp. 195–199.

———. "Hunter Midtown Library: The Closing of an Open Door." *Journal of Academic Librarianship* 2 (Nov. 1976): 235–237.

———. "Library Instruction for the Disadvantaged." *LACUNY Journal* 3 (Spring 1974): 14–16.

———. "The SEEK Librarian, Present, Past, and Future." *American Libraries* 2 (Sept. 1971): 776–777.

Fox, Peter K. "Library Handbooks: An International Viewpoint." *Libri* 27 (Dec. 1977): 296–304.

———. *Reader Instruction Methods in Academic Libraries*, 1973 (Cambridge University Library, Librarianship Series, no. 1). Cambridge: University Library, 1974. 70 pp.

"Freshman English Teachers and Librarians at the University of Arizona Have Joined in an Effort to Equip New Students with That Necessary Skill: How to Use a University Library." *College and Research Library News*, no. 11 (Dec. 1977), p. 332.

Frick, Elizabeth. "Information Structure and Bibliographic Instruction." *Journal of Academic Librarianship* 1 (Sept. 1975): 12–14.

Comment by K. J. Stranger. *Journal of Academic Librarianship* 1 (Jan. 1976): 23.

Frost, William J. Comment on article by Joseph Rosenblum. *See* Rosenblum, Joseph. "Overdue: The Future of Reference Service."

Fruedenthal, Juan R. "Bibliographic Instruction: A New Library Movement." *The Library Scene* 9 (Dec. 1974): 18–19.

Furneaux, Barbara. "I Do Not Know Where to Look." *The Times Educational Supplement* 2,698 (Feb. 3. 1967): 345.

Gains, Derek. "Libraries and Other Information Sources for Open University Students on Higher Level Courses in 1976." *Teaching at a Distance*, no. 11 (May 1978), p. 65–69.

Galloway, Sue. "Nobody is Teaching the Teachers." *Booklegger Magazine*, 3 (Jan. 1976): 29–31; combined issue with *Emergency Librarian*, 3 (Jan. 1976): 29–31.

Galloway, Sue, and Sherwood, Virginia. "Essentials for an Academic Library's Instructional Service Program." *California Librarian* 37 (April 1976): 44–49.

Gardner, Jeffrey J. "Point-of-Use Library Instruction." *Drexel Library Quarterly* 8 (July 1972): 281–285.

Garen, Robert J. "Library Orientation on Television." *Canadian Library* 24 (Sept. 1967): 124–126.

Gattinger, F. Eugene. "Orienting the Freshman to the Library." *Canadian Library* 21 (March 1965): 390–394.

Gebhard, Patricia. "How to Evaluate Library Instructional Programs." *California Librarian* 37 (April 1976): 36–43.

Gee, Ralph D. "The Information Worker in His Environment." *Aslib Proceedings* 26 (Jan. 1974): 28–46.

Genung, Harriet. "Can Machines Teach the Use of the Library?" *College and Research Libraries* 28 (Jan. 1967): 25–30.

Gibbons, Andy. "Freshman Library Orientation." *Mountain/Plains Library Association Quarterly* 18 (Spring 1973): 8–9, 14.

Gibson, Colleen. "Introducing the Reader to the Library." *Library Association of Alberta Bulletin* 1 (July 1969): 19–23.

Givens, Johnnie E. "The Use of Resources in the Learning Exerience." In *Advances in Librarianship*, Vol. 4 N.Y.: Academic Press, 1974, pp. 149–174.

Glogoff, Stuart J., and Seeds, Robert S. "Interest among Librarians to Participate in Library-Related Instruction at the Pennsylvania State University Libraries." *Pennsylvania Library Association Bulletin* 31 (May 1976): 55–56.

Gore, Daniel. "Course in Bibliography for Freshmen at Asheville-Biltmore College." *North Carolina Libraries* 23 (Spring 1965): 78–81.

———. "Teaching Bibliography to College Freshmen." *Educational Forum* 34 (Nov. 1969): 111–117.

"Graduate Bibliographic Instruction in the U of M Library." *Journal of Academic Librarianship* 1 (May 1975): 24–25.

Greaves, F. Landon, Jr., and Yates, Dudley V. "Library Orientation: Varied Approaches to a Common Problem." *Louisiana Library Association Bulletin* 31 (Summer 1968): 61–64.

Greig, J. S.; Arnott, F.; and Newton, H. "Reader Education for Engineers." *Australian Academic and Research Libraries* 4 (Sept. 1973): 119–122.

———. "Reader Education for Engineers: A progress Report." *Australian Academic and Research Libraries* 6 (Sept. 1975): 133–134.

Griffin, Lloyd W., and Clarke, Jack A. "Orientation and Instruction of Graduate Students in the Use of the University Library: A Survey." *College and Research Libraries* 33 (Nov. 1972): 467–472.

Griffith, Alice B. "Library Handbook Standards." *Wilson Library Bulletin* 39 (Feb. 1965): 475–477.

Grundt, Leonard. "Program of Instructional Services at Nassau Community College Library." *Odds and Bookends* 53 (Winter 1967): 7–10.

Gruner, Charles R. "A Library-Research Assignment." *The Speech Teacher* 22 (March 1973): 158–159.

Guidelines for Library Handbooks. Washington, D.C.: Federal Library Committee, 1972. 7 pp.

Gunselman, Marshall. "Learning by Doing with Media." *Learning Today* 6 (Winter 1973): 41–47.

Guss, Margaret; Symons, Ann; and Voit, Irene. "Advice on Making a College Orientation Video-Tape." Unpublished paper. Corvallis: Oregon State University Library, 1973. 9 pp. (ERIC Doc. #: ED 082 781).

Gwinn, Nancy E. "The Faculty-Library Connection." *Change* 10 (Sept. 1978): 19–21.

Haag, D. E. "The Teaching Function of the University Library." *South African Libraries* 37 (April 1970): 272–279.

Hackman, Martha. "Proposal for a Program of Library Instruction." *Drexel Library Quarterly* 7 (July/Oct. 1971): 299–308.

Haider, S. Jalaluddin. "Library Services: Education for Librarians and Library Users: Particular Requirements in Asian Countries." In IFLA Worldwide Seminar, Seoul, Korea, May 31–June 5, 1976. *Proceedings.* Seoul,

Korea: Korean Library Association, 1976, pp. 102–112.

Hall, Audrey W. "One Use of Audio-Cassettes for Library Instruction." *Education Libraries Bulletin* 20 (part 1, 1977): 29–31.

Hall, Virginia B., et al. "Slide-Tape Program for Beginning Pharmacy Students: Effect on Learning." *Bulletin of the Medical Library Association* 65 (Oct. 1977): 44–445.

Hammond, Nancy. "Teaching Library Use." In John Cowley, *Libraries in Higher Education: The User Approach to Service.* Hamden, Conn.: Shoe String Press (Linnet Books), 1975, pp. 83–101.

Hanlon, Peter F. "Needed: Student Key to Library Resources." *Canadian Library* 23 (Jan. 1967): 270–271.

Hansen, Janet H. "A Comparative Study of Programmed Text and Audio-Visual Modular Programs for Library Orientation/Instruction." Ph.D dissertation. Washington, D.C.: Catholic University of America, 1975. 216 pp.

Hansen, Lois N. "Computer-Assisted Instruction in Library Use: An Evaluation." *Drexel Library Quarterly* 8 (July 1972): 345–355.

Hardesty, Larry L. *Survey of the Use of Slide/Tape Presentations for Orientation and Instruction Purposes in Academic Libraries.* Greencastle, Ind.: DePauw University Library, 1976. 183 pp. (ERIC Doc. #: ED 116 711).

———. *Use of Slide/Tape Presentations in Academic Libraries.* New York: Jeffrey Norton Publishers, 1978. 222 pp.

———. "Use of Slide-Tape Presentations in Academic Libraries: A State-of-the-Art Survey." *Journal of Academic Librarianship* 3 (July 1977): 137–140.

Harley, Jessie M. "Some Aspects of Advanced Reader Assistance at Swinburne." In Library Association of Australia. Conference, 1971, Sydney. *Proceedings.* Surry Hills, N.S.W.: Library Association of Australia, 1972, pp. 514–516.

Haro, Robert Peter. "College Libraries for Students." *Library Journal* 94 (June 1, 1969): 2207–2208.

Harrelson, Larry E. "Large Libraries and Information Desks." *College and Research Libraries* 35 (Jan. 1974): 21–27.

Harrington, Jan. "SAM—Sources and Materials; IU's Undergraduate Library Course." *Focus on Indiana Libraries* 27 (Spring 1973): 23.

Harris, Colin. "Educating the User: Traveling Workshops Experiment." *Library Association Record* 79 (July 1977): 359–360.

> Comment by L. Shores and J. B. Fusaro. *Learning Today* 10 (Fall 1977): 51–52.
> Comment by H. B. Rader Delgado. *Learning Today* 11 (Winter 1978): 18.

———. "Illuminative Evaluation of User Education Programmes." *Aslib Proceedings* 29 (Oct. 1977): 348–362.

Harrison, Orion. *Library Service Enhancement Program. First Quarterly Progress Report to the Council on Library Resources.* Statesboro, Ga.: Georgia Southern College, 1977. 51 pp. (ERIC Doc. # ED 148 366).

———. *Library Service Enhancement Program. Second Quarterly Progress Report to the Council on Library Resources for the Period December 1, 1977–February*

28, 1978. Statesboro, Ga.: Georgia Southern College, 1978. 17 pp. (ERIC Doc. #: ED 156 111).

Hartley, Audrey A. "Hey That's Love Story!" *North Carolina Libraries* 34 (Spring 1976): 23–24.

Hartz, Frederic R. "Freshman Library Orientation: A Need for New Approaches." *College and Research Libraries* 26 (May 1965): 227–231.

Hatt, Frank. "A Day in the Life of the Tutor-Librarian." *Assistant Librarian* 60 (March 1967): 38.

―――. "My Kind of Library-Tutoring." *Library Association Record* 70 (Oct. 1968): 258–261.

Haywood, C. Robert. "The Teacher-Historian and the Library-Teacher." *Liberal Education* 55 (May 1969): 288–295.

Heaps, Doreen M., and Pavars, Mara Karnupe. "A Survey of Canadian User Education in Science and Technology Sources." In International Federation for Documentation. *Users of Documentation: FID International Congress on Documentation, Buenos Aires, 21–24 September 1970.* The Hague: author, 1970, Paper II.8, 21 pp.

Heberger, K., and Balazs, J. "Educating the Students as Library Users in Hungarian Technical Universities." In International Association of Technological University Libraries. Conference, 1970, Loughborough. *Educating the Library User; Proceedings of the Fourth Triennial Meeting, April 1–3, 1970.* Loughborough, Leicestershire, England: Loughborough University of Technology Library, 1970, pp. C1–C17. Also *IATUL Proceedings* 5 (Dec. 1970): 83–94.

Heineke, Charles D. "Library Orientation and Closed-Circuit TV at Midwestern Unniversity." *Texas Library Journal* 44 (Winter 1968): 167.

"Helping Users Find Their Way." *Wisconsin Library Bulletin* 73 (July 1977): 145–166.

Henne, Frances E. "Instruction in the Use of the Library and Library Use by Students." In *Conference on the Use of Printed and Audio-Visual Materials for Instructional Purposes: First Report.* New York: Columbia University, School of Library Service, 1966, pp. 164–190.

Henning, Patricia A. "Council on Library Resources Activities." *Drexel Library Quarterly* 7 (July/Oct. 1971): 343–345.

―――. "Research on Integrated Library Instruction." *Drexel Library Quarterly* 7 (July/Oct. 1971): 339–341.

Henning, Patricia A., and Shapiro, Joyce, eds. "Library Instruction: Methods, Materials, Evaluation." *Drexel Library Quarterly* 8 (July 1972): 219–365.

Henning, Patricia A., and Stillman, Mary E., eds. "Integrating Library Instruction in the College Curriculum." *Drexel Library Quarterly* 7 (July/Oct. 1971): 171–378.

Hering, Millicent B. "Library as a Lab." *Sourdough* 9 (July 1972): 3–6.

Herner, Saul. "An Experimental Course in Information Gathering for Scientists and Engineers." *Journal of Chemical Documentation* 9 (May 1969): 99–102.

Hernon, Peter. "Library Lectures and Their Evaluation: A Survey." *Journal of Academic Librarianship* 1 (July 1975): 14–18.

―――. " 'Pathfinders'/Bibliographic Essays and the Teaching of Subject Bibliography." *RQ* 13 (Spring 1974): 235–238.

Hernon, Peter, and Pastine, Maureen. "Floating Reference Librarian." *RQ* 12 (Fall 1972): 60–64.

Hicks, Joan Tomay. "Computer-Assisted Instruction in Library Orientation and Services." *Bulletin of the Medical Library Association* 64 (April 1976): 238–240.

Hilker, Helen-Anne. "Electronic Librarian: Institute on Newer Methods and Media for Library Orientation." *Library of Congress Information Bulletin* 25 (July 14, 1966): 409–410.

Hill, George. "National Package Omits Personal Approach." *Library Association Record* 80 (Aug. 1978): 405.

Hill, M. W. "Cooperation Between Libraries in Organizing Discipline Oriented Instruction." In International Association of Technological University Libraries. Conference, 1970, Loughborough. *Educating the Library User; Proceedings of the Fourth Triennial Meeting, April 1–3, 1970.* Loughborough, Leicestershire, England: Loughborough University of Technology Library, 1970.

Hills, Philip J. "Library Instruction and the Development of the Individual." *Journal of Librarianship* 6 (Oct. 1974): 255–263.
     Comment by M. B. Stevenson. *Journal of Librarianship* 7 (Jan. 1975): 66–68; Rejoinder. *Journal of Librarianship* 7 (Oct. 1975): 16–18.

———. "The Production of Tape/Slide Guides to Library Services." *Visual Education* (June 1972): 21–22.

———. "Tape-Slide to Teaching Package: The Place of the SCONUL Tape-Slide Scheme in Educating the Library User." *IATUL Proceedings* 9 (1977): 23–29.

Hills, Philip J., et al. "Formative Evaluation of Tape/Slide Guides to Library Instruction." In Lionel Evans and John Leedham, eds., *Educational Technology for Continuous Education. (Aspects of Educational Technology,* (vol. 9) London: Kogan Page, 1975, pp. 218–225.

Hobbins, John. "Challenge to Teach: Instruction in Academic Libraries." *Argus* 5 (May–Aug. 1976): 44.

Holler, Frederick. "Library Material Without Instruction: A Disaster?" *Journal of Education for Librarianship* 8 (Summer 1967): 38–48.

Holley, Edward G. "Academic Libraries in 1876." *College and Research Libraries* 37 (Jan. 1976): 15–47,

Horton, Allan. "Early Attempts at Reader Education at the University of New South Wales." *IATUL Proceedings* 5 (Dec. 1970): 54–60.

Horton, John J. "Library Liaison with Social Scientists: Relationships in a University Context." *Aslib Proceedings* 29 (April 1977): 146–157.

Horton, Weldon J. "From Problems to Opportunities." *Learning Today* 8 (Summer 1975): 22–23.

———. "Painless Professional Library Tour; Day or Night." *Unabashed Librarian*, no. 23 (Oct. 1977); p. 10.

Hostrop, Richard W. *Education Inside the Library Media Center.* Hamden, Conn.: Shoe String Press (Linnet Books), 1973. 178 pp.

Houghton, Beth. "Whatever Happened to Tutor Librarianship?" *Art Library Journal,* 1 (Winter 1976): 4–19.

Howison, Beulah C. "Simulated Literature Searches." *Drexel Library Quarterly*

7 (July/Oct. 1971): 309–320.

Howison, Beulah C., et al. *Self-Paced instructional Packages on Utilizing Library Resources. Final Report.* Stout, Menomonie: University of Wisconsin, Media Retrieval Services, 1974. 48 pp. (ERIC Doc. #: ED 098 999).

Hsu, Martha. "Library Orientation for Undergraduates —a New Look." *The Bulletin of Cornell University Libraries* 202 (Oct.–Dec. 1976): 16–18.

Hudspeth, Patricia. "Report on Reader Education Seminar." *Australian Academic and Research Libraries* 4 (March 1973): 25–28.

Hughes, J. Marshal. "A Tour of the Library by Audiotape." *Special Libraries* 65 (July 1974): 288–290.

Hutchinson, Harold, and Kibbey, Ray Anne. "Library Lectures—Learning the Library." *RQ* 11 (Summer 1972): 335–337.

Hyland, Anne. "Instructional Standards." *Ohio Association of School Librarians Bulletin* 28 (Oct. 1976): 36–39, and *Educational Media in Ohio* 5 (Oct. 1976): 36–39, [special joint issue].

Illinois Clearinghouse for Academic Library Instruction Council. *Methods of Administering Library Instruction Programs in Large Academic Libraries.* Urbana, Ill.: author, 1977.

———. *Techniques for Institutional Support of Library Instruction.* Urbana, Ill.: author, 1977.

Instruction in the Use of the College and University Library: Selected Conference Papers, July 13–14, 1970 Conference/Workshop. Berkeley: University of California. School of Librarianship, 1970. 29 pp. (ERIC Doc. #: ED 045 103).

International Association of Technological University Libraries. Conference, 1970, Loughborough. *Educating the Library User; Proceedings of the Fourth Triennial Meeting, April 1–3, 1970.* Loughborough, Leicestershire, England: Loughborough University of Technology Library, 1970. 138 pp. (ERIC Doc. #: ED 044 126).

Issacson, David. "Reaction: The Academic Library in a 'Schooled' Society" ("On My Mind" column). *Journal of Academic Librarianship* 4 (March 1978): 27.

Jackson, Eugene B. "The Engineer a Reluctant Information User—A Remedial Plan." In International Conference on Training for Information Work, Rome, November 15–19, 1971. *Proceedings.* Rome: Italian National Information Institute; The Hague: International Federation for Documentation, 1972, pp. 430–434.

Jahoda, Gerald. "Introduction to Symposium on Training Chemists in the the Use of Chemical Literature." *Journal of Chemical Documentation* 9 (May 1969): 91.

Jebb, M. "Computer Assisted Instruction: A Look at the Future." *Cornell University Library Bulletin* 180 (Nov. 1972): 6–7.

Jeffries, John. "TV Can Teach Readers Best." *Library Association Record* 78 (Jan. 1976): 18.
    Comment by Barbara G. Smith. *Library Association Record* 78 (April 1976): 177.

Jernigan, Elizabeth Thorne. "Computer-Assisted Instruction for Library Purposes." *Special Libraries* 58 (Nov. 1967): 631–633.

Johnson, Gertrude W. "Library orientation of College Freshmen." *PNLA*

Quarterly 34 (Oct. 1969): 4–8.

Johnson, John M. "Study of United States Medical School Library Orientation Programs for Medical Students: A Survey with a Suggested Program." M.S. in L.S. thesis. Chapel Hill: University of North Carolina, Graduate School of Library Science, 1967. 55 pp.

Johnson, Peter T. "The Latin American Subject Specialist and Bibliographic Instruction." *SALALM,* 19 (April 1974).

Jolly, Caryl. "Teaching Information-Use to Science Students." *Library Association Record* 77 (Feb. 1975): 41.
  Comment. *Library Association Record* 77 (April 1975): 95.
  Comment. *Library Association Record* 77 (May 1975): 124.

Jones, Anona M., and Theidling, Ernie C. "Reference Skills on Line; A Computer Assists Individually Planned Instruction." *Wisconsin Library Bulletin* 72 (May 1976): 103–104.

Jones, David E. "Information Resources for the Social Sciences: A Library Seminar for University Teaching and Research Staff." *Education Libraries Bulletin* 17 (Summer 1974): 27–35.

Jones, Norah E. "An Undergraduate Library—for Undergraduates! The UCLA Experience." *Wilson Library Bulletin* 45 (Feb. 1971): 584–590.

Jørgensen, F. "User Education at the National Technology Library of Denmark (DTB)." *IATUL Proceedings* 9 (1977): 66–69.

Joyce, Beverly A. "Library Instruction" [Sixth Annual Conference]. *Oklahoma Librarian* 26 (July 1976): 21–23.

Justis, Lorraine, and Wright, Janet S. "Who Knows What? An Investigation." *RQ* 12 (Winter 1972): 172–174.

Kaser, David. E. "Famine in a Land of Plenty." *Southeastern Librarian* 17 (Summer 1967): 74–80.

Katz, William A. "The Reference Librarian as an Educator." In *Introduction to Reference Work,* Vol. 2. New York: McGraw-Hill, 1974, pp. 61–66.

Kaul, B. K. "College Library and Instruction." *Herald of Library Science* 8 (July 1969): 203–209.

Kazemek, F. E. "Library Handbooks and Orientation in Illinois Community College Libraries." *Illinois Libraries* 57 (May 1975): 354–355.

Keever, Ellen H., and Raymond, James C. "Integrated Library Instruction on the University Campus: Experiment at the University of Alabama." *Journal of Academic Librarianship* 2 (Sept. 1976): 185–187.

Keller, C. Warren. "Monsanto Information Center's Audio-Visual Orientation Program." *Special Libraries* 57 (Nov. 1966): 648–651.

Kennedy, James R. "Integrated Library Instruction." *Library Journal* 95 (April 15, 1970): 1450–1453.

Kennedy, James R., Jr.; Kirk, Thomas G.; and Weaver, Gwendolyn. "Course-Related Library Instruction; A Case Study of the English and Biology Departments at Earlham College." *Drexel Library Quarterly* 7 (July/Oct. 1971): 277–297.

Keroack, Ann. *A Basic Behavioral Objectives Library Package.* Berlin, N.H.: New Hampshire Vocational Technical College, 1977. 18 pp. (ERIC Doc. #: ED 136 819).

Kibbey, Ray Anne, and Weiner, Anthony M. "USF Library Lectures, Revisited." *RQ* 13 (Winter 1973): 139–142.

Kies, Cossette Nell. "Handbook Designer: Consideration of Design in Planning a Library Handbook." *Mountain-Plains Library Quarterly* 12 (Winter 1968): 17–20.

Kinney, Lillie C. "Librarians as Educators." *Community and Junior College Journal* 47 (May 1977): 10–11, 27.

Kirk, Thomas. "A Comparison of Two Methods of Library Instruction for Students in Introductory Biology." M.A. thesis. Bloomington, Ind.: Indiana University, 1969. 62p.

———. "A Comparison of Two Methods of Library Instruction for Students in Introductory Biology." *College and Research Libraries* 32 (Nov. 1971): 465–474.

———. *The Development of Course Related Library and Literature Use Instruction in Undergraduate Science Programs.* Richmond, Ind.: Earlham College, 1977. 4 vols.: 120p., 82p., 93p., 95p. (ERIC Doc. #: ED 152 230–233).

———. "Past, Present and Future of Library Instruction." *Southeastern Librarian* 27 (Spring 1977): 15–18.

Kirk, Thomas, et al., eds. *Academic Library Bibliographic Instruction: Status Report 1972.* Chicago: Association of College and Research Libraries, 1973. 75p. (ERIC Doc. #: ED 072 823).

Kirk, Thomas; Lossing, Sharon; and Stoffle, Carla J. *Bibliographic Instruction in Academic Libraries; Edited Transcript of a Panel Discussion* (Conference-Workshop on Bibliographic Instruction for Library Users). Cambridge, Mass.: Association of College and Research Libraries, New England Chapter, Nov. 1974. 26p. (ERIC Doc. #: ED 112 946).

Kirk, Thomas, and Lynch, Mary Jo. "Bibliographic Instruction in Academic Libraries: New Developments." *Drexel Library Quarterly* 8 (July 1972): 357–365.

Kirkendall, Carolyn B., ed. "Library Instruction: A Column of Opinion." See issues of *Journal of Academic Librarianship*, starting with the Sept. 1976 issue.

———. *See also* Conference on Library Orientation for Academic Libraries, Seventh.

Kluth, Rolf. "University Library Activities in Modern Higher Education." In *University Library problems. (Acta Bibliothecae R. University Upsaliensis*, vol. 19). Stockholm, Sweden: Almqvist and Wiksell, 1975, pp. 85–90.

Knapp, Patricia B. *Experiment in Coordination between Teaching and Library Staff for Changing Student Use of University Library Resources.* Metuchen, N.J.: Scarecrow Press, 1966. 293 pp.

———. "Guidelines for Bucking the System: A Strategy for Moving toward the Ideal of the Undergraduate Library as a Teaching Instrument." *Drexel Library Quarterly* 7 (July/Oct. 1971): 217–221.

———. "Independent Study and the Academic Library." In *An Approach to Independent Study* (New Dimensions in Higher Education, no. 13). Washington, D.C.: U.S. Office of Education, 1965, pp. 25–33.

———. "Library-Coordinated Instruction at Monteith College." In Byron Lamar Johnson, ed. *The Junior College Library; A Report of a Conference Sponsored by the University of California, Los Angeles, the American Association of Junior Colleges, the American Library Association, and the Accrediting Commission for Junior Colleges of the Western Association of Schools and*

Colleges, July 12–14, 1965 (Occasional Report #8). Los Angeles: University of California School of Education, Junior College Leadership Program, Jan. 1966, pp. 31–36. (ERIC Doc. #: ED 021 606).
——. "The Library, the Undergraduate and the Teaching Faculty." Unpublished paper presented at the Institute on Training for Service in Undergraduate Libraries. San Diego: University of California Libraries, August 17–21, 1970. 50 pp. (ERIC Doc. #: ED 042 475). (Published in part as "Guidelines for Bucking the System. . . ." *Drexel Library Quarterly* 7 (July/Oct. 1971): 217–221.
——. "The Library's Response to Innovation in Higher Education." *California Librarian* 29 (April 1968): 142–149.
——. "The Meaning of the Monteith College Library Program for Library Education." *Journal of Education for Librarianship* 6 (Fall 1965): 117–127.
——. *The Monteith College Library Experiment.* Metuchen, N.J.: Scarecrow Press, 1966. 293 pp.
Koppelman, Connie. "The Metamorphosis of an Idea." *ARLIS/NA Newsletter* 2 (Feb. 1974): 26.
——. "Orientation and Instruction in Academic Art Libraries." *Special Libraries* 67 (May/June 1976): 256–260.
Koren, Stephanie. "Some Thoughts on Bibliographical Instruction." *New York Library Association Bulletin* 23 (Oct. 1975): 1.
Koster, Gayl E. "Librarian in the Classroom." *Drexel Library Quarterly* 8 (July 1972): 223–229.
Kouns, Betty. "Thirteen Steps to Library Orientation." *School Library Journal* 23 (March 1977): 125.
Kraus, W. Keith. *Murder, Mischief, and Mayhem: A Process for Creative Research Papers.* Urbana, Ill.: National Council of Teachers of English, 1978. 148 pp. (ERIC Doc. #: ED 154 415).
Kubeck, Ralph D. "Training the Business Information User." In International Conference on Training for Information Work, Rome, November 15–19, 1971. *Proceedings.* Rome: Italian National Information Institute; The Hague: International Federation for Documentation, 1972. pp. 435–437.
Kuo, Frank F. "Comparison of Six Versions of Science Library Instruction." *College and Research Libraries* 34 (July 1973): 287–290.
Kusnerz, Peggy Ann, and Miller, Marie, comps. *Audio-Visual Techniques and Library Instruction.* Ann Arbor: University of Michigan, Library Extension Service, 1975. 33 pp. (ERIC Doc. #: ED 118 106).
LaBrant, Lou, and Richards, Violet. "A Study for the Future at Dillard University: A Summary Report." Mimeographed. New Orleans: Dillard University, June 1, 1969.
Laclemendiere, Jean de. "For What and Why to Train and Educate?" In International Conference on Training for Information Work, Rome, November 15–19, 1971. *Proceedings.* Rome: Italian National Information Institute; The Hague: International Federation for Documentation, 1972, pp. 438–448.
Lamprecht, Sandra J. "The University Library Map Room Orientation." *SLA Geography and Map Division Bulletin* 98 (Dec. 1974): 31–33.
Lancaster, Frederick Wilfrid. "User Education: The Next Major Thrust in

Information Science?" *Journal of Education for Librarianship* 11 (Summer 1970): 55–63.

Lane, David O. "The City University of New York and Open Enrollment." *Bookmark; News about Library Services* 31 (Jan./Feb. 1972): 73–75.

Larson, Dale M. *Library Instruction in the Community College: Toward Innovative Librarianship.* Fullerton: California State College, 1971. 30 pp. (ERIC Doc. #: ED 054 765).

————. *A Systems Approach to Individualized Library Instruction.* Fullerton: California State College, 1972. 48 pp. (ERIC Doc. #: ED 071 681).

Larson, Thelma E. "The Public Onslaught: A Survey of User Orientation Methods." *RQ* 8 (Spring 1969): 182–187.

Lasher, Edward, and Hibbs, Jack. "Creating a Slide Tape Library Orientation Program." *Ohio Media Spectrum* 30 (Jan. 1978): 76–77.

Lee, John W., and Read, Raymond L. "The Graduate Business Student and the Library." *College and Research Libraries* 33 (Sept. 1972): 403–407.

————. "Making the Library Good for Business." *Learning Today* 6 (Spring 1973): 36–41.

Lee, Sul H., ed. *See* Conference on Library Orientation, First and Second.

Lenski, Sally. "Library Orientation—A Way of Hope for Users and Staff." *Illinois Libraries* 59 (April 1977): 293–295.

LeUnes, Arnold D. "The Developmental Psychology Library Search: Can a Nonsense Assignment Make Sense?" *Teaching of Psychology* 4 (April 1977): 86.

Lewis, May Genevieve. "Library Orientation for Asian College Students." *College and Research Libraries* 30 (May 1969): 267–272.

"Library Instruction Information Exchange." *North Carolina Libraries,* 35 (Summer–Fall 1977): 77–78.

"Library Instruction Materials Bank (LIMB)." *Bibliography, Documentation, Terminology* 17 (Nov. 1977): 367.

"Library Instruction—The Right Time and Place." *Journal of Academic Librarianship* 4 (May 1978): 92–93.

"Library Orientation and Library Use at the University of Alabama" (Also Miles and Mobile Colleges). *Alabama Librarian* 26 (Nov./Dec. 1974): 13.

"Library Orientation and Use Instruction." *Alabama Librarian* 26 (Sept./Oct. 1975): 8, 10.

"Library Orientation Film." *Special Libraries* 56 (May 1965): 340.

"Library Orientation in South Carolina." *South Carolina Librarian* 17 (Fall 1972): 22–28.

"Library Service Enhancement Program Leaders Work to Improve Library Service." *CLR* (Council on Library Resources). *Recent Developments* 6 (April 1978): [3–4].

"Library Use Instruction in Academic and Research Libraries." *ARL Management Supplement,* vol. 5 (Sept. 1977). 6 pp.

Liebesny, F. "Education." In *Storage and Retrieval of Information: A User-Supplier Dialogue. Proceedings 18–30 June 1968.* Neuilly-sur-Seine: North Atlantic Treaty Organization, Advisory Group for Aerospace Research and Development, 1968, pp. 179–186.

Lincoln, Cynthia Mary, ed. *See* International Association of Technological University Libraries. Conference, 1970, Loughborough.

Lindberg. A. "Teaching Library Users at Linköping University Library." *IA-TUL Proceedings* 9 (1977): 76–78.

Linden, Ronald O. "Tutor-Librarianship: A Personal View." *Library Association Record* 69 (Oct. 1967): 351–355, 357.

Linderman, Winifred B., ed. *The Present Status and Future Prospects of Reference/Information Service: Proceedings of the Conference Held at the School of Library Science, Columbia University, March 30–April 1, 1966.* Chicago: American Library Association, 1967. 195 pp.

Line, Maurice B. *The College Student and the Library; Report of a Survey in May 1964 of the Use of Libraries and Books by Students in Five Teacher Training Colleges.* Southampton, England: University of Southampton, Institute of Education, 1965. 64 pp.

————. Comment on article by Gerald M. Smith. *See* Smith, Gerald M. "Library-Based Information Services in Higher Education."

————. "Information Services in Academic Libraries." In International Association of Technological University Libraries. Conference, 1970, Loughborough. *Educating the Library User; Proceedings of the Fourth Triennial Meeting, April 1–3, 1970.* Loughborough, Leicestershire, England: Loughborough University of Technology Library, 1970. Also in *IATUL Proceedings.* 5 (May 1970): 28–34.

————. "Information Services in University Libraries." *Journal of Librarianship* 1 (Oct. 1969): 211–224.

Line, Maurice B., and Tidmarsh, Mavis. "Student Attitudes to the University Library: A Second Survey at Southampton University." *Journal of Documentation* 22 (June 1966): 123–135.

Lipow, Anne Grodzins. "User Education and Publicity for On-line Services." In Peter G. Watson, ed. *On-line Bibliographic Services—Where We Are, Where We're Going.* Chicago: American Library Association. Reference and Adult Services Division, 1977, pp. 67–77.

Lolley, John L. "Educating the Library User; the Evolution of Individualized Library Instructional Program at Tarrant County Junior College." *Texas Library Journal* 51 (Spring 1975): 30–32.

Lubans, John, Jr. *Educating the Library User.* New York: R. R. Bowker, 1974. 435 pp.

————. "Educating the Library User in England." *Mountain-Plains Library Association Newsletter* 20, no. 5 (1975–76): 3.

————. "Evaluating Library User Education Programs." *Drexel Library Quarterly* 8 (July 1972): 325–343.

————. "In Pursuit of the Educated Library User: A Dilemma." *Ohio Association of School Librarians Bulletin* 28 (Oct. 1976): 7–9, and *Educational Media in Ohio* 5 (Oct. 1976): 7–9 [special joint issue].

————. "A Look at Library Use Instruction Programs: The Problems of Library Users and Non-users." Report to the Council on Library Resources on a Fellowship Awarded for 1971/72. Mimeographed. Boulder: University of Colorado Library, 1972. 23 pp. (ERIC Doc. #: ED 093 311).

————. "Nonuse of an Academic Library." *College and Research Libraries* 32 (Sept. 1971): 362–367.

————. "On Non-use of an Academic Library: A Report of Findings." In New York Library Association, College and University Libraries Section. *Use, Mis-use and Non-use of Academic Libraries.* Woodside, N.Y.: author, 1970, pp. 47–70. ERIC Doc. #:ED 046 419).

————. *Program to Improve and Increase Student and Faculty Involvement in Library Use; First Annual Progress Report, Sept. 1, 1973–Aug. 31, 1974.* Boulder:' University of Colorado Libraries, 1974. 14 pp. (ERIC Doc. #: ED 097 864).

————. *Program to Improve and Increase Student and Faculty Involvement in Library Use; Second Annual Progress Report, September 1, 1974–August 31, 1975.* Boulder: University of Colorado Libraries, 1975. 28 pp. (ERIC Doc. #: ED 114 097).

Lubans, John, Jr., ed. *Progress in Educating the Library User.* New York: R. R. Bowker, 1978. 230 pp.

Lunin, Lois F. "Directions in Education for Information Science: The Rationale and Planning for an Information Science Course in a 'Foreign' Discipline: Medicine." *Information,* Part 2, 2, no. 4 (1973): 21–28.

Lunin, Lois F., and Catlin, Francis I. "Information Science in the Medical School Curriculum: A Pioneer Effort." In American Society for Information Science. *Proceedings of the 33rd Annual Meeting, Philadelphia, October 11–15, 1970;* vol. 7: *The Information Conscious Society.* Washington, D.C.: The Society, 1970, pp. 37–39.

Lupoi, Maurizio. "University Training of Jurists in Information Work." In International Conference on Training for Information Work, Rome, November 15–19, 1971. *Proceedings.* Rome: Italian National Information Institute, The Hague: International Federation for Documentation, 1972, pp. 241–245.

Lynch, Mary Jo. "A New Approach to the Guided Tour." *RQ* 11 (Fall 1971): 46–48.

Lynch, Sister Mary Dennis. "U.S. by Bus: Or, What is Going on in B. I. Land?" See issues of *Catholic Library World,* beginning with Oct. 1977.

McComb, Ralph W. "Orientation and Library Instruction." *Drexel Library Quarterly* 2 (July 1966): 248–249.

McGowan, Owen T. P. "Library Instruction Needed" (High school). *Catholic Library World* 48 (Nov. 1976): 185.

MacGregor, John, and McInnis, Raymond G. "Integrating Classroom Instruction and Library Research; the Cognitive Functions of Bibliographic Network Structures." *Journal of Higher Education* 48 (Jan.–Feb. 1977): 17–38.

Mackenzie, A. Graham. "Reader Instruction in Modern Universities." *Aslib Proceedings* 21 (July 1969): 271–279.

McKinn, Emma J. "Survey of Instruction in the Use of the Library in Medical Schools." Unpublished research project. Columbia: University of Missouri, School of Library and Information Science. 1969.

McKinney, Richard W. "Workshop Course Teaches Students Use of Resources." *Journalism Educator* (Oct. 1977): 5759.

Macleod, Beth. "Special Projects in Academic Libraries." *Michigan Librarian* 38 (Summer 1972): 5–6.

Maginnity, Gerald. F. *A Personalized System of Instruction in Library Use.* Monterrey, Mexico: Instituto Tecnologico de Monterrey, 1976. 14 pp. (ERIC Doc. #: ED 125 530).

Malley, Ian. "Library Instruction Materials Bank." *Aslib Proceedings* 30 (July 1978): 271–276.

Mallory, Mordine. "SEEK Program at Queens College." In Institute on a New College Student: The Challenge to City University Libraries, 1969, Brooklyn College. *Papers.* Rockway Park, N.Y.: Scientific Book Service, 1969, pp. 32–40.

Mangión, Marion B. "Need for Expanded Library Education Programs." *Maine Library Association Bulletin* 30 (May 1969): 3–5.

Mann, Peter H. "Communication About Books to Undergraduates." *Aslib Proceedings* 26 (June 1974): 250–256.

Manning, D. J., ed. "Report of a Committee of the University and College Libraries Section of the Library Association of Autralia Appointed to Examine the Requirements for Reader Education Activities in Universities and Colleges." *Australian Academic and Research Libraries* 4 (Dec. 1973): 19 pp. supplement.
  Review by Dorothy W. Freed *New Zealand Libraries* 37 (June 1974): 139.

Marie Martha, Sister. "Relevant Research." *Catholic Library World* 41 (April 1970): 505–507.

Marklund, K. "Library Integration into Technical Education at the University of Lulea." *IATUL Proceedings* 9 (1977): 79–85.

Marshall, Albert Prince. *Library Orientation—What's That?* Ypsilanti, Mich.: Annual Conference on Library Orientation for Academic Libraries, 1975. 8 pp. (ERIC Doc. #: ED 108 710).

———. "Library Outreach: The Program at Eastern Michigan University." *Drexel Library Quarterly* 7 (July/Oct. 1971): 347–350.

———. "This Teaching/Learning Thing: Librarians as Educators." In Herbert Poole, ed. *Academic Libraries by the Year 2000; Essays Honoring Jerrold Orne.* N.Y.: Bowker, 1977, pp. 50–63.

Martin, Dean F., and Robison, Dennis E. "Who's Teaching Chemical Literature Courses These Days?" *Journal of Chemical Documentation* 9 (May 1969): 95–99.

Martin, Jess A., et al. "Teaching of Formal Courses by Medical Librarians." *Journal of Medical Education* 50 (Sept. 1975): 883–887.

Martindale, James, and Hardesty, Larry. *Library Service Enhancement Program, DePauw University. Grant Proposal and Quarterly Reports.* Greencastle, Ind.: DePauw University, 1977. 195 pp. (ERIC Doc. #: ED 145 839).

Martinelli, James. "Bilingual Slide Tape Library Orientation." *Audiovisual Instruction* 21 (Jan. 1976): 55–56.

Martins, Barbara, comp. *Bibliographic Instruction.* Bethany, W. Va.: West Virginia Library Association, 1977. 52 pp. (ERIC Doc. #: ED 144 582).

Maxwell, Monty M., and Tullis, Carol. "UGL's Library Instruction Program at Indiana University." *LOEX News* 2 (March 15, 1975): 2–5.

Melum, Verna V. "Library Instruction in a University." *Illinois Libraries* 51 (June 1969): 511–521.

———. "Library Orientation in the College and University: A Survey to Aid

Your Fall Planning." *Wilson Library Bulletin* 46 (Sept. 1971): 59–66.

———. "1971 Survey of Library Orientation and Instructional Programs." *Drexel Library Quarterly* 7 (July/Oct. 1971): 225–253.

Mews, Hazel. "Library Instruction Concerns People." *Library Association Record* 72 (Jan. 1970): 8–10. Also in Seminar on Human Aspects of Library Instruction, University of Reading, Dec. 9, 1969. *Proceedings.* Cardiff, Wales: Standing Conference on National and University Libraries, 1970, pp. 44–49.

———. "Library Instruction to Students at the University of Reading." *Education Libraries Bulletin* 32 (Summer 1968): 24–34.

———. *Reader Instruction in Colleges and Universities: Teaching the Use of the Library.* Hamden, Conn.: Shoe String Press (Linnet Books), 1972. 111 pp.

———. "Teaching the Use of Books and Libraries with Particular Reference to Academic Libraries." In *British Librarianship and Information Science, 1966–1970.* London: The Library Association, 1972, pp. 581–609.

Midwest Federation of Library Associations. Conference, 1975, Detroit, Michigan. *Writing Objectives for Bibliographic Instruction in Academic Libraries; a Summary of the Proceedings . . . October 1–2, 1975.* [University of Wisconsin, Parkside. Library, Kenosha] author, 1976. 234 pp.

Mikhailov, A. I. "The Training of Information Users in the USSR." In International Federation for Documentation. *Users of Documentation: FID International Congress on Documentation, Buenos Aires, 21–24 September 1970.* The Hague: author, 1970, Paper II.9, 7 pp.

———. "The Training of Users of Information." In International Conference on Training for Information Work, Rome, November 15–19, 1971. *Proceedings.* Rome: Italian National Information Institute; The Hague: International Federation for Documentation, 1972, pp. 403–406.

Milby, T. H. "A Study of Instructional Programs in the Use of Biological Literature at Selected U.S. Universities." Mimeographed. Report to the Council on Library Resources for a Fellowship. Washington, D.C.: The Council, 1971.

Miller, Lawrence. "Liaison Work in the Academic Library." *RQ* 16 (Spring 1977): 213–215.

Miller, Michael M. "North Dakota State University Library Uses New Technology in Library Use Instruction." *Mountain-Plains Library Association Newsletter* 20, no. 2 (1975–76): 12.

Miller, Stuart Wayne. "Library Use Instruction in Selected American Colleges." M.A. thesis. Chicago: University of Chicago, 1976. 91 pp.

Millis, Charlotte Hickman. "The Wabash Project: A Centrifugal Program." *Drexel Library Quarterly* 7 (July/Oct. 1971): 365–374.

Millis, Charlotte Hickman, and Thompson, Donald E. "Wabash College Library Project." *Library Occurrent* 23 (Feb. 1971): 311–316, 332.

Mills, Lawrence. "College Librarian As Teacher." *Maryland Libraries* 33 (Fall 1966): 26–28.

Mills, Robin K. "Legal Research Instruction in Law Schools, the State of the Art; or, Why Law School Graduates Do Not Know How to Find the Law. *Law Library Journal* 70 (Aug. 1977): 343–348.

Moon, Eric E. "A-V Showtime: Preconference Institute on Library Orientation Programs." *Library Journal* 91 (Aug. 1966): 3640–3642.

Morris, Jacquelyn M., and Webster, Donald F. *Developing Objectives for Library Instruction.* [Workshop] sponsored by College and University Section of NYLA and New York Library Instruction Clearinghouse. Syracuse, N.Y.: New York Library Instruction Clearinghouse, 1976. 26 pp.

Mortimer, A. W. B. "Succeeded to Dragons: Library Tutorial Programmes." *Australian Library Journal* 20 (Sept. 1971): 22–26.

Motley, Drucilla. "Old Wine, New Bottles." *Library Journal* 93 (Oct. 15, 1968): 3932–3933; *School Library Journal* 15 (Oct. 1968): 118–119.

Myatt, A. G. "Experience in Educating the User at the NLL." In International Association of Technological University Libraries. Conference, 1970. Loughborough. *Educating the Library User; Proceedings of the Fourth Triennial Meeting, April 1–3, 1970.* Loughborough, Leicestershire, England: Loughborough University of Technology Library, 1970.

National Conference on the Implications of the New Media for the Teaching of Library Science, Chicago, 1963. *Proceedings,* Harold Goldstein, ed. (University of Illinois Graduate School of Library Science Monograph Series, no. 1). Urbana: University of Illinois Graduate School of Library Science. 1963. 233 pp.

Neal, Kenneth W. "Training Students in the Use of a Library." *Assistant Librarian* 59 (August 1966): 164–165.

Neelameghan, A. "Doctoral Candidates: Orientation in the Use of Documents and Documentation Service: Report on a Workshop." *Library Science with a Slant to Documentation* 10 (Sept. 1973): 428–438.

Neil, A. G. "Library Tutoring." *Educational Libraries Bulletin* 42 (Autumn 1971): 9–14.

Nelson, Jerold. "Faculty Awareness and Attitudes toward Academic Library Reference Services: A Measure of Communication." *College and Research Libraries* 34 (Sept. 1973): 268–275.

Nettlefold, Brian A. "A Course in Communication and Information Retrieval for Undergraduate Biologists." *Journal of Biological Education* 9 (Oct. 1975): 201–205.

"Nevada High Schoolers Get University Orientation." *Library Journal* 102 (Aug. 1977): 1552.

[A New Approach to Freshman Library Instruction . . . at Colorado State University.] *The Colorado Academic Library* 3 (Winter 1966): 22–23.

Newell, Matthias G. "GP in the Academic Library." *Catholic Library World* 43 (April 1972): 453–456.

"New Library Orientation Course at College of Charleston." *South Carolina Librarian* 18 (Spring 1974): 34.

Newman, John. "Library Orientation in the Community College." *Wilson Library Bulletin* 46 (May 1972): 856.

New York Library Association. College and University Libraries Section. *Use, Mis-use and Non-use of Academic Libraries.* Woodside, N.Y.: author, 1970. 129 pp. (ERIC Doc. #: ED 046 419).

New York Library Instruction Clearinghouse. *Developing Objectives for Library Instruction. See* Morris, Jacquelyn M., and Webster, Donald F.

———. *Developing Printed Material for Library Instruction.* See Elkins, Elizabeth, and Byman, Judith A.

"New York Library Instruction Clearinghouse." *Information Hotline* 8 (Sept. 1976): 10.

"New York Library Instruction Clearinghouse Has Been Established at the F. Franklin Moon Library, SUNY College of Environmental Science and Forestry in Syracuse, New York." *College and Research Library News* 3 (March 1976): 70.

Nielsen, Erland Kolding. "On the Teaching of Subject Bibliography in History: Some Experiences and Views on a Methodological Approach to the Discipline with Specific Reference to Danish Conditions." *Libri* 24, no. 3 (1974): 171–208.

"North Dakota State University is Solving its Library Orientation Problem." *Mountain-Plains Library Quarterly* 17 (Spring 1972): 22–24.

NVBF Anglo-Scandinavian Seminar on Library User Education, November 2–4, 1976, Gothenburg. Sweden. *Proceedings.* (CTHB—Publikation #12) Gothenburg. Sweden: Chalmers University of Technology Library, 1977.

Nwoye, S. C., and Anafulu, J. C. "Instructing University Students in Library Use.: The Nsukka Experiment." *Libri* 23, no. 4 (1973): 251–259.

Oakley, Adeline Dupuy. "Content Analysis of Student Responses in Topic-Centered Library Orientation." Ph.D. dissertation. Boston, Mass.: Boston University, School of Education, 1978. 254 pp.

Oberman-Soroka, Cerise, ed. *See* Southeastern Conference on Approaches to Bibliographic Instruction, Charleston, S.C., March 16–17, 1978, *Proceedings.*

O'Connor, Elizabeth C. "College Library Preceptorial Instruction Program." *Bookmark; News about Library Services* 31 (Jan./Feb. 1972): 76–79.

"Off on a LIMB" [Library Instruction Materials Bank]. *Library Association Record.* 80 (July 1978): 325.

Olafioye, A. Olu. "The University Library and Its Community." *Lagos Librarian* 3 (Dec. 1968): 28–33.

Olaniyan, B. F., et al. "Instructing Students in the Use of the Library in the University of Lagos. *Nigerian Libraries* 11 (April–Aug. 1975): 123–133.

Olevnik, Peter P. *A Media-Assisted Library Instruction Orientation Program Report.* Brockport: State University of New York College at Brockport. 1976. 55 pp. (ERIC Doc. #: ED 134 138).

Oppenheim, George. "User Education." Comment on article by M. B. Stevenson. *Journal of Documentation* 33 (Sept. 1977): 243–244.

O'Reilly, Shirley. "Reader Education (1): A Readers' Advisor's Programme." *Australian Academic and Research Libraries* 1 (Autumn 1970): 16–20.

Orgren, Carl F. *Production of Slide-Tape Programs.* Iowa City: University of Iowa, School of Library Science, 1972.

"Orientation Clearinghouse Set Up at SUNY-Syracuse." *Library Journal* 101 (March 1, 1976): 649–650.

"Orientation Programs in Colorado Academic Libraries." *Colorado Academic Library* 4 (Autumn 1968): 15–23.

Orna, Elizabeth. "Should We Educate Our Users?" *Aslib Proceedings* 30 (April 1978): 130–141.

Owen, Edith M. "Closed Circuit Television in the Library." *Education Libraries Bulletin* 27 (Autumn 1966): 24–27.

Page, B. S., and McCarthy, Stephen A. "Library Provision for Undergraduates." *College and Research Libraries* 26 (May 1965): 219–224.

Palandri, Guido. "Overdue: Beyond Vuturism: Back to Academic Librarianship." Comment on an article by R. Vuturo. *Wilson Library Bulletin* 52 (March 1978): 568–569.

Palmer, Millicent C. "Academic Library Instruction—Problems and Principles." *Tennessee Librarian* 25 (Winter 1973): 11–17.

——. "Creating Slide-Tape Library Instruction: The Librarian's Role." *Drexel Library Quarterly* 8 (July 1972): 251–267.

——. "Library Instruction at Southern Illinois University, Edwardsville." *Drexel Library Quarterly* 7 (July/Oct. 1971): 255–276.

——. "Problems in Academic Library Instruction Our Own Creation?"*Catholic Library World* 43 (April 1972): 447–452.

Parker, Franklin. "Library Resources for Educational Leaders: A Class Discussion." *Library-College Journal* 3 (Summer 1970): 31–36.

Parsons, Christopher James. *Library Use in Further Education.*London: Edward Arnold & Co., 1973. 75 pp.

Paterson, Ellen R. "An Assessment of College Student Library Skills." *RQ* 17 (Spring 1978): 226–229.

Patterson, Margaret C. "Ivory Towers and Note Cards." Paper presented at the Annual Meeting of the Modern Language Association, 1976. 9 pp. (ERIC Doc. #: ED 137 801).

——. "Library Literacy—A Cumulative Experience." *Literary Research Newsletter* 2 (Oct. 1977): 180–186.

Paugh, Sharon L., and Marco, Guy A. "The Music Bibliography Course: Status and Quo." *Notes (Music Library Association)* 30 (Dec. 1973): 260–262.

Paulson, Bruce L. *Junior College Library Orientation Innovations.* Los Angeles: University of California at Los Angeles, 1968. 34 pp. (ERIC Doc. #: ED 019 058).

Peacock, P. G., and Cameron, Kenneth J. "The Open University Summer School at the University of Stirling: A Report on Library Usage." *Library Association Record* 74 (Dec. 1972): 237–238.

Pearce, B. L. "Tuition in Library Use as a Part of Open University Preparatory Courses." *Library Review* 25 (Autumn 1976): 254–256.

Peck, Theodore. "The Engineering Library as an Applied Learning Laboratory." *Engineering Education* 67 (April 1977): 723–724.

Peck, Theodore P. "Reference Librarian Recast in a New Role." *RQ* 11 (Spring 1972): 212–213.

Peele, David Arnold. "Hook Principle; or, How to Get the Faculty to Listen to Your Library Lecture with Some Other Practical Hints for Introducing the 'I Want My Students to Know Something About the Library' General Lecture." *RQ* 13 (Winter 1973): 135–138.

Penland, Patrick. "Library Use, Instruction In." In *Encyclopedia of Library and Information Science*, vol. 16, pp. 113–147. New York: Marcel Dekkar, 1975.

Penney, Barbara. "Planning Library Instruction." In John Cowley, *Libraries in Higher Education: The User Approach to Service.* Hamden, Conn.: Shoe String Press (Linnet Books), 1975, pp. 137–149.

Perkins, Ralph. *The Prospective Teacher's Knowledge of Library Fundamentals: A Study of the Responses Made by 4,170 College Seniors to Tests Designed to Measure Familiarity with Libraries*. Metuchen, N.J.: Scarecrow Press, 1965. 202 pp.

———. "Realistic Library Orientation—A Necessity." *Library-College Journal* 3 (Fall 1970): 20-27.

Perry, Emma Bradford. "A Study to Determine the Effectiveness of a Library Instruction Course in Teaching the Use of the Library to Upward Bound Students." Ed.S. thesis. Kalamazoo: Western Michigan University. 1974. 94 pp.

Peterman, Edward, and Holsclaw, Jim. "Library Orientation in a New Mode." *Audiovisual Instruction* 16 (Feb. 1971): 46–47.

Phillips, Linda. "Making Library Instruction More Palatable." *American Vocational Journal* 52 (April 1977): 57–58.

Phipps, Barbara H. "Library Instruction for the Undergraduate." *College and Research Libraries* 29 (Sept. 1968: 411–423.

Pierce, Preston E. "Make Your Own Library Skill Reinforcers." *Audiovisual Instruction* 17 (Jan. 1972): 58.

Pierson, Robert M. "A Jaundiced Approach to the Guided Tour." *RQ* 11 (Fall 1971): 55–58.

Piróg, Wojciech. "Training of Documentation and Information Users." *Unesco Bulletin for Libraries* 24 (Sept./Oct. 1970): 266–272, 275.

———. "Training of Students in Academic Schools." In International Federation for Documentation. *Users of Documentation: FID International Congress on Documentation, Buenos Aires, 21–24 September, 1970*. The Hague: author, 1970, Paper II.1, 7 pp.

Pitts, Ben E. *Using Educational Research in Teaching Teachers*. Cookeville: Tennessee Technological University Library, 1977. 11 pp. (ERIC Doc. #: ED 156 652).

Poole, Jay Martin, et al. *Preliminary Paper toward a Comprehensive Program of Library Orientation/Instruction for the Libraries of the State University of New York at Buffalo*. Buffalo: State University of New York Libraries, 1974. 37 pp. (ERIC Doc. #: ED 092 137).

Porter, John. "The Travelling Workshops Experiment in the Use of Biological Literature." *Journal of Biological Education* 11 (June 1977): 143–144.

Powell, Ronald H. "Library Orientation." *RQ* 11 (Winter 1971): 147–148.

Poyer, Robert K. "Improved Library Services through User Education." *Bulletin of the Medical Library Association* 65 (April 1977): 296–297.

"The President Views the Campus Library." *Journal of Academic Librarianship* 3 (Sept. 1977): 192–199.

Pritchard, Hugh C. "Library Orientation." *RQ* 7 (Fall 1967): 9–11.

———. "Pre-arrival Library Instruction for College Students." *College and Research Libraries* 26 (July 1965): 321.

"Program Alert: Educating the User; New Approaches Tried." *Library Journal* 103 (Feb. 15, 1978): 424, 427.

Comment. *Learning Today* 11 (Spring 1978): 28–29.

"Prospective Teachers Found Ignorant of Library Use and Resources." *Library Journal* 90 (May 15, 1965): 2348–2349; *School Library Journal* 12 (May 1965): 44–45.

Pugh, L. C. "Library Instruction Programmes for Undergraduates: Historical Development and Current Practice." *Library World* (March 1970): 267–273.

———. "Tutor-Librarianship: A Reappraisal." *Library World* 72 (Jan. 1971): 206–208.

Quon, Frieda Seu. "Study of Library Handbooks and a Gudie to the Resources and Services of the University of Mississippi Library." M.L.S. thesis. University, Miss.: University of Mississippi. 1965. 172 pp.

Rader, Hannelore B. *Five-Year Library Outreach Orientation Program; Final Report.* Ypsilanti: Eastern Michigan University Library, 1975. 168 pp. (ERIC Doc. #: ED 115 265).

———. "The Humanizing Function of the College Library; or, Providing Students with Library Know-How." *Catholic Library World* 49 (Feb 1978): 278–281.

———. *Instructing the Community College Library User: The Michigan Experience.* 1977. 16 pp. (ERIC Doc. #: ED 152 331).

———. "Reaching Out to Freshmen." *Michigan Librarian* 37 (Autumn 1971): 11–13.

Rader, Hannelore B., ed. *See also* Conference on Library Orientation for Academic Libraries, Fourth, Fifth, and Sixth.

Rader, Hannelore B.; Weber, Hans H.; and Boes, Warren N., eds. *A Guide to Academic Library Instruction.* Foundations in Library and Information Science Series, vol. 7. Greenwich, Conn.: Jai Press, 1978. 300 pp. (approx.).

Ramey, James W. "Classroom Dynamics: or, Is There a Teacher in the House?" *Drexel Library Quarterly* 8 (July 1972): 237–244.

Ramsay, O. Bertrand. "An Audio-Visual Guide to the Chemical Literature." *Journal of Chemical Documentation* 9 (May 1969): 92–95.

Ranganathan, Shiyali Ramamrita. "Productivity and Partnership in University Education." *Library Herald* 10 (April 1968): 1–18.

Rao, Paladugu. "Library Orientation: A Multimedia Approach at Eastern." *Audiovisual Instruction* 15 (May 1970): 83–84.

Rawlinson, Stephen. "A Role for the Academic Library in Library Instruction." *Physics Education* 12 (Nov. 1977): 432–433.

"Reader Education, Two Comments." *Australian Academic and Research Libraries* 6 (June 1975): 92–95.

"Reader Services." In Sarah Katharine Thomson, *Learning Resource Centers in Community Colleges; a Survey of Budgets and Services.* Chicago: American Library Association, 1975, pp. 101–105.

Reid, Bruce J. "Bibliographic Teaching in French and Politics at the University of Leicester." *Journal of Librarianship* 5 (Oct. 1973): 292–303.

Reitan, E. A. "New Perspectives on Using the Library in History Teaching." *American Historical Association Newsletter* 16 (April 1978): 5–6.

Renaud, Ivan G. "The Training of Users of the French Scientific and Technical Information Centres." In International Conference on Training for Information Work, Rome, November 15–19, 1971. *Proceedings.* Rome: Italian National Information Institute; The Hague: International Federation for Documentation, 1972, pp. 454–458.

Renford, Beverly L. "A Self-Paced Workbook Program for Beginning College Students." *Journal of Academic Librarianship* 4 (Sept. 1978): 200–203.

Renwick, K. D. "Production or Protraction?" *Audiovisual Librarian* 4 (Autumn 1977): 23–24.

"Research Methods Mini-course." *NYLA Bulletin* 22 (April 1974): 6.

Revill, D. H. "Teaching methods in the Library: A Survey from the Educational Point of View." *Library World* 71 (Feb. 1970): 243–249.

Reynolds, C. J. "Discovering the Government Documents Collection in Libraries." *RQ* 14 (Spring 1975): 228–231.

Rhodes, R. G., and Evans, A. J. "Educational Role of the University Library and the Provision of Information Services." *IATUL Proceedings* 7 (July 1973): 11–25.

Richnell, D. T. "Library and Undergraduate: 2. The Hale Committee Report and Instruction in the Use of Libraries." *Library Association Record* 68 (Oct. 1966): 357–361.

Rickwood, Peter C. "Introducing University Students to the Geological Literature." *Journal of Geological Education* 23 (May 1975): 103–106.

Ridgeway, Patricia, ed. "Orientation Instruction Round-Up." Column. See issues of *South Carolina Librarian*, starting with Fall 1977.

Riley, Louise Elise. "A Study of the Performance on a Library Orientation Test in Relation to the Academic Achievement and Scholastic Aptitude of a Selected Group of Freshman College Students at Tuskegee Institute." *ACRL Microcard Service*, 145 (1964). 35 leaves.

Roach, Jeanetta C. "A Good Library Needs an Interested Faculty." *Mississippi Library News* 38 (March 1974): 25–26.

Roberts, Anne. *A Study of Ten SUNY Campuses Offering an Undergraduate Credit Course in Library Instruction.* Albany: State University of New York, Albany. Libraries, 1978. 81 pp. (ERIC Doc. #: ED 157 529).

Robson, John; Kacena, Carolyn; and Peters, Charles. "Plato IV Comes of Age." *Network* 1 (July 1974): 12–14.

Rodda, Reddy R. "Questions Most Often Asked in Our Science Library." *Unabashed Librarian*, no. 23 (1977), p. 22.

Ronkin, R. R. "A Self-Guided Library Tour for the Biosciences." *College and Research Libraries* 28 (May 1967): 217–218.

Rooker, Margaret. "Tools and Tactics, the Framework for an Experiment in Introducing Students to the College Library." *Education Libraries Bulletin* 22 (Spring 1965): 29–41.

Rosenblum, Joseph. "Overdue: The Future of Reference Service: Death by Complexity?" *Wilson Library Bulletin* 52 (Dec. 1977): 300–301, 350.
    Comment by William J. Frost. "Complexity in Indexes: The Real Culprit." *Wilson Library Bulletin* 52 (March 1978): 571.

Ross, Woodburn O. "The Academic Library: A Personal View." *Library-College Journal* 1 (Fall 1968): 34–46.

Rossoff, Martin. "The Forgotten Key." *Library Journal* 91 (Oct. 15, 1966): 5126–5128, 5141.

Roth, Dena L. "The Needs of Library Users." *Unesco Bulletin for Libraries* 28 (March/April 1974): 92–95.

Rowlett, Russell J., Jr. "Training Chemists in the Use of Chemical Abstracts'

Services." *Journal of Chemical Documentation* 9 (May 1969): 103–105.

Ruckman, Bonita, and Barnes, Ida. "A Need, an Idea, a Project." *Journal of Reading* 14 (April 1971): 473–474.

Rutstein, Joel S. *Access to U.S. Government Statistics through Course-Related Instruction.* Fort Collins: Colorado State University Libraries, 1976. 17 pp. (ERIC Doc. #: ED 134 211).

Rzasa, Philip V., and Moriarity, John H. "The Types and Needs of Academic Library Users." *College and Research Libraries* 31 (Nov. 1970): 403–409.

Sable, Martin H. "Needed: Libraries Skills, Teaching, Bibliography in Academic Libraries." *Wisconsin Library Bulletin* 70 (Nov./Dec. 1974): 305–306.

Sabol, Cathy. *Librarian in the Classroom.* Manassas, Va.: Northern Virginia Community College, 1977. 11 pp. (ERIC Doc. #: ED 150 985).

Sadow, Sandra, and Beede, Benjamin R. "Library Instruction in American Law Schools." *Law Library Journal* 68 (Feb. 1975): 27-32.

Samuels, Marilyn S. "A Mini-Course in the Research Paper." *College English* 38 (Oct. 1976): 189–193.

Sanacore, Joseph. "Locating Information: The Process Method." *Journal of Reading* 18 (Dec. 1974): 231–233.

Sandock, Mollie. "A Study of University Students' Awareness of Reference Services." *RQ* 16 (Summer 1977): 284–296.

Scherer, Henry. "The Faculty and the Librarian." *Library-College Journal* 3 (Nov. 1970): 37–43.

Schiller, Anita R. "Reference Service: Instruction or Information?" *Library Quarterly* 35 (Jan. 1965): 52–60.
Comment by C. Evans. "Research without Result." *Catholic Library World* 36 (May 1965): 629–631.

Schmidmaier, Dieter. "New University Library Buildings and Library Instruction." *IATUL Proceedings* 8 (1976): 29–36.

———. "Selective Dissemination of Information and User Training in the German Democratic Republic." In International Association of Technological University Libraries. Conference, Copenhagen, 1973. *Computer-based Information Services: Practical Experience in European Libraries.* Loughborough, Leicestershire, England: Loughborough University of Technology Library, 1974, pp. 69–73.

———. "Some Effects of the 'Science of Science' on the Education of the Library User in the D.D.R." *IATUL Proceedings* 5 (May 1970): 35–50. Also in International Association of Technological University Libraries. Conference, Loughborough, 1970. *Educating the Library User,* pp. E1–E18.

———. "User Education and Selective Dissemination of Information (SDI) in Technological University Libraries—A Summary of Problem and Solution." *IATUL Proceedings* 9 (1977): 37–46.

Schnucker, R. V. "A Method and an Appraisal: For New Stars through Learning." *Learning Today* 6 (Fall 1973): 55–64.

Schwarz, Philip John. "Instruction in the Use of Microform Equipment." *Wisconsin Library Bulletin* 67 (Sept./Oct. 1971): 341–343.

———. "Learning to Use Microform Equipment: A Self-Instructional Approach." *Microform Review* 4 (Oct. 1975): 262–265.

Schwob, Elizabeth. "Orientation: Library Program Shows 'Gratifying' Results." *Feliciter* 23 (Feb. 1977): 3.

"Scientists Need Training in Library Use." *The Times Educational Supplement,* 2,677 (Sept. 9, 1966): 481.

Scott, David B. "Training for Educational Self-Reliance." *Australian Library Journal* 19 (Oct. 1970): 329–333.

Scrivener, J. E. "Instruction in Library Use.: The Persisting Problem." *Australian Academic and Research Libraries* 3 (June 1972): 87–119.

Seminar on Human Aspects of Library Instruction, University of Reading, Dec. 9, 1969. *Proceedings.* Mimeographed. Cardiff, Wales: Standing Conference on National and University Libraries, 1970. 68 pp. (ERIC Doc. #: ED 047 764).

Seminar on User Education Activities, the State of the Art in Texas. Houston, Texas, April 1976. *Proceedings.* Houston: Texas Library Association, 1977. 43 pp. (ERIC Doc. #: ED 138 247).

Seyer, Brian. "The Tutor Librarian." In *Progress in Library Science, 1965.* Washington, D.C.: Butterworths, 1965, pp. 192–194.

Shain, Charles H. *"Filming Narrative" for Library Instruction Film "You Don't Have to be a Hero to Use the U. C. Library."* Berkeley; University of California Berkeley Library, 1976. 32 pp. (ERIC Doc. #: ED 134 215).

Sharplin, C. D. "Library Orientation: What Is It Worth in Alberta?" *Library Association of Alberta Bulletin* 5 (Oct. 1974): 110–112.

Sherman, Steve. "Do It Yourself for Under $100." *Film Library Quarterly* 2 (Spring 1969): 46–48.

Shipps, Harold S. "A Pre-College Program in Library Skills for Minority Students." *Mountain-Plains Library Quarterly* 16 (Fall 1971): 24–27.

Sim, Yong Sup (Sam). *An Individualized Library Orientation Program in Mercer County Community College Library; Curriculum Development.* Ed.D. Practicum. Fort Lauderdale, Fla.: Nova University, May 1975. 28 pp. (ERIC Doc. #: ED 119 651).

———. *A Self-Guided Library Tour Method at Mercer County Community College. The Learning Theory and Applications Module.* Trenton, N.J.: Mercer County Community College, 1976. 37 pp. (ERIC Doc. #: ED 135 342).

Simmons, Beatrice Downin. "Librarian: Instructional Programmer." *Drexel Library Quarterly* 8 (July 1972): 247–250).

Simon, Dorothy Byron. "A More Human Approach to Instruction in the Use of Academic Libraries." In Elonnie Junius Josey, ed., *New Dimensions for Academic Library Service.* Metuchen, N.J.: Scarecrow, 1975, pp. 169–174.

Simpson, J. S. "Electrical Experiment; Students of the Higher National Certificate Course Given a Library Project." *Scottish Library Association News* 97 (May 1970): 77–79.

Sinha, K. M., and Deo, M. S. "User's Initiation." *Herald of Library Science* 12 (Jan. 1973): 31–34.

"Sixth-Form Library Visits." *Library Association Record* 77 (April 1975): 79–81.

Sizemore, W. Christian. "Experimental College Programs and Implications for Library Service." *Southeastern Librarian* 22 (Spring 1972): 34–40.

Slajpah, M. "Education of Students as Users of Scientific and Technical Information in Yugoslavia (with Special Regard to Conditions in Slovenia)." *IATUL Proceedings* 9 (1977): 47–55.

Smalley, Topsy N. "Bibliographic Instruction in Academic Libraries: Questioning Some Assumptions." *Journal of Academic Librarianship* 3 (Nov. 1977): 280–283.

Smith, Gerald M. "Cause for Concern." *New Library World* 78 (Oct. 1977): 189–190.

    Comment by I. Winship *New Library World* 78 (Dec. 1977): 241; Rejoinder. *New Library World* 79 (Feb. 1978): 34.

Smith, Gerald M. "Library-Based Information Services in Higher Education: Towards a Reappraisal." *Aslib Proceedings* 27 (June 1975): 239–246.

    Comment by I. Winship and J. Lambert. *Aslib proceedings* 27 (Nov./ Dec. 1975): 480–481.

    Comment by M. B. Line. *Aslib Proceedings* 28 (Jan. 1976): 36–38.

Snider, Feliz E. "Relationships of Library Ability to Performance in College." Ph.D dissertation. Urbana: University of Illinois, Graduate School of Library Science, 1965. 215 pp.

Southeastern Conference on Approaches to Bibliographic Instruction, Charleston, S.C., March 16–17, 1978. *Proceedings.* Charleston, S.C.: Continuing Education Office, College of Charleston, 1978. 136 pp.

Spaulding, Carl. "Teaching the Use of Microfilm Readers." *Microform Review* 6 (March 1977): 80–81.

Spencer, Karen L. "Legal Research in a Slide Carousel." *Law Library Journal* 71 (Feb. 1978): 156–157.

Spencer, Robert C. "The Teaching Library." *Library Journal* 103 (May 15, 1978): 1021–1024.

Standing Conference on National and University Libraries (SCONUL). *See* Seminar on Human Aspects of Library Instruction, University of Reading, Dec. 9, 1969.

Sternberg. Marilyn. "There Are No Stupid Questions: A University Library Film." *Unabashed Librarian* 18 (Winter 1976): 27–28.

Stevens, Charles H.; Canfield, Marie P.; and Gardner, Jeffery T. "Library Pathfinders: A New Possibility for Cooperative Reference Service." *College and Research Libraries* 34 (Jan. 1973): 40–46.

Stevens, R.; Hacker, B.; and Fachan, K. *AIMLO: Auto-Instructional Media for Library Orientation, Final Report.* Ft. Collins: Colorado State University Libraries, 1974. 27 pp. (ERIC Doc. #: ED 105 882).

Stevenson, Malcolm B. Comment on article by P. J. Hills. *See* Hills, Philip J. "Library Instruction and the Development of the Individual."

———. "Education in the Use of Information in University and Academic Environments" (with discussion). *Aslib Proceedings* 28 (Jan. 1976): 17–21.

———. "Education of Users of Libraries and Information Services." *Journal of Documentation* 33 (March 1977): 53–78.

    Comment by C. Oppenheim, with rejoinder. *Journal of Documentation* 33 (Sept. 1977): 243–244.

———. "Evaluation of Tape/Slide Presentations." In *Exploitation of Library Resources: A Systems Approach; a Workshop at the Hatfield Polytechnic, April 22nd, 1972.* Hatfield, England: Hatfield Polytechnic, 1972, pp. 25–30.

———. "User Education in the United Kingdom." *IATUL Proceedings* 9 (1977): 5–10.

———. *User Education Programmes: A Study of Their Development, Organization, Methods and Assessment.* Research and Development Reports, no. 5320 HC. London: British Library Research and Development Department, 1977. 44 pp.

Stewart, Alva. W. "Independent Study and Library Use." *American Libraries* 2 (Jan. 1971): 17.

Stewart, Barbara C. *An Evaluation of a Course in Library Instruction at Ball State University.* Muncie, Ind.: Ball State University Library, 1976. 56 pp. (ERIC Doc. #: ED 138 246).

Stillerman, Sophia J. "Format for Library Instruction; Stated Student Preferences at a Community College." Final paper. South Orange, N.J.: Seton Hall University, June 1975. 35 pp. (ERIC Doc. #: ED 115 294).

Stillman, Mary E. "A Program for Action." *Drexel Library Quarterly* 7 (July/Oct. 1971): 375–378.

Stobart, R. A. "Use of Library—or G.C.E. Bibliographical Knowledge." *Library World* 70 (Sept. 1968): 55–63.

Stoffle, Carla J. "How Much Time for Library Instruction?" *Wisconsin Library Bulletin* 69 (June 1973): 176.

Stoffle, Carla J., and Bonn, Gabriella S. "Academic Library Instruction in Wisconsin." *Wisconsin Library Bulletin* 69 (March/April 1973): 99–100.

———. "Inventory of Library Orientation and Instruction Methods." *RQ* 13 (Winter 1973): 129–133.

Stoffle, Carla J., and Larson, Julie. "Academic Library Skills, How Do Wisconsin Academic Libraries Teach Library Use?" *Wisconsin Library Bulletin* 73 (July-Aug. 1977): 157–158.

Stoffle, Carla J., and Pryor, Judith. "Parkside Teaches Library Use from Orientation to Competency Requirements." *Wisconsin Library Bulletin.* 73 (July–Aug. 1977): 159–160.

Stubbs, Marion. "Tutor-Librarians, a Definition." *Assistant Librarian* 60 (Nov. 1967): 241.

    Comment by B. A. J. Winslade. *Assistant Librarian* 60 (Nov. 1967): 242–243.

    Comment by A. E. Standley. *Assistant Librarian* 61 (Jan. 1968): 20–21.

    Comment by G. W. J. Wheatley. *Assistant Librarian* 61 (April 1968): 93–94.

Sullivan, Peggy, ed. *Realization: The Final Report of the Knapp School Libraries Project.* Chicago: American Library Association, 1968. 398 pp.

Sutton, Lee. "Teaching Technique for Library Centered Courses." *Library-College Journal* 1 (Summer 1968): 20–25.

Suzuki, Yukihisa. "Library Services: Education for Librarians and Library Users in a Multi-lingual, Multi-ethnic Environment." In IFLA Worldwide Seminar, Seoul, Korea, May 31–June 5, 1976. *Proceedings.* Seoul, Korea: Korean Library Association, 1976, pp. 96–101.

Tacey, William S. "Bibliosearch: Exercise in Library Use." *Pennsylvania Library Association Bulletin* 21 (May 1966): 192–195.

Tanzer, T. J. "Training Engineering Students to Use the Library." *IATUL Proceedings* 9 (1977): 59–65.

Taylor, Robert S. "Orienting the Library to the User." In New York Library Association, College and University Libraries Section. *Use, Mis-use and Non-use of Academic Libraries.* Woodside, N.Y.: author, 1970, pp. 5–19. (ERIC Doc. #: ED 046 419).

———. "Orienting the Library to the User at Hampshire College." *Drexel Library Quarterly* 7 (July/Oct. 1971): 357–364. (Different from preceding article.)

Taylor, T. K. "School Libraries and the Academic Progress of Students. *Australian Academic and Research Libraries* 7 (June 1976): 117–122.

"Teaching Library at Sangamon State University." *Journal of Academic Librarianship* 1 (Sept. 1975): 28–29.

"Term Paper Clinic." *Journal of Academic Librarianship* 1 (March 1975): 24–25.

Tevis, Ray. "Academic Library Instruction: The Need for a New Breed." *Catholic Library World* 45 (May/June 1974): 480–484.

Thomson, Mollie. "Macquarie University Chemistry Library Project." In Library Association of Australia, Conference, 1969, Adelaide. *Proceedings.* Surry Hills, N.S.W.: Library Association of Australia, 1971, pp. 568–572.

Thomson, Mollie. and Wilkinson, Eoin H. "Learning to Use a University Library Subject Catalogue." *Australian Academic and Research Libraries* 9 (June 1978): 71–80.

Tidmarsh, Marvis N. "Instruction in the Use of Academic Libraries." In Wilfred L. Saunders, ed. *University and Research Library Studies.* London: Pergamon Press, 1968, pp. 39–83.

Tietjen, Mildred C. "Library Instruction Improvement Association." *Library Scene* 4 (June 1975): 12–13.

Tiffany, Constance J., and Schwartz, Philip J. "Need More Ready in Your Reference? — KWOC It." *RQ* 16 (Fall 1976): 39–43.

Ting, Robert N. "Library Workshops for Engineers: The Buffalo Experiment." *Special Libraries* 66 (March 1975): 140–142.

Toy, Beverly J., ed. "The Role of the Academic Librarian: A Symposium." *Journal of Academic Librarianship* 4 (July 1978): 129–138.

Toy, Beverly M. *Library Instruction at the University of California; Formal Courses.* Berkeley: University of California Libraries, 1975. 9 pp. (ERIC Doc. #: ED 116 649).

Trinkner, Charles L., comp. *Teaching for Better Use of Libraries.* Hamden, Conn.: Shoe String Press, 1970. 344 pp.

Tripp, Edward. "On Library Panic." *Library Journal* 90 (Oct. 15, 1965): 4514–4516.

Trivedi, B. I. "Evolving Facet of Technical Education in a Varying Culture." *Herald of Library Science* 11 (April 1972): 144–147.

Tucker, Ellis E. " A Study of the Effects of Using Professional Library Staff as Co-instructors in an Instructional Program." Ph.D dissertation. Tallahassee: Florida State University, 1974. 192 pp.

Tucker, John Mark. "An Experiment in Bibliographic Instruction at Wabash College." *College and Research Libraries* 38 (May 1977): 203–209.

Tucker, Mark. *Five-Year Report and Evaluation on Project CLR No. 486 Presented to the Council on Library Resources.* Crawfordsville, Ind.: Wabash College Library, 1975. 198 pp. (ERIC Doc. #: ED 126 940).

"Two Approaches to Instruction of Library Patrons in Research Materials." *Mountain-Plains Library Association Newsletter* 20, no. 2 (1975–76): 12.

"UM [University of Mississippi] Library Initiates Outreach Programs." *Mississippi Library News* 41 (Dec. 1977): 208.

University of Bath. Library. "Experimental Information Service in the Social Sciences, 1969–1971: Final Report." Mimeographed. Project Director, Maurice B Line. Bath, England: author, 1972. 162 pp.

University of California at Berkeley, School of Librarianship. 1970 Conference/Workshop. See *Instruction in the Use of the College and University Library.* . . .

University of Denver Conference on the Evaluation of Library Instruction, 1973. *Evaluating Library Use Instruction.* Ann Arbor, Mich.: Pierian Press, 1975. 97 pp.

University of Kentucky Libraries. *College Library Program: Second Annual Progress Report to the Council on Library Resources and the National Endowment for the Humanities, for the Year July 1, 1975–June 30, 1976.* Lexington: author, 1976. 30 pp. (ERIC Doc. #: ED 126 900).

University of Texas at Austin. General Libraries. *A Comprehensive Program of User Education for the General Libraries, The University of Texas at Austin.* Austin: author, 1977. 115 pp. (ERIC Doc. #: ED 148 401).

University of Wisconsin—Parkside. Library/Learning Center. *Bibliographic Instruction Program.* Kenosha: University of Wisconsin Libraries, 1976. 62 pp. (ERIC Doc. #: ED 126 937).

Urquhart, Donald John. "Developing User Independence." *Aslib Proceedings* 18 (Dec. 1966): 351–356. Reply by Ir. D. J. Maltha follows on pp. 357–362.

> Comment by D. V. Arnold. *Aslib Proceedings* 19 (Feb. 1967): 63–64.

Uuttu, L. K. "User Instruction at Helsinki University of Technology Library— a Case Study." *IATUL Proceedings* 9 (1977): 70–75.

Van Burgh, Nora. "Conference on Library Orientation for Academic Librarians." *Wyoming Library Roundup* 27 (June 1972): 27–28.

Van Dijk, C. "Education and Training for Information Users and Intermediaries." *Open* 2 (Oct. 1970): 651–654.

Vasilakes, Mary. "Video as a Service in Special Libraries." *Special Libraries* 64 (Sept. 1973): 351–354.

Vernon, Christie. "An Individualized Program for Learning Resource Center Orientation." Ed. D. Practicum. Fort Lauderdale, Fla.: Nova University, June 1975. 66 pp. (ERIC Doc. #: ED 114 086).

"Videotape for Orientation at University of Washington." *Library Journal* 93 (Oct. 15, 1968): 3740.

> Comment by G. N. Hartje. *Library Journal* 93 (Dec. 15, 1968): 4594.

Vilentchuk, Lydia. "First Steps in Users Training." In International Conference on Training for Information Work, Rome, November 15–19, 1971. *Proceedings.* Rome: Italian National Information Institute; The Hague: International Federation for Documentation, 1972, pp. 397– 402.

Vogel, J. Thomas. "A Critical Overview of the Evaluation of Library Instruction." *Drexel Library Quarterly* 8 (July 1972): 315–323.

Vuturo, Robert. "Beyond the Library Tour: Those Who Can, Must Teach." *Wilson Library Bulletin* 51 (May 1977): 736–740.
> Comment by June A. Biermann. "Technological Tools and Toys." *Wilson Library Bulletin* 52 (Sept. 1977): 26.
> Also, for an article that takes issue, see G. Palandri: *Wilson Library Bulletin* 52 (March 1978): 568–569.

Vutoro, Robert A., and Cowdrick, Charles E. "Recycling the College Library: Staffroom Interchange." *College Composition and Communication* 28 (Feb. 1977): 57–58.

Wagner, Walter. "On Integrating Libraries and Classrooms; An Experiment Worth Continuing." *Learning Today* 6 (Winter 1973): 48–62.

Walker, Jerry. "Knapp School Libraries Project: What Do Student Teachers Know about Libraries?" *School Libraries* 16 (Winter 1967): 17–18, 23.

Walser, Katina P., and Kruse, Kathryn W. "A College Course for Nurses on the Utilization of Library Resources." *Bulletin of the Medical Library Association* 65 (April 1977): 265–267.

Ward, James E. "Library and Bibliographic Instruction in Southeastern Academic Libraries." *The Southeastern Librarian* 26 (Fall 1976): 148–159.

Wasi, Muriel. "A Learning Experience." *New Frontiers in Education* 4 (Jan./March 1974): 74–82.

Watkins, David R. "Role of Instruction in the Academic Library." *LACUNY Journal* 2 (Spring 1973): 8–10.
> Comment by D. A. Peele. *LACUNY Journal* 2 (Spring 1973): 10–11.
———. "Some Notes on 'Orienting the Library to the User.'" In New York Library Association. College and University Libraries Section. *Use, Misuse and Non-use of Academic Libraries*. Woodside, N.Y.: author, 1970, pp. 43–45.

Weatherford, John. "Temples and Confessional Booths." *Library Journal* 91 (Jan. 1, 1966): 70.

Weir, Katherine M. "Teaching Library." *SLA Geography and Map Division Bulletin*, no. 109 (Sept. 1977); pp. 34–39.

Wendt, Paul R. "New Library Materials and Technology for Instruction and Research." *Library Trends* 16 (Oct. 1967): 197–210.
———. "Programmed Instruction for Library Orientation." *Illinois Libraries* 45 (Feb. 1963): 72–77.

Wendt, Paul R., and Rust, Grosvenor. "Pictorial and Performance Frames in Branching Programmed Instruction." *Journal of Educational Research* 55 (June/July 1962): 430–432.

Wendt, Paul R., and Woelflin, Leslie. *Simulation of Computer-Assisted Instruction*. St. Ann, Mo.: Central Midwestern Regional Educational Laboratory, Inc., 1968. 23 pp. (ERIC Doc. #: ED 032 758).

Wendt, Paul R., et al. *To Test Refinements in Intrinsic Programming in Pictorial, Audio, and Performance Frames to Maximize the Probability of Desired Terminal Behavior*. Carbondale: Southern Illinois University, 1965. 88 pp. (ERIC Doc. #: ED 003 235).

Werking, Richard Hume. *Lawrence University's Library Service Enhancement*

Program: A Report on the Planning Year. Appleton, Wis.: Lawrence University, 1977. 102 pp. (ERIC Doc. #: ED 144 576).

———. *The Library and the College: Some Programs of Library Instruction.* Appleton, Wis.: Lawrence University Library, 1976. 32 pp. (ERIC Doc. #: ED 127 917).

———. "Library Service Enhancement." *Wisconsin Library Bulletin* 73 (Nov. 1977): 279.

Wheeler, Helen Rippier. "Current Community College Library Practice: IV. Instructional Experiences in Library Usage are Provided as Needed by the Community College Student Body." In *The Community College Library; A Plan for Action.* Hamden, Conn.: Shoe String Press, 1965. 170 pp.

Whildin, Sara Lou. "Library Instruction in Pennsylvania Academic Libraries: A Survey Summary." *Pennsylvania Library Association Bulletin* 31 (Jan. 1976): 8.

———. "Plimpton Prepares: How to Win the Library Instruction Game." *Drexel Library Quarterly* 8 (July 1972): 231–235.

Whitbeck, George W., and Hernon, Peter. "Bibliographic Instruction in Government Publications: Lecture Programs and Evaluation in American Academic Depository Libraries." *Government Publications Review* 4, no. 1 (1977): 1–12.

White, Dorothy H. "Librarian as Teacher." *Scottish Library Association News* 84 (March 1968): 52–54.

  Comment by J. M. Allan. *Scottish Library Association News* 85 (May 1968): 95–96.

Wiesenberger, Ivan. "The Organization of Training and Curriculum for Students as Future Users of Information." In International Conference on Training for Information Work, Rome, November 15–19, 1971. *Proceedings.* Rome: Italian National Information Institute; The Hague: International Federation for Documentation, 1972, pp. 459–464.

Wiggins, Marvin E. "The Development of Library Use Instructional Programs. *College and Research Libraries* 33 (Nov. 1972): 473–479.

———. "For the Student's Sake: Sounding Out New Direction." *Utah Libraries* 14 (Spring 1971): 21–23.

Wiggins, Marvin E., and Low, D. Stewart. "Use of an Instructional Psychology Model for Development of Library-Use Instructional Programs." *Drexel Library Quarterly* 8 (July 1972): 269–279.

Wilkinson, E. H., et. al. *The Use of a University Library's Subject Catalogue: Report of a Research Project.* North Ryde, Australia: Macquarie University, 1977. 99 pp. (ERIC Doc. #: ED 142 231).

Will, L. D. "Finding Information: A Course for Physics Students." *Physics Bulletin* 23 (Sept. 1972): 539–540.

Williams, Margaret P. "Library Skills Taught at Jacksonville." *Alabaman Librarian* 17 (Jan. 1966): 23.

Williamson, John G. "Swarthmore College's 'Teaching Library' Proposals." *Drexel Library Quarterly* 7 (July/Oct. 1971): 203–215.

Wilson, John H. "Librarians — Introverted or Integrated." *Australian Academic and Research Libraries* 8 (June 1977): 87–93.

Wingate, Henry W. "The Undergraduate Library: Is it Obsolete?" Section captioned "The Flaw in the Concept." *College and Research Libraries* 39 (Jan. 1978): 29–33.

Winship, Ian. "Physics Students and Information Sources." *Physics Education* 11 (July 1976): 362–364.

Woelflin, Leslie E. Instruction in the Undergraduate Library-College." *Learning Today* 5 (Winter 1972): 40–48.

Woelflin, Leslie E., and Pelley, Shirley. "Effective and Efficient Use of the Education Index." In *Evaluating the Group and Individual Use of the Audiovisual Teaching Machine Program.* Research Grant, Faculty Research Committee. Norman, Okla.: University of Oklahoma, 1969.

Wójcik, Maria. "Academic Library Instruction." *College and Research Libraries* 26 (Sept. 1965): 399–400.

Wood, D. N. "Instruction in the Use of Scientific and Technical Literature." *Library Association Record* 70 (Jan. 1968): 13.

———. "Library Education for Scientists and Engineers." *Bulletin of Mechanical Engineering Education* 8, no. 1 (1969): 1–9.

———. "Training Scientists and Technologists to Handle Information." In International Federation for Documentation. *Users of Documentation: FID International Congress on Documentation, Buenos Aires, 21–24 September 1970.* The Hague: author, 1970, Paper II. 10, 24 pp.

Wood, D. N., and Barr, K. P. "Courses on the Structure and Use of Scientific Literature." *Journal of Documentation* 22 (March 1966): 22–32.

"Wood Exhibits at SELA." *Mississippi Library News* 40 (Dec. 1976): 228.

Woolpy, Jerome H. "Information Retrieval for Introductory Science Courses." *American Biology Teacher* 39 (March 1977): 162–164, 171.

Wright, Sylvia Hart. "A Pre-college Program for the Disadvantaged." *Library Journal* 95 (Sept. 1970): 2884–2887.

Wyatt, H. V., and Bottle, Robert T. "Training in the Use of Biological Literature." *Aslib Proceedings* 19 (April 1967): 107–110.

Wyatt, R. W. P. "The Production of Video-Tapes for Library Instruction— An Account of Experience at Brunel University." In International Association of Technological University Libraries. Conference, 1970, Loughborough. *Educating the Library User; Proceedings of the Fourth Triennial Meeting, April 1–3, 1970.* Loughborough, Leicestershire, England: Loughborough University of Technology Library, 1970, pp. 21–25.

———. "Video Tapes in Brunel University Library." In *Exploitation of Library Resources: A Systems Approach; A Workshop at the Hatfield Polytechnic, April 22nd, 1972.* Hatfield, England: Hatfield Polytechnic, 1972, pp. 31–37.

Yagello, Virginia E. "Model Library Program of Project INTREX." *American Journal of Pharmaceutical Education* 36 (Dec. 1972): 752–757.

Yamada, Ken. "Instruction in the Effective Use of Library Resources." *Tennessee Librarian* 25 (Winter 1973): 27–30.

Young, Arthur P., et al. "Survey of User Education in New York State Academic Libraries." Mimeographed. New York: New York Library Association, College and University Libraries Section, 1971. 22 pp. (ERIC Doc. #: ED 055 621).

Young, R. D. E. "Instructing Freshmen in a Nigerian University on How to Make the Best use of Their Library." *Education Libraries Bulletin* 26 (Summer 1966): 10–27.

Young, Shirley M. *Chemical Reference Literature*. Washington, D.C.: American Chemical Society (Chemical Literature Division), Sept. 13, 1971. 33 pp. (ERIC Doc. #: ED 054 812).

Ziegler, H. "Certain Problems Faced in the Training of Users of Information." In *Symposium on Communication of Scientific and Technical Information for Industry, Rome, 21–22 October, 1969*. Cogenhagen: International Federation for Documentation Study Committee, Information for Industry (FID/II), Paper D6 (29). 19 pp.

Index